Erectile Dysfunction

Integrating Couple Therapy, Sex Therapy, and Medical Treatment

ALSO BY GERALD WEEKS

Promoting Change Through Paradoxical Therapy
Treating Couples: The Intersystem Model of the Marriage Council of Philadelphia

with R. DeMaria and L. Hof
Focused Genograms: Intergenerational Assessment of Individuals, Couples, and Families

with L. Hof
Integrating Sex and Marital Therapy: A Clinician's Guide
The Marital-Relationship Therapy Casebook: Theory and Application of the Intersystem Model
Integrative Solutions: Treating Common Problems in Couples Therapy

with L. L'Abate
Paradoxical Psychotherapy: Theory and Practice with Individuals, Couples, and Families

with R. Sauber and L. L'Abate
Family Therapy: Basic Concepts and Terms

with R. Sauber, L. L'Abate, and W. Buchanan
Dictionary of Family Psychology and Therapy

with S. Treat
Couples in Treatment

Erectile Dysfunction

Integrating Couple Therapy, Sex Therapy, and Medical Treatment

⌘⌘⌘⌘⌘

GERALD R. WEEKS, PH.D.
NANCY GAMBESCIA, PH.D.

W. W. Norton & Company
New York • London

For information about permission to reproduce selections
from this book, write to
Permissions, W. W. Norton & Company, Inc., 500 Fifth Avenue,
New York, NY 10110

Composition by Bytheway Publishing Services
Manufacturing by Haddon Craftsmen

Library of Congress Cataloging-in-Publication Data

Weeks, Gerald R., 1948–
    Erectile dysfunction : integrating couple therapy, sex therapy, and medical
treatment /
Gerald R. Weeks, Nancy Gambescia.
        p.   cm.
    Includes bibliographical references and index.
    ISBN 0-393-70330-4
    1. Impotence. 2. Marital psychotherapy. 3. Sex therapy. I. Gambescia,
Nancy. II. Title.

RC889.W385   2000
616.6'9206—dc21   99-058041

W. W. Norton & Company, Inc., 500 Fifth Avenue, New York, N.Y. 10110
www.wwnorton.com

W. W. Norton & Company Ltd., 10 Coptic Street, London WC1A 1PU

1 2 3 4 5 6 7 8 9 0

Acknowledgments

The authors would like to thank several people who helped to bring this book to a successful completion. We deeply appreciate our many clients, colleagues, and other staff members at Penn Council for Relationships, Philadelphia, Pennsylvania. They have enriched our lives, both personally and professionally. Most notably, Shirley Jacoby and Liz Clark provided outstanding organizational and administrative support. Melinda Biddle, Carol Beth Wolfe, GiGi Smith, and Sherrie Buchanan generously contributed their editorial assistance. Jacob Mathai helped us keep the computers whirling, resolving the many glitches we helplessly encountered. Drs. Devan Gabale and Davis Ellis, urologists, have been valued colleagues over many years and provided information regarding the latest medical developments in their field. Our editors at Norton, Susan Munro and Deborah Malmud, provided excellent support and feedback on the manuscript. We are deeply grateful for the support and understanding of Kathy Weeks, Gerald's wife, and Michael Chenet, Nancy's partner. Finally, special appreciation is offered to Lauren and Matt Gambescia for their patience while their mother worked on the manuscript.

Contents

Acknowledgments   v
Preface   ix

1. Overview of Issues and Concerns   1
2. Medical Aspects of Erectile Dysfunction   14
3. Psychological Aspects of Erectile Dysfunction   39
4. Assessment of Psychological Risk Factors   62
5. Sex Therapy with Couples: Basic Principles
   and Strategies   88
6. Sex Therapy with Couples: Basic Techniques   118
7. Integrating Psychological and Medical Treatments   144
8. Pitfalls in Dealing with Couples' Problems   156
9. Dealing with Couples' Problems: Common Issues   164

References   182
Index   191

Preface

ERECTILE DYSFUNCTION HAS BEEN ESTIMATED to affect up to 30 million men in the United States. As the baby boomers enter their fifties and grow older during the next few decades, many more men will be affected by this problem. Erectile dysfunction increases with the age of the male: The prevalence rate for men who are 40 years of age is 39%, dramatically increasing to 67% for men who are 70 (Feldman, Goldstein, Hatzichriston, Krane, & McKindlay, 1994). The widespread prevalence of this dysfunction means that clinicians are likely to encounter this problem in their individual or couple psychotherapy practices. Unfortunately, most clinicians have had little training in the physiological aspects of human sexuality or functioning or in the therapeutic principles and practices of sex therapy. Typically, a cursory assessment is made and the client then referred to a physician or a sex therapist.

The purpose of this volume is to provide clinicians with the principles and practices of the state-of-the-art treatment of erectile dysfunction. Many changes in our understanding and treatment of this problem have occurred during the last five years. Some of these changes are in the psychological arena and others are medical. Unlike the few earlier books that have been published on this topic (Eid & Pearce, 1993; Kaplan, 1974; Rosen & Leiblum, 1992b), our text presents an integrated approach that examines both the organic and psychological factors contributing to erectile dysfunc-

ix

tion, and describes both the medical and the psychological therapies available, and finally, presents a new treatment model synthesizing both the medical and psychological therapies.

This book follows the treatment principles proposed in earlier volumes on marital and sex therapies. The intersystemic approach (Weeks & Hof, 1995) proposes that every problem be viewed in terms of its individual, interactional, and intergenerational components, where the individual component is seen as including both the biological (medical) and psychological factors. This volume also stresses the role of the couple's relationship as a contributing factor in the etiology and treatment of erectile dysfunction. The dysfunction affects the couple, and the couple's attitude toward the problem further affects performance. Relational risk factors are discussed and therapy techniques described.

We have many years of experience in treating erectile problems and other types of sexual dysfunctions. Because we are not only sex therapists but also couple therapists who routinely integrate these two fields when working with couples, we have been able to transcend the usual professional, organizational, and academic boundaries. We are also interested in the medical aspects of this problem and believe that medical and psychological treatments can mutually enhance outcome.

This volume provides the clinician with an understanding of the various treatment options and what to expect from them. Clinicians who are interested in working with these problems can utilize this volume as a clinical guidebook to help them with their clients and physicians in designing effective treatment programs. We have devoted considerable attention to describing both the process and content of treatment. Clinicians who are not interested in providing sex therapy for erectile dysfunction will learn how to assess this problem and make an appropriate referral.

Our experience and most of the literature about treating erectile dysfunction has been focused on heterosexual couples. This volume assumes a heterosexual relationship; however, we have successfully applied the same principles to working with homosexual couples.

Chapter 1 lays the theoretical foundation for the book. The psychological factors of erectile dysfunction delineated in the *DSM-IV* are described and the prevalence of the disorder is reviewed. Since this disorder is always conceptualized by the authors as a couple's problem, this chapter discusses how the couple's relationship may contribute to its origin, how it is often associated with other sexual disorders, and how the couple must work together to resolve the problem. Many clients with this problem are reluctant to mention it, let alone seek help for it. The factors that inhibit couples from getting help are listed and some of the common myths about erectile dysfunction explored.

Chapter 2 provides the most current information needed by sex therapists in order to integrate current medical and psychological approaches to treating erectile dysfunction. The anatomy and physiology of an erection and the sexual response cycle are reviewed. Particular attention is given to the medical assessment and the oral, transurethral, and injection treatments. Sex therapists with an outlook to the future are introduced to the rapidly changing modalities that impact clinical practice.

Chapter 3 utilizes our intersystemic approach in reviewing the psychological risk factors associated with erectile dysfunction. Personality factors such as anxiety, depression, and fears of intimacy are linked to erection problems. The impact of relational conditions such as impending divorce, marital conflict, anger, and power and control struggles are discussed. Intergenerational components such as receiving negative sexual messages about sexuality, experiencing sexually-related trauma (incest, rape), and the impact of religious training are covered.

Chapter 4 reviews techniques such as the therapeutic reframe and underscores the importance of developing the therapeutic alliance in working with the couple. The intersystemic model is used to provide structure to the three major areas of assessment: the individual, the couple, and family-of-origin issues. The overlap of assessment and treatment of erectile dysfunction is also examined.

Chapter 5 is the first of two chapters that deals specifically with the treatment of sexual dysfunction and focuses on the basic principles and processes of treatment. It covers areas such as establishing a therapeutic relationship with the couple, dealing with their fears and anxieties, framing the problem, beginning an incremental program of therapy, developing a treatment plan with their participation, and integrating the work on the erectile dysfunction with other sexual work as needed.

Chapter 6 continues a comprehensive overview of the psychoeducational, behavioral, cognitive, and affective techniques that can be useful in resolving erectile dysfunction. Sexual myths and negative attitudes are explored from a cognitive perspective. Behaviorally-oriented techniques such as sensate focus exercises and learning to lose and regain an erection are used to reduce sexual anxiety. The couple is also coached on how to create an erotic environment, rather than an environment filled with fear and the anticipation of failure.

Chapter 7 brings together the medical and psychological approaches to treatment, discussing the treatment of those cases that require both modalities. Some of these cases involve organic causes, while others illustrate refractory or difficult problems in which a medical approach on a short-term basis is useful. Processes involved in referring and working with physicians, as well as issues arising once medical intervention is used are clearly described. Clients have many misconceptions regarding medical remedies and are often reluctant to actually use the method prescribed. Attention is given to client resistance, especially in refractory sex therapy cases.

Chapter 8 provides guidelines on how to begin working with couples and identifies and describes some of the common treatment pitfalls as well as how to avoid them. Assessing the couple's overall relationship is also discussed in terms of how to formulate a case from the intersystemic perspective.

Chapter 9 covers some of the fundamental problems we encounter when doing sex therapy, including communication difficulties, differences in expectations, and unresolved anger and conflict.

The last two chapters can stand alone as a brief overview of working with the couple relationship.

Erectile Dysfunction

Integrating Couple Therapy, Sex Therapy,
and Medical Treatment

1

⌘ ⌘ ⌘ ⌘ ⌘

Overview of Issues
and Concerns

THE TREATMENT OF ERECTILE DYSFUNCTION in the field of sex therapy (not medical therapy) has progressed very little since the original work of Masters and Johnson (1970). Although numerous texts have been published about assessment and treatment, the fundamental behavioral principles developed by Masters and Johnson (1970) are still at the core of the major sex therapy programs in use today.

Unlike the field of sex therapy, medical therapies for erectile dysfunction have developed at an ever-accelerating pace in the last 20 years. Physicians can now offer different types of corrective surgeries, penile implants, vacuum pumps and venous flow devices, penile injections, transurethral insertions, and oral medications. We will describe how the latest developments in the medical field can be used in conjunction with sex and couple therapy. Our approach to treating erectile dysfunction requires a working knowledge of the latest medical interventions as well as sex therapy techniques. Clinicians need to know when and how the various treatment modalities are indicated, when to seek a medical consultation, and how to discuss medical as well as behavioral treatment options.

In 1998, the release of Viagra (sildenafil), an oral medication that promotes erectile functioning, revolutionized the way couples view erectile dysfunction. Viagra sparked intense interest in the popular media: talk shows, news broadcasts, leading news magazines, and even stock market reports covered it. The entire country was blanketed with information about Viagra as the instant cure for erectile dysfunction. In our practices, the topic of Viagra has already become commonplace. Couples discuss whether or not the man should use it to enhance sexual functioning. Sometimes, the woman discovers that the man has been using Viagra secretly for a period of time. We have even encountered couples in which the man angrily insists that his partner try Viagra to increase her desire! Not surprisingly, the introduction of Viagra to the couple system stirs up underlying issues and offsets the homeostasis that had previously existed, often creating a crisis that the couple must address. We see this kind of crisis as an opportunity to enhance the level of intimacy in a relationship and thereby increase overall satisfaction.

In the decade prior to Viagra's emergence, two drugs were gaining popularity in the medical treatment of erectile dysfunction. First, Caverject (alprostadil), a medication injected into the penis and causing dilation of the blood vessels, was used by urologists. Then, in 1997, just prior to the release of Viagra, MUSE (again alprostadil), a pellet inserted into the penile urethra, was released as a medication. Both the injection and the penile suppository contained the same effective drug that causes erections in most men. Physicians now had numerous treatment options to offer to patients. In our experience, some of the older physicians still preferred the surgical methods, while the younger and more progressive physicians preferred the newer, less invasive procedures. Patients often would receive conflicting information about which treatment method would be the best choice for them depending upon whom they consulted for treatment. Each physician typically had a favorite option. The more popular treatments, such as MUSE, may have lost favor after a period of initial promise as the clinical results did not match physicians' expectations.

The development of Viagra, Caverject, and MUSE has had a very powerful effect. Erectile dysfunction has become a thoroughly medicalized problem. That is, it is seen as having a medical cause that will respond to medical treatment. This view has an insidious effect. Hope is extended that every erectile problem can be simply treated with the right medication. This promotes a kind of magical thinking that precludes any awareness of the development and maintenance of erectile problems; it removes the man's emotions and his intimate relationship from his sexual response "equations." This exclusionary medical focus is a trend mental health professionals have also witnessed in the field of psychiatry. Many of the leading psychiatric training programs in the country today have all but abandoned courses in "talk therapy," focusing instead on the new generation of psychoactive medications. The lay person now believes erectile problems are strictly medical, and the answer is in an injection, or better yet, a pill.

The medical model of illness postulates an organic cause, tends to be reductionistic, and is individualistic. In relation to creating and maintaining the erectile dysfunction, the patient is viewed as an individual rather than a member of a couple. A physician can treat a man's penis when it doesn't function and may be successful in getting the penis to become tumescent, even if the causes for the problem are not addressed. The medical model approach to treating erectile dysfunction creates a set of problems that serves to isolate the penis and focus on making *it* work again. Such an approach does not include an awareness that a man uses his penis to express a part of his sexuality, or that he has any need to feel sexual intimacy within the context of a loving relationship. And without a doubt, the medical treatment does not consider the sexual or relational needs of the man's partner. We believe treatment must address the functioning of the physical system, the sexuality of each partner, and the quality of the relationship.

A COUPLES' PROBLEM

The fields of sex therapy and couple/marital therapy have also contributed to ineffective treatment of erectile dysfunction by remaining polarized in their approaches. The two fields are seen as professionally, academically, and organizationally separate. Each field has its own professional organizations, which determine training and credentialing standards, thereby creating further fragmentation. Training programs in sex and couple therapies stress one to the virtual exclusion of the other, and clinicians tend to identify themselves as sex therapists *or* as couple therapists. Sex therapists, like their physician counterparts today, have generally focused on restoring sexual functioning without attending to the couple's relationship. Couple therapists have generally focused on improving the couple's relationship but have received little training in dealing with sexual problems.

In 1987, the senior author published the first professional textbook that advocated the integration of sex and marital therapies. From a clinical perspective, the fragmentation in these fields simply does not make sense. The theoretical foundation of this model was a triangular theory of love proposed by Sternberg (1986) based on research in interpersonal attraction and social psychology. According to his theory, an adult loving relationship has three major components: commitment, intimacy, and passion. Commitment is the ability to form and sustain a relationship; intimacy consists of a sense of closeness, mutual respect, well-being, and bondedness; passion is the desire to *be with* the other person, sharing both affection and sex. Sex therapists have generally claimed passion as their "territory" or part of the love triangle, and couple therapists have claimed intimacy and commitment as their domain.

A relationship in which there is love, however, has all three components. It would be absurd to say that a couple is in love except that they aren't committed, or don't share any intimacy, or lack passion. How can we approach couples while holding a professional attitude that one part is not connected to another part? How can we ignore our professional responsibilities to treat the whole person and the whole relationship? It is our contention that erectile problems are multicausal phenomena and must be treated at multiple levels. More and more of the cases we evaluate have organic, psychogenic, *and* relational components. The treatment approach must be holistic; clearly, clinicians are in the best position to manage a comprehensive treatment approach to erectile dysfunction.

Our treatment model, which integrates sex and marital therapies, considers all components of erectile dysfunction without fragmenting the assessment or treatment processes. The erectile dysfunction, as a physical system, must be treated. The man's experience of his sexuality, his risk factors for erectile dysfunction, and his relationship to his partner must all be considered. The partner should be an active participant in the treatment. Her experience of her sexuality and her relationship to him must be considered. A fundamental assumption of our approach is that sexuality includes both passion and intimacy. We must strive to help the couple comprehend the richness, complexity, and interconnectedness of their sexual relationship.

The task is challenging. Couples are ambivalent about how they view their sexuality. Typically, men would like to believe their problem has some simple physical cause that can be fixed medically. Women also accept this simplistic explanation. The idea that the problem is physical removes any personal responsibility on their parts. They do not have to confront the fact that their sexual problem may have something to do with their own psyches or with how they relate to one another. Nor do they have to involve themselves in the work of repairing their intimate and sexual relationship. Their desired treatment is a quick fix. The penis magically becomes erect again through the use of a device or a pill.

If sexuality were this simple, then good sex would make for good relationships. But even as couples subscribe to these simplistic notions of sexuality, they also understand that their sexuality is more than the sum of their sexual interactions. Couples intuitively understand that sex has meaning beyond the physical act. Good sex requires the capacity for commitment and intimacy as well as passion. Unfortunately, most couples are unable to have deep and genuine dialogues about issues such as these. Sexual communication is especially difficult for most couples. In the absence of communication, the act of sex lacks deeper meaning because the underlying thoughts and feelings are not expressed. The lack of communication about sex is a result of cultural attitudes that restrict and limit real sexual dialogue. The fact that we are surrounded by superficial sexual messages in the media has contributed to the idea that we are an open society sexually, when in fact nothing could be further from reality.

In today's culture of quick fixes, managed care, and now a new "erection industry" headed by powerful drug companies, the notion that sexuality involves more than functioning is undervalued. In such a culture, which does not promote thoughtful, deep, and controversial discussions about sex, our task is to facilitate couples' needs for sexual growth. The couples we have treated for sexual dysfunction, including erectile dysfunction, sometimes tell us they accomplished much more than they had expected from their treatment. They express appreciation for being more sexually aware and for being able to talk about sex, to express their feelings and needs, and to relate to each other more effectively. They learn to reach a deeper level of sexual and emotional intimacy with fewer obstacles or barriers. Couples are willing to reach great depths of intimacy and passion when they have the right road map and the right guides.

DEFINING ERECTILE DYSFUNCTION

The conceptualization of erectile problems has changed significantly since its introduction in the American Psychiatric Association's (APA) *Diagnostic and Statistical Manual of Mental Disorders (DSM)* in 1954. The initial term used, "impotence," referred to a range of sexual difficulties, including desire, arousal, and orgasm dysfunctions. Besides being an imprecise term, it also has demeaning and pejorative meanings. In *DSM-III* (APA, 1980), "impotence" was replaced by "inhibited sexual arousal," and in the revised edition, *DSM-IIIR* (APA, 1987), the term became "male erectile disorder." The latter diagnostic descriptor is more accurate and is in use in the current diagnostic system.

The definition of male erectile disorder offered in the latest edition of the *Diagnostic and Statistical Manual of Mental Disorders* (DSM-IV; APA, 1994) is the "persistent or recurrent inability to attain or maintain an adequate erection until completion of sexual activity" (p. 302). Furthermore, there must be "marked distress or interpersonal difficulty" to meet criteria for the diagnosis. This definition is intended to suggest that the disorder is primarily sexual and psychological; the diagnosis is not to be used if the dysfunction could be accounted for by another Axis I disorder, or if it is a direct effect of a medication, a medical condition, or substance abuse.

The definition encompasses several types of erectile dysfunction. The first two types are *lifelong* or *acquired*. Lifelong (primary) would mean the man has always had an erectile dysfunction. This is an extremely rare presentation and tends to require longer-term psychotherapy. More commonly, acquired (secondary) erectile dysfunction occurs in men who have had the experience of successful intercourse with an erection. Typically, acquired dysfunction follows a period of normal functioning that may extend for years or decades. At some later time, these men have consistent difficulty keeping or getting an erection. The prognosis for an acquired dysfunction is much better than lifelong and the length of treatment is much shorter.

The second two types of erectile dysfunction are *generalized* or *situational*. Men with a generalized pattern of erectile dysfunction are not able to sustain an erection with anyone. In some cases, these men cannot maintain an erection even during masturbation. A situational presentation is the more common pattern for erectile dysfunction. If he is in a monogamous relationship, he may have erectile problems in certain situations or at certain times, not others. In the nonmonogamous man, a situational erectile dysfunction occurs with some partners and not others, or only in some situations. The situational group is generally easier to treat.

The problem of erectile dysfunction presents in a variety of ways in both of the types mentioned above. A few patterns are common. One of these patterns is for the man to be able to obtain a partial erection, usually for a brief period of time, but not a full, firm, usable erection. He may be able to achieve penetration under ideal circumstances, but the erection never becomes fully tumescent. Another pattern is for the man to achieve a firm erection but to lose it just before or after penetration. These men typically have a great deal of performance anxiety at this moment, which disrupts their erectile ability. Other men find they can achieve erections during masturbation but not while trying to engage in intercourse with a partner. Finally, some men are so unaware of their own bodies that they aren't sure about the quality of their erections, but know that having intercourse is problematic.

PREVALENCE OF ERECTILE DYSFUNCTION

Many men experience difficulty in obtaining an erection from time to time. They may have been overly fatigued, had too much to drink, or just not have been in the mood. Sometimes these men overreact to this normative occurrence, whereby it becomes a much more significant and clinical problem. Obtaining good reliable and accurate data on men who have this disorder is challenging. It requires a standardized definition, effective assessment, and data collection from a large group of men. In spite of the methodological flaws that can be found in the following studies, they are useful indicators of how common this type of erectile dysfunction is in the population.

Kinsey and his associates were among the first to offer statistics on the prevalence of erectile dysfunction (Kinsey, Pomeroy, & Martin, 1948). They found that less than 1% of males younger than 19 had an erectile problem, but by the age of 75 the rate was 25%. Frank, Anderson, and Kupfer (1976) reported that 36% of men presenting for sex therapy had an erectile dysfunction. Renshaw (1988) reported that 48% of the men in her sex therapy clinic had an erectile problem. In an excellent review of the literature, Spector and Carey (1990) found that the most common complaint reported by men in sex therapy clinics was erectile dysfunction. Fifty percent of the men who received treatment at the Masters and Johnson Institute were diagnosed with acquired or secondary erectile dysfunction, and 8% were diagnosed with lifelong or primary erectile dysfunction. The frequency with which the problem is reported in sex therapy institutes is known to be high. Given the advent of specialized treatment centers ("impotence centers") and the proliferating number of urologists who specialize in this problem, it is not surprising that these types of clinics would have a very high rate of men seeking help.

Several studies have attempted to answer the question of how common the problem is in the general population. Frank, Anderson, and Rubinstein (1978) asked 100 "normal" couples to report any sexual problems. Their sample consisted of well-educated, mostly white men and women in different age groups. They found that 7% of men had trouble getting an erection, and 9% had trouble maintaining an erection. In this study, almost one out of five men reported an erectile dysfunction. Two other studies stand out for their attempt to gain samples in a methodologically rigorous way. The Massachusetts Male Aging Study (Feldman et al., 1994) assessed men from ages 40 to 70. Of the 1,290 men in the study, 52% reported some degree of erectile difficulty. Total failure was reported by 9.6% of the men. The second study, known as the *Sex in America* study (Michael, Gagnon, Laumann, & Kolata, 1994), reported that 10% of men had an erectile dysfunction for at least a period of twelve months prior to being questioned. This study consisted of 3,432 subjects, 44.6% of them men.

SEXUAL DYSFUNCTION IN THE COUPLE

We contend that erectile dysfunction in a man should be viewed in the context of his relationship. The relationship may be a factor in the etiology of the problem, and it is definitely a factor in being able to resolve the problem and establish a mutually satisfying sexual relationship. The prevalence of sexual problems in couples suggests that many couples who present with an erectile dysfunction are also experiencing other problems. The data from the study by Frank and others (1978) showed that 40% of men and 50% of women had a major sexual dysfunction, and 50% of men and 77% of women reported "minor difficulties." Because the study was conducted prior to hypoactive sexual desire being considered a major problem, lack of desire was considered to be a "minor difficulty." The statistical probability of each partner having a sexual problem is therefore quite high. In our clinical experience, we frequently find that the couple is struggling with at least two distinct but interrelated problems. Solving just one problem does not solve the other; in fact, solving only one of the problems often exacerbates the significance of the other because the equilibrium that had been established in the sexual relationship is disturbed. The classic example would be to help a man with an erectile dysfunction overcome his problem only to find that his partner has a lack of sexual interest or experiences pain during sex. Solving his problem is not viewed as a help by his partner, who does not have to confront her problem as long as he is having a problem.

This situation has occurred in many of our treatment cases. The men become excited about the possibility of restored potency, only to find that their partners share little excitement about the possibility of renewing the sexual relationship. Some women are also angry that their newly potent partners are now attaining orgasm during intercourse, whereas they are not. Another common complaint of middle-aged and older couples is that intercourse now lasts too long and is irritating or painful due to the fact that they are not adequately lubricated.

Wincze and Carey (1991) reviewed a number of studies reporting a high incidence of sexual dysfunction in women. Frank and colleagues (1978) found that 48% of the women in their study had difficulty getting sexually excited, 33% had difficulty maintaining excitement, 11% reached orgasm too quickly, 46% had difficulty reaching an orgasm, and 15% were unable to have an orgasm. Their sample consisted of 100 couples that were not in treatment. The large-scale *Sex in America* study (Michael et al., 1994) of almost 4,000 respondents showed that about 33% of women lacked sexual desire, 24% were unable to have an orgasm, 21% did not experience sex as pleasurable, 15% experienced pain, 12% were concerned about performance, 10% climaxed too early, and almost 20% had trouble lubricating. It should be noted that these researchers only asked about sexual problems during the preceding 12 months.

Treating just the erectile dysfunction without considering the overall sexual relationship would be misguided and unproductive. We frequently find that we are treating the sexual dysfunction(s) in both the partner and the overall couple relationship. Later in this volume we present material on some of the issues that pertain to improving the couple relationship.

BARRIERS TO SEEKING HELP

Individuals with sexual dysfunctions generally wait several years before seeking professional help. In our practices men with erectile dysfunction often delay getting help for four to five years from the onset of the problem. Several reasons account for the fact that men wait so long before they seek help. Men are often reluctant to seek *any* kind of medical help, hoping the problem will somehow disappear. The same is true of erectile problems; men will rationalize (hope) that the problem will take care of itself. In addition, men cannot imagine how seeing a therapist and *talking* about the problem could help. The fact is, they are right, but this is due to a misconception about the nature of the therapy. Just talking about the problem will not help. The treatment must involve an active behavioral component that includes homework exercises to be performed with one's partner. Most men, of course, do not know that this is a part of the treatment. Moreover, even if they did, they would be skeptical that such a process could work. In a later chapter, we address the issue of how to deal with men's skepticism and pessimism at the beginning of treatment.

Unfortunately, some men have had the experience of seeing a therapist for this problem and received inappropriate treatment. Approximately half the men we treat for an erectile problem have seen one other therapist who provided either "talk" therapy or a poorly constructed attempt at sex therapy. These men now re-enter therapy with little hope or with the idea that we are their "last" hope. The first issue in treatment is to deal with the inappropriate therapy they received—why it didn't work and what will be different during the new course of therapy.

Many men believe their problem is unique or at least uncommon. This is a variation of considering oneself to be "abnormal." They believe that a problem that is uncommon would be difficult to treat, because not much would be known about it. They believe themselves to be beyond help. With the recent reports regarding the new oral medication, Viagra, men have now gotten the message that the problem is much more common than most had believed; but they now think it is *just* a medical problem that can be treated with a medication.

Shame and embarrassment are two other powerful reasons men do not get help with erectile difficulties. They do not want to admit they have this problem for fear of how they will appear to others. They are concerned about appearing weak or incompetent to their partners. The problem raises questions about their virility and whether they are attracted to their partners. Some men we have treated have sought medical solutions, injection therapy, or Viagra without telling their partners, especially if they are dating. Since these issues make confronting the problem difficult, men adapt by avoiding sexual interactions and conversations about the problem.

Finally, finding help can be an obstacle. The number of qualified sex therapists in this country relative to the number of individuals with sexual problems is highly disproportionate. In many parts of the country, especially rural areas, it is virtually impossible to find a sex therapist. The therapists who are available are in demand and do not belong to managed care organizations, which means their fees are often beyond the reach of many consumers. Our premise is that the ideal therapist is well trained in both couple therapy and sex therapy. Unfortunately, the number of therapists with this type of training is very small and most are in urban areas. Therefore, only a limited number of clients will be successful in finding a therapist of this caliber and training.

Misconceptions about Erections

The lack of adequate sex education has led to the development and perpetuation of many misguided ideas about sex. Many of these misconceptions deal with erections. A man or a couple who believes these notions are true may experience a variety of sexual difficulties. Anxiety and worry generated by misconceptions may contribute directly to the development of the problem. Misconceptions may also dictate how partners relate to each other sexually or change the meaning of a behavior from one that is normal to one that is viewed as dysfunctional. Zilbergeld (1992b) and others have delineated a number of myths about sex and erections. We have detected the following common misconceptions in the couples we have worked with over the last 20 years.

1. *An erection is necessary in order to have sex.* This myth reflects the idea that sex must involve intercourse. In fact, many couples may enjoy nonpenetration sex. Furthermore, many women prefer that some sexual encounters do not involve intercourse. Most women need some form of noncoital stimulation in order to have an orgasm. While penetration is pleasurable, it may not provide the correct alignment for adequate clitoral stimulation to orgasm.

2. *An erection is an indication of sexual desire.* This myth equates desire with performance. In reality, a man may feel tremendous sexual desire without having an erection. The context may not be conducive for an erection, or he may have an erectile dysfunction that precludes an erection, yet he still experiences desire for his partner.

3. *The erection should occur almost instantly, regardless of circumstances.* Younger men are capable of getting erections very quickly under almost any circumstance. With increasing age, however, it takes longer to get an erection in general and, in particular, after ejaculating. This is called the refractory period, and it increases with age. Young men have short refractory periods and are usually able to get an erection quickly after ejaculation. As a man ages, it takes longer and longer (sometimes days) before he is able to get another erection. Many men

notice an increase in the refractory periods at around age 40, and if they are uninformed about normal sexual functioning, they become anxious.

4. *The erection should get hard and stay hard until ejaculation.* This is another myth that pressures men to believe that the sexual response never fluctuates. Getting an erection is an inconsistent process. It will begin to occur, then be lost partially, and then become more erect. The penis does not fill up consistently, like a balloon being inflated. It waxes and wanes until fully erect.

5. *The erection must be completely firm or hard in order to have intercourse.* A rock-hard erection is not necessary for intercourse. The penis must be firm enough to achieve and maintain penetration, but it does not have to be completely firm.

6. *An erection is necessary in order to ejaculate.* Actually, erection and ejaculation are separate processes. Usually, the two go hand-in-hand when everything is working properly, but a man can certainly ejaculate with a flaccid penis if he receives enough stimulation. Ejaculation without an erection will happen when he is anxious or afraid that he is not going to have an orgasm.

7. *When erections aren't as firm as they used to be it means something must be terribly wrong.* As a man ages, the firmness of his erection will diminish. This process is normal.

8. *Women like a large erection.* Most women could not care less about the size of a man's penis. What counts is the sexual technique and the relationship. A large penis will not compensate for what is missing in these two areas.

9. *If the erection is lost during sex, the penis will not regain tumescence.* Erections come and go under normal conditions. A man may lose and regain his erection several times during a sexual encounter. Trying to force the penis to stay erect continually goes against nature.

10. *Every time a man has an erection, he must have sex.* Unfortunately, both men and women subscribe to this myth which forces men into the role of "sex machines." They may also attempt to convince their partners that each erection must be relieved through sexual intercourse. The fact is a man can sustain an erection and choose not to have an orgasm without risking physical or psychological damage. Furthermore, satisfying sex does not have to follow a prescribed formula, beginning with an erection and ending with coitus. Men can enjoy many erections without having intercourse or even an orgasm because each is always a choice, not an obligation.

11. *An erection during sleep or upon wakening must mean the man was dreaming about something sexual.* Erections occur during sleep on a

regular basis and have nothing to do with sex. They are part of the dream sleep or the REM sleep pattern that occurs cyclically. A man may attain and lose several erections throughout the night without necessarily having an erotic dream.

12. *Losing an erection one time must be a sign of impotence.* This belief is an unfortunate interpretation of what it means to lose an erection. Men do experience erectile failures. These experiences are normal and nothing to worry about if they are occasional. Unfortunately, many men and/or their partners panic about these normal occurrences and create anxiety that only worsens the situation.

13. *Men begin to lose their ability to get erections in their early 40s.* The fact is that if a man is in good health, erectile ability is never lost.

14. *An erection problem must be either physical or psychological.* It could be either one, or it may be a mix of the two. For older men, it is often a mix.

15. *Firm erections are essential in a relationship.* Many men give up on dating because they don't feel they can perform well enough sexually. They avoid relationships fearing they will fail to perform sexually and as a result be rejected.

16. *If a man can't get an erection, it's because he's not trying hard enough.* An erection can't be willed or forced. It can only happen when the conditions are right. The harder men try to force an erection, the less likely it will happen.

17. *The woman should not initiate sexual contact if a man has an erection problem.* This myth that the partner's initiation will put too much pressure on the man could not be further from the truth. If the woman never initiates, he may begin to think she is not interested, and if he thinks she isn't interested, it will be harder for him to get aroused.

18. *As soon as the erection is hard enough for intercourse, the man should proceed with penetration.* This idea is a set-up for failure. A newly formed erection can dissipate easily. Allowing the erection to persist for a few minutes helps to more firmly establish it.

In addition to the myths solely about erections, there are many other myths and negative sexual attitudes which compound matters. Zilbergeld (1978) discussed several other myths that are common in men. Some of these were:

- Men should not have or express certain feelings.
- The man is responsible for initiating and taking charge of sex.

- A man always wants sex and is always ready.
- The purpose of physical contact is to have sex.
- Sex and intercourse are the same.
- Good sex always leads to an orgasm.
- Sex is a natural and spontaneous process.

The chapter in his book in which the myths are found is called "It's Two Feet Long, Hard as Steel, and Goes All Night." This title reflects the high level of expectation to which men hold themselves about being sexual supermen. It is the male idea that more is better, bigger is better, longer is better, and performance is everything. Moreover, many of the couples we have seen in our practices also hold negative sexual attitudes which (1) make doing therapy difficult, and (2) create guilt and anxiety for the couple. A few of these beliefs are:

- Sex is bad, wicked, and sinful.
- Masturbation is bad, wicked, and sinful.
- Sex is only for procreation.
- Sex should not be enjoyed (too much).
- Something bad will happen if I am too sexual.
- Good sex is for other people.
- Good sex can only be enjoyed with bad women.
- Good women don't like sex.
- Women just submit to sex.
- Women use sex to manipulate men.
- Women just use men.
- A good marriage can't have sexual problems.

An erectile dysfunction is a disorder caused by many factors that arise from three basic sources: the individual's vulnerabilities, interactional (dyadic) issues, and intergenerational (family-of-origin) factors. We give special emphases to the role of the couple in this problem in determining both the etiology and the treatment. This dyadic emphasis coupled with our interdisciplinary perspectives set our model apart from the earlier approaches and existing literature on erectile dysfunctions (Kaplan, 1974; Masters & Johnson, 1970; Rosen & Leiblum, 1992b).

2

⌘ ⌘ ⌘ ⌘ ⌘

Medical Aspects of Erectile Dysfunction

SEX THERAPISTS ARE CHALLENGED TO INTEGRATE the individual, relational, and familial factors that predispose a man toward an erectile dysfunction with the ever-changing medical understanding of the dysfunction and the new medical therapies. Medical issues related to the causes and treatment of erectile dysfunction can be daunting, particularly for therapists without specialized training. In the last decade, the medical advances in treatment alone have dramatically changed the nonmedical approach to treating erectile dysfunction. Now sex therapists need a working knowledge of the advantages and disadvantages associated with the various medical treatments as well as the latest information about sex therapy. This chapter summarizes some of the medical information needed by sex therapists when treating erectile dysfunction: how to integrate sex and medical therapies; when and how to involve medical experts in the diagnosis and treatment processes; and how to talk intelligently about popular current medical treatments.

Ultimately, this medical information will increase the therapist's knowledge and comfort level and impact favorably on the treatment of the man and his partner.

THE SEXUAL RESPONSE CYCLE

Sexual response can be conceptualized as a cycle having beginning, middle, and end phases. Masters and Johnson (1966) were the first to scientifically investigate the physiology of the human sexual response, describing in detail the many bodily changes that occur during sexual arousal and orgasm. Kaplan (1979) expanded our understanding of the human sexual response by focusing on the importance of sexual desire and fantasy in the development and maintenance of the sexual appetite, arousal, and orgasm. This triphasic model of the sexual response cycle includes the distinct phases of *desire, arousal,* and *orgasm.*

Sexual desire, or the appetite for sex, is the trigger for the remaining phases of the sexual response. Through desire, the individual experiences erotic feelings and creates sexual fantasies that fuel the pump for sexual arousal. Sexual desire is a psychological process, involving the individual's ability to recognize his or her sexual needs, feel deserving of sexual pleasure (McCarthy, 1995), and value intimacy in a relationship (Schnarch, 1991, 1997). Physiological arousal (or excitement) is triggered by the individual's ability to experience sexual desire, thereby activating genital as well as extragenital responses. It is during the phase of sexual arousal that penile tumescence and vaginal lubrication occur. Orgasm follows the arousal phase provided there is ongoing stimulation, both physically and through continued focus on erotic feelings.

According to the *DSM-IV*, an erectile dysfunction involves an inhibition at the second phase of the sexual response cycle, the stage of sexual arousal (APA, 1994). This inhibition can be caused by psychogenic factors such as depression or anxiety. For instance, if a man becomes worried about sustaining his erection, in effect he is distracting himself from the natural flow of erotic images as well as enjoyment of his partner. The physiological responses necessary for maintaining erectile tumescence will therefore be inhibited, causing a partial or complete detumescence. Also, certain physical conditions, such as diabetes or vascular disease, can make a man vulnerable to an erectile dysfunction. These conditions can interfere with sexual arousal directly by reducing the blood supply to the penis. Lastly, erectile functioning can be adversely affected by a combination of organic and psychogenic factors, discussed later in this chapter.

THE PHYSIOLOGY OF AN ERECTION

The complicated psychological factors that can have an impact on erectile functioning will be explored in subsequent chapters using the intersystems model described by Weeks (1994). In regard to physiology, the "bottom line" for maintaining penile tumescence throughout the duration of sexual activity is a structurally and functionally intact sexual system. That is, the central nervous system (brain and spinal cord) and both vascular and hormonal systems need to be operating optimally. Any disruption in the activity of any one of these systems will interfere with the quality of an erection.

The Central Nervous System

Sexual thoughts and fantasies trigger the beginning of physiological sexual arousal. An intact central nervous system is required for translating erotic thoughts into physical responses. Through a system of cranial nerves and fibers, sexual impulses travel from the cerebral cortex to the limbic system within the brain to the spinal cord. These sensitive fibers and nerves then journey from the sacral area of the spinal cord along the back and sides of the prostate, ultimately penetrating the delicate tissues of the penis (Rosen & Leiblum, 1992b). The arteries of the penis respond by dilating, allowing the blood flow into the penis to increase.

Physical touch to the genitals can also activate sexual arousal. Sensory receptors within the skin and delicate tissue of the genitals carry impulses from the nerves and fibers to the reflex centers in the lower portion of the spinal cord. Then, they are interpreted by the higher centers in the brain as erotic or pleasurable, signaling the genitals to respond through vasodilatation.

Erections are often present during rapid eye movement (REM) sleep and also when the man awakens from sleep with a full bladder. These nonsexual erections are entirely involuntary and are seen with a greater frequency in younger men and boys. As the man gets older, he has fewer nocturnal erections. Segraves and Schoenberg (1987) have observed that awakening with a robust erection is a good indicator of sexual health. In most instances, one can assume that the physiological systems that support the maintenance of tumescence are intact if he awakens from sleep with an erection, and that the cause of the erectile problem is most likely psychogenic. There are some exceptions to this "rule," however. In these cases of organically caused erectile dysfunction, the man's erection may be firm upon awakening but it rapidly diminishes if he attempts to have sexual relations.

The Vascular System

The genital and extragenital physiological responses that occur during the normal arousal phase in men are produced through the processes of *vasocongestion* (increased blood supply) and *myotonia* (muscle tension). These responses were skillfully measured by Masters and Johnson (1966) and reported in their text, *Human Sexual Response*. Through vasocongestion, the arterial supply to the penis allows a relatively large amount of blood to be delivered within seconds or minutes. The blood enters three chambers of erectile tissue, which extend throughout the length of the penis. The erectile tissue contains veins, arteries, smooth muscle, and fibrous and spongy tissue. The larger two chambers, or the *corpora cavernosa*, are surrounded by a smooth membrane called the *tunica albuginea*, which actually relaxes during erection, allowing for increased blood flow to enter the membranes, resulting in tumescence (Kaplan, 1974; Masters & Johnson, 1966). When the erectile tissue expands, it presses against the walls of the tunica albuginea, mechanically preventing the flow of blood out of the penis through veins and capillaries (Wagner & Kaplan, 1993). As long as the smooth membrane surrounding the corpora cavernosa remains relaxed, blood will remain trapped within the penis, sustaining tumescence. Thus, the erection actually involves two hydraulic processes: an increased inflow of blood through the penile arteries as well as decreased venous outflow. Both of these processes are necessary for the integrity of an erection. If a psychological or physical problem interferes with this delicate balance, the erection will be interrupted either partially or completely.

During sexual arousal, the testes are drawn upward toward the *perineum* (the area between the scrotum and the anus) of the pelvis. This is accomplished through the process of myotonia or tensing of the *cremasteric* muscle that supports the testes. In addition, the spermatic cord shortens, further helping to elevate the testes toward the pelvis. Mobility of the testes decreases as they are held closer to the body. Due to vasocongestion, the testes become at least 50% larger than their nonstimulated size during sexual arousal. Both elevation and engorgement of the testes become more pronounced as sexual arousal continues. The scrotum responds to sexual arousal by constricting and thickening in order to support the testicular elevation of the advanced state of sexual arousal.

Extragenital responses to sexual arousal caused by systemic vasocongestion as well as myotonia vary from individual to individual. According to Kolodny, Masters, and Johnson (1979), in many men, the nipples become erect and a "sex flush" is noted on the chest, neck, and face. Muscle tone of the body increases, causing contraction of the muscles of the trunk, pelvis, and extremities. Heart rate, blood pressure, and respiratory rate also increase in response to sexual arousal.

The Hormonal System

A comprehensive review of the neurology and endocrinology of the sexual response is provided by Crenshaw and Goldberg (1996) in *Sexual Pharmacology*. They carefully assess the delicate equilibrium of certain naturally occurring substances within the body and how the brain responds to these substances to promote sexual arousal. Key hormones such as testosterone and other neurotransmitters are discussed in depth.

Testosterone is produced primarily in the testes, and, to a lesser degree, in the adrenal glands. The correlation between circulating levels of testosterone and sexual desire has been clearly established (Crenshaw & Goldberg, 1996; Kaplan, 1995; Rako, 1996). Testosterone both stimulates the brain to develop and maintain a sexual appetite and promotes the physical conditions necessary for sexual functioning. The effects of testosterone on sexual arousal are less clearly understood, however. In addition to testosterone, sexual arousal appears to involve many factors such as cognitions, feelings, and the degree of physical stimulation provided. According to the studies reviewed by Davidson and Rosen (1992), testosterone promotes sexual arousal in men and is believed to contribute to erectile robustness. Some of these conclusions are inferential, based on studies of men with clinically low testosterone levels (Vermeulen, 1991). For example, men with testosterone deficiency suffer from lack of desire as well as erectile dysfunction. Testosterone also affects sexual functioning indirectly because it promotes overall strength and vigor, muscle mass, and bone density (Vermeulen, 1994).

Other hormones also affect sexual arousal although none is as significant as testosterone. For instance, *dehydroepiandrosterone* (DHEA), produced in the adrenals, facilitates the production of testosterone, thereby enhancing sexual arousal as well as desire. Because DHEA rises precipitously in adolescence and declines with aging, it is believed to be involved in sexual functioning. Yet the direct effect of DHEA on sexual arousal is not clearly understood and the review of the literature conducted by Crenshaw and Goldberg (1996) suggests that the results are inconclusive. DHEA indirectly promotes sexual arousal by increasing energy and physical strength.

According to Crenshaw and Goldberg (1996), peptides are known to mediate the sexual response in various excitatory ways. *Oxytocin*, produced by the pituitary, is excreted in high amounts during sexual arousal. *Vasopressin* potentiates male sexual arousal directly and by stimulating the production of other hormones such as testosterone; primarily, it allows sexual arousal to remain consistent throughout the duration of sexual activity. *Prostaglandins*, found in genital tissue, are directly responsible for maintenance of erections by facilitating vasodilatation, the process responsible for penile tumescence. Various injection drugs for the treatment of erectile dysfunction contain prostaglandins.

AGE-RELATED CHANGES IN SEXUAL FUNCTIONING

Sexual Desire

Normative age-related changes in sexual functioning are noticeable at each of the three stages of the sexual response cycle. Sexual appetite decreases throughout the life span although there is a wide range of variability among men. Men generally require more erotic stimulation as they age to compensate for the gradual decrease in sexual desire. There is a gradual ebb in sexual frequency after age 50 with a more precipitous decline after age 70 (Pfeiffer, 1974). Probably the most important factor in the age-related decrease in sexual desire is the reduction in the production of testosterone and, to a lesser extent, DHEA, beginning at about age 40. The older man is less controlled by the hormones that were plentiful in his younger years. In effect, he is less driven by sexual desire and therefore potentially more sensitive to his sexual partner. If he is not intimidated by the changes he is experiencing, he can look forward to a lifetime of enjoyable sex. Provided the man is informed that certain physiological changes are normal and predictable, he will not become anxious about his sexual performance when they occur.

One unusual case history exemplifies the notion that sometimes the exception becomes the rule. A couple arrived for conjoint therapy complaining about a severe discrepancy in sexual desire and the frequency of sexual activity, although neither was troubled by the quality of their contact. They were in a committed relationship and both were in their mid-seventies. The man was upset that his partner did not desire sexual intimacy every day! She was satisfied with a frequency of two to three times a week. Neither suffered from serious medical or relational problems. Needless to say, the psychotherapy addressed ways in which the couple could reach a satisfactory comfort zone in terms of frequency. In less than eight sessions, the couple was helped to discuss their expectations and work out a compromise that was acceptable to each. Essentially, he accepted that she was not responsible for every orgasm he experienced. This couple also enjoyed bibliotherapy that further helped to normalize their predicament and promoted active discussion of sexuality. Two books were particularly valuable, *For Each Other* (Barbach, 1982) and *The New Male Sexuality* (Zilbergeld, 1992b).

Sexual Arousal

Although erections are less firm with advancing age, normally a man can expect to enjoy sexual activity to completion throughout his life span, although it will have qualitative differences. The older man may have moments of rigid tumescence, but he cannot expect to sustain the kind of robustness he experienced when he was younger. This age-related instability of penile tumescence occurs because the muscles and blood vessels supplying the penis gradually deteriorate over time (Davidson & Rosen, 1992). The sexually enlightened older man can experience sexual relations in a relaxed, nondemanding fashion, no longer driven by orgasm-focused sex but, instead, able to enjoy a greater variety of coital as well as noncoital stimulation.

Another normal sexual alteration throughout the life cycle is the reduction in the number of spontaneous erections experienced by most men. An older man no longer has the luxury or the burden of having an erection at the mere thought of erotic material. With age, men require more physical and erotic stimulation to produce and sustain erections. In fact, as men age, the penis becomes less exquisitely sensitive to physical stimulation (Kaplan, 1995). Since penile sensitivity is related to testosterone production as well as vascular and muscle robustness, it is understandable that penile tumescence is less consistent although still fully enjoyable with age (Kaplan, 1995; Segraves & Segraves, 1992).

Without a doubt, the incidence of erectile dysfunction is age-related, gradually increasing with age (Laumann, Gagnon, Michael, & Michaels, 1994). This is due to a combination of factors, such as the normal physiologic changes of aging just mentioned, compounded by the mounting incidence of cardiovascular disease and the impact of anxiety on erectile function. More than half of all men between the ages of 40 and 70 suffer from some degree of erectile dysfunction. By the age of 70, over 65% of men experience mild to moderate erectile problems (Feldman et al., 1994).

It is not unusual to encounter clients who feel they are abnormal because they have noticed some subtle, age-related changes in sexual arousal. Some men may even ascribe an inaccurate cause to explain the changes they notice, suddenly doubting their sexual orientation, fearing they are becoming homosexual. Sometimes the man makes matters worse by avoiding intimate contact with his partner. He creates so much performance anxiety that he experiences psychogenic erectile dysfunction. In these instances, the psychotherapy addresses the normative physical changes that accompany aging, increasing his knowledge base and thereby decreasing anxiety. It is helpful to include the partner in the sessions to more thoroughly dispel myths and encourage joint resolution of the problem. Typically, this kind of issue, ignorance of age-related changes in sexual functioning, is treated in fewer than five sessions.

Orgasm

In addition to experiencing a less compelling sexual appetite and less robust and consistent arousal, there are changes related to orgasm that may further impact the man's level of sexual arousal. First, as they get older, men require more time after an ejaculation before they are able to sustain another erection. As noted previously, his increasing refractory period is a normal consequence of aging and not a sign of dysfunction. Also, the stage of ejaculatory inevitability becomes briefer or absent in some instances. There is less semen in the ejaculate, which reduces its volume. The ejaculate is not expelled with the projectile vigor of the younger man. In fact, at times, the ejaculate seeps rather than surges from the penis. Orgasm thus becomes less intense with age. If the man and his partner have realistic expectations about these normal age-related sexual changes, they can plan for a lifetime of enjoyable sexual relations.

Physical Changes and Anxiety

These normative age-related changes in sexual functioning can cause the man to become more vulnerable to the effects of anxiety. At a younger age, he might have been able to tolerate a greater degree of stress without having it impact his erections. This is due to the overall resilience of the vascular and nerve supply to the penis and to the power of circulating testosterone which compels the younger man to remain more focused on orgasm. As he approaches 50, the man notices that stress or anxiety can more readily interfere with his sexual arousal and the quality of his erections. Crenshaw and Goldberg (1996) believe that this vulnerability actually makes the older man more sensitive to the sexual needs of his partner. Kaplan (1995) reported being "positively impressed" by the ability of most men in her clinical sample to adapt to the normal physiological changes without much impairment in their sexual enjoyment.

ORGANIC CAUSES OF ERECTILE DYSFUNCTION

As stated previously, certain organic conditions or physiological vulnerabilities are predisposing factors in erectile dysfunction. For our purposes, these conditions can be grouped into the three categories mentioned previously in the discussion of the physiology of erectile functioning. Although psychotherapists might not have medical or nursing degrees, a general knowledge of the organic causes of erectile dysfunction is essential.

Central Nervous System Problems

Any disease that impairs brain functioning can potentially interfere with tumescence. For instance, Parkinson's disease, brain tumors, strokes, dementia, or surgical manipulation of the brain or spinal cord are a few of the many conditions that can interfere with the conduction of impulses from the brain through the spinal cord to the penis. Diseases of the spinal cord (such as multiple sclerosis) or spinal injuries or tumors can potentially interfere with erectile functioning because the severed nerves cannot carry impulses to the penis. Surgery to the genitals or rectum, such as the removal of the prostate for the treatment of prostate cancer, can cause erectile dysfunction if delicate nerve endings are inadvertently cut during surgery.

Trauma to or compression of the delicate nerve endings of the genitals or perineum can cause transient or permanent erectile problems. An enlarged prostate can interfere with erectile functioning by compressing the nerves that supply the penis. This condition is known as *benign prostatic hyperplasia*, and it occurs more frequently as men reach the sixth decade of life. Medical researchers have noted that trauma resulting from recreational injuries or prolonged biking practices have been associated with organic erectile dysfunction (Anderson & Bovim, 1997; Mellion, 1991). These studies made recommendations for recreational practices and biking equipment designed to reduce the pressure on penile arteries, veins, and nerve endings.

Central nervous system depressants, such as alcohol, can have an inhibitory effect on erectile functioning. In small quantities, alcohol can serve to reduce anxiety, but it is certain to create erectile problems if the amount ingested is too high. This is due to the direct depressant effect of alcohol on the brain. Both prescription and nonprescription drugs can also inhibit sexual arousal although the reasons are varied and more complicated. The following drug groups are notorious for causing erectile problems: antidepressants (in particular, the selective serum serotonin reuptake inhibitors); centrally acting antihypertensive medications; central nervous system depressants such as the benzodiazepenes, phenothiazines, butyrophenes; beta blockers; and any drug with an anticholinergic effect. Men who are being treated for depression, anxiety, heart disease, or hypertension often report side effects related to diminished or absent sexual arousal. These side effects are more common at the beginning of treatment and can often be interrupted by changing the dose or by using another drug. An ongoing relationship with the treating physician and the therapist is essential, especially if drug substitutions are to be attempted. Consult Crenshaw and Goldberg (1996) for a comprehensive discussion of sexual pharmacology.

Vascular Problems

Any disease process that interferes with the circulation of blood throughout the body will inevitably cause a reduction in the penile blood supply required for the maintenance of an erection. The arteries pump the blood away from the heart to the organs throughout the body. During sexual stimulation, the penile arteries dilate, increasing the circulation to the corpora cavernosa of the penis.

A sedentary lifestyle combined with a high-fat diet often results in clogged arteries, eventually leading to vascular changes that restrict the blood flow in the veins and arteries throughout the body. Ultimately, the adverse vascular changes will impact the amount of blood supply to the penis. Vascular disease is not an expected consequence of aging, nor is erectile dysfunction. Unfortunately, these two preventable conditions are seen all too often as men get older.

Medical conditions that cause or contribute to *arterial* circulation problems associated with erectile dysfunction include arteriosclerosis (hardening of the arteries), elevated blood pressure, high cholesterol, and diabetes (Gill, 1997). Although not a medical condition per se, smoking causes arterial changes that contribute to organ and vascular disease. In these instances, the arterial blood flow throughout the entire body is compromised; the penile arteries cannot dilate sufficiently to maintain an erection. The vascular disturbances associated with these medical conditions constitute the presenting problems of a significant number of men and their partners seen by the authors for psychotherapy.

Since an intricate network of veins carries blood away from body organs back to the heart, *venous* problems can interfere with erectile functioning. For example, with a venous outflow problem, the blood flows *out* of the penis as tumescence occurs, rather than remaining trapped within the corpora cavernosa (Eid & Pearce, 1993; Wagner & Kaplan, 1993). The arteries pump the blood into the penis but it "leaks" out again. Because the outflow occurs in veins close to the surface of the skin, sometimes a tourniquet applied to the base of the penis can help.

Certain injuries, surgeries, tumors, or diseases of the penis can contribute to structural or circulatory problems that interfere with erection (Jarrow & Lowe, 1997). Peyronie's disease is an illness of unknown etiology in which plaques of fibrous tissue grow inside the dorsal portion of the penis, causing strictures, curvature of the erect penis, and pain during erection. Sometimes, erectile difficulties can be the first sign of a disease process such as Peyronie's. When conducting a sex history, it is prudent to include questions about the onset and pattern of the erectile dysfunction as well as asking about any changes in the physical appearance of the penis.

Hormonal Problems

Physical examination and blood studies are recommended for all adults on an annual basis. It is especially important to recommend a referral to a physician specializing in internal medicine or urology when a man experiences an erectile dysfunction to rule out the numerous possible physical causes, especially those that are hormonal in nature. The body regulates a delicate balance in the production of hormones required for an erection.

Too much or too little of certain hormones can contribute to erectile diffi-culties. According to Gill (1997), some of these hormones include: *thy-roxin*, produced by the thyroid gland; *prolactin*, produced in the pituitary gland within the base of the brain; *steroids* and *adrenalin*, produced in the adrenal glands above the kidneys; and *testosterone*, produced in the testes.

The only way to know for certain if the difficulty in obtaining and main-taining an erection is hormonal in origin is to have a blood test prescribed by a physician. The authors typically ask the client to schedule an appoint-ment with his personal physician. Sometimes the client is asked to obtain a specific laboratory test, for example, to measure his testosterone levels, before we proceed with the therapy.

MEDICAL EVALUATION

Initial Assessment

In order to determine the extent of organic pathology present, the therapist begins the assessment with medical questions. Later, psychological factors related to the individual, the couple, and the family of origin are addressed. Finally, the therapist assesses the extent to which the etiology is organic, psychogenic, or combined. The therapist conducts the first step in the eval-uation of organic factors when s/he inquires about the man's medical history. These questions may be asked either in a conjoint or individual session, depending on the availability of the man's partner. Of course, if he is married or in a relationship, the authors prefer the joint format be-cause both partners are encouraged in the early phases of therapy to share a collective perspective, rather than making the man the identified patient. Also, it is more comprehensive if the man's partner is present to provide additional information about the onset and persistence of the erectile prob-lem as well as any additional medical data the man may have overlooked or withheld. Each partner contributes factual information about overall health, past medical history, medications taken, and onset of the erectile difficulties. An evaluation by a physician will also be necessary if there is a suspicion that the etiology is organic.

First, determine the date of the man's last physical examination that included blood and urine studies, an electrocardiogram, and a rectal exami-nation of the prostate. We explain to clients who are not in the habit of obtaining annual medical evaluations, especially those who are 40 or older, that many potentially dangerous diseases can begin insidiously and remain undetected without medical intervention. Next, ask for a list of any pre-scription drugs the client is taking, length of time he has been on the medication, and dosage. As already noted, certain medications can cause or contribute to erectile problems, particularly if they are taken for several months or years. Moreover, prescribed medications automatically add information about the disease being treated. Inquire about why the man is taking each medication. Ask about nonprescription drugs as well, especially those taken for allergies and sleep problems. In addition, because erectile competence is associated with good health, general, matter-of-fact questions about diet, exercise, smoking history, and recreational drug usage such as alcohol or marijuana reveal information about overall health. Erectile dysfunction is associated with smoking, drinking, elevated cholesterol, diabetes, and cardiovascular disease. Also inquire about any medical problems in the past for which he was treated medically or surgically. Finally, ask about the structure of the penis, if there are curvatures, injuries, or other abnormalities. Determine if excessive exercise such as bicycling, trauma, stress, or occupational activities such as lifting are currently placing him at risk for erectile dysfunction.

Within the last year, the authors have seen several men who have self-medicated with Viagra or other prescription drugs. Typically, these men are physicians themselves who have decided to try Viagra to see if it works, or they are nonphysicians who have engaged in the dangerous practice of obtaining Viagra over the Internet without a medical examination. Even though it might be difficult to convince a physician to be examined medically, the therapist must nonetheless firmly enlist his cooperation before undertaking a course of psychotherapy for erectile dysfunction. Obviously, it is unacceptable to proceed with psychotherapy unless the man complies with the requirement for a medical examination to rule out the presence of underlying diseases that would contraindicate the use of Viagra.

Sometimes an erectile dysfunction can be an early symptom of a greater underlying medical problem, such as diabetes or cardiovascular disease. In such cases, men typically report greater than normative age-related changes in erectile capacity over a period of months or years. Usually, when there is organic etiology, the man has experienced a psychological overlay of anxiety by the time he seeks treatment, making it difficult to distinguish the degree to which the dysfunction is caused by organic pathology versus the effects of performance anxiety. Most cases of erectile dysfunction have a mixed etiology and it is impossible to be absolutely certain of the extent of organic pathology without a medical examination.

Unless the therapist suspects that the erectile dysfunction is purely psychogenic, a medical consultation is necessary. Although it is more customary to require a medical work-up, in some instances questioning alone can determine if the dysfunction is psychogenic. For instance, if the man is younger than 40, denies medical problems, has no difficulty sustaining an

erection during masturbation, and reports robust erections upon awakening from sleep, proceed with psychotherapy. If the erectile dysfunction does
not remit with psychological treatment, require a medical evaluation even
though the presumed etiology is psychogenic.

Physical Examination

The next phase of the medical evaluation is conducted by the general prac-
titioner or internist, who will order laboratory tests to determine if there
are any neurological, vascular, or hormonal problems. Sometimes a referral
to a urologist is necessary, but this always follows the general medical
examination. In our experience, it is not uncommon for the man to report
that he has not had a medical examination in several years; therefore, he
might need help in selecting a physician or discussing a plan of action. His
partner can be very helpful in this process provided that s/he has been
a part of the therapeutic alliance. Sometimes the man is referred to the
psychotherapist by a urologist who has already performed the necessary
diagnostic tests. In this case, the therapist needs to assess if the man is a
reliable informant or if the physician needs to be involved in a discussion
of the man's medical condition. Of course, a signed release is necessary if
the therapist intends to consult with the physician.

During the physical examination, the physician observes skin coloring,
pupillary reflexes, and neurological indices such as balance and coordination in an effort to assess overall circulatory, cardiac, and neurological
functioning. Due to the nature of the presenting problem, the genitals are
examined for the presence of any abnormalities that could interfere with
erection, such as Peyronie's disease, testicular atrophy, injury, scarring, or
previous surgery. In addition, the penile nerves are evaluated superficially
by checking the bulbocavernosus reflex. This is performed by squeezing the
glans of the penis while the man is in the supine position, noting the reflex
contraction of the anal sphincter. This enables a cursory evaluation of the
ability of penile nerves to provide adequate sensation to the penis, an important requirement for erectile functioning.

Laboratory Tests and an Electrocardiogram

Blood and urine tests are used to measure hormone levels, such as testosterone and prolactin, which need to be in proper balance for normal erectile
functioning. Cholesterol and triglyceride levels are indicators of cardiac
function; elevated indices can signal the presence of or potential for cardiovascular disease. An electrocardiogram, also a part of a normal physical
examination, gives the doctor information about the conduction of electri-

cal activity within the heart muscle. Through this noninvasive test, many cardiac and cardiovascular problems can be discovered. Elevated blood sugar levels or urine glucose can signal the presence of underlying diabetes.

Rectal Examination

A rectal examination is performed to check for the presence of blood in the stool, which can be a sign of a more serious colorectal condition. Also, the physician can check for prostatitis, an inflammation of the prostate, during the rectal examination by palpating the prostate to determine if there is hypertrophy or enlargement (which can either be a malignant or benign condition). In either instance, the enlarged prostate may compress the delicate nerves and blood vessels that supply the penis, thereby contributing to erectile problems. Pain or discomfort from prostatitis or hypertrophy can also interfere with sexual activity.

Sleep Monitoring

Normally, erections occur during REM sleep and upon awakening from sleep. If sleep erections do not occur, it may be because the blood or nerve supply to the penis is interrupted. The nocturnal penile tumescence (NPT) study monitors the frequency, rigidity, and girth of erections during REM sleep. This is usually performed in a sleep laboratory because the man needs to be connected to sensitive instruments that measure penile tumescence and the cyclical sleep stages. Sometimes a portable monitor can be used at home, but the results tend to be less accurate. The testing is typically performed over two or three nights in order to obtain the most representative results. The diagnostic value of the NPT is questionable, though, because many variables need to be considered when using the test (Schiavi, 1988). For instance, some normal men have been found to have abnormal results and men with physical problems sometimes have normal results. Since the man's penis and scalp are connected to machines, understandably he might not sleep well and the results will be inaccurate. Also, the NPT study is expensive and time-consuming. Schiavi (1992) offers a thorough discussion of the NPT and other tests used in the diagnosis of erectile dysfunction.

Two simple noninvasive devices used to screen for sleeping erections are: Snap-Gauge and RigiScan. Both contain tensiometric loops that record changes in penile tumescence and rigidity. There is some question about the reliability of these tests, though, because the results are often imprecise (Allen & Brendler, 1990). More recently, Karadeniz, Topsakal, Aydogmus, and Beksan (1997) found that RigiScan reliably differentiated organic from psychogenic impotence. However, the authors recommend a multidisciplinary diagnostic approach in order to increase reliability.

The nocturnal penile rigidity tests are of little value in classifying the etiology or determining the severity of an erectile problem. Their value is solely in determining the *absence* of erectile functioning. However, the man can still have underlying medical problems while being able to have one good erection per night.

Penile Blood Pressure

The blood pressure within the six penile arteries can be measured noninvasively by using an inflatable blood pressure cuff, which is wrapped around the base of the penis, in conjunction with an ultrasound flow detector. However, this test is time-consuming and often inaccurate because the cavernosal arteries, which are primarily responsible for tumescence, are difficult to record (Schiavi, 1988).

Other Urology Tests

Once it is determined that an erectile dysfunction has an organic cause, the urologist uses a variety of tests to determine the etiology and extent of the problem. The physical examination and laboratory sleep studies help to guide the urologist in deciding which further diagnostic tests are necessary. Some of the tests are noninvasive, such as the strain gauge plethysmography and the pulse wave assessment of penile blood flow. It is beyond the scope of this book to discuss these procedures; detailed reviews are offered by Broderick (1998) and Schiavi (1992).

Other tests involve the injection of a medication into the corpora cavernosa, such as papaverine, which stimulates penile erection. Prior to and during tumescence, the penile arteries and corpora cavernosa are evaluated for unrestricted blood flow. The ultrasound investigation discussed below is an example of an invasive test that provides information about the cause and severity of an erectile dysfunction.

Ultrasound Investigation

In some instances, the urologist performs ultrasound studies when vascular problems of the penis are suspected. An instrument called a Doppler is used in conjunction with the ultrasound test to measure blood flow within the arteries of the penis. The ultrasound is a noninvasive, painless test used to measure the diameter of the penile arteries in a resting state by scanning the vessels for the presence of strictures or lesions, such as plaque deposits or actual hardening of the arteries that could impede circulation. After the initial ultrasound is performed, a vasodilating drug is injected into one or more of the penile arteries. A normal artery will dilate in response to the stimulation of the vasodilator. (Once the artery is dilated after the injection, the blood flow will increase provided there is no disease within the artery.) This is relatively painless, although there can be mild discomfort at the injection site. After the injection, the artery is again measured by ultrasound for the most reliable results (Lue, Hricak, Schmidt, & Tanagho, 1986). In addition, the corpora cavernosa are also scanned for the presence of scarring or fibrotic lesions that can potentially restrict tumescence (Eid & Pearce, 1993).

Another medical condition that can be detected with these tests is the venous flow problem discussed earlier. If there is a venous leak, the arteries will dilate normally and blood will flow into the penis, although there will be no erection because the blood is simultaneously emptied through the many superficial veins.

Cavernosography and Cavernosometry

The next level of diagnostic tests involves a more invasive examination of the corpora cavernosa within the penis. These tests are recommended when vascular problems are detected through the ultrasound studies and additional clarification of intensity and significance is needed.

Neurological Testing of the Penis

Although vascular disturbances are the most common etiological factor in organic erectile dysfunction, there may be a neurological etiology in the form of an interruption or disruption in the delicate web of nerves that supply the penis. The neurological measurement of penile nerves has not been standardized and there is conflicting evidence about the diagnostic value of any of these tests (Broderick, 1998). Nevertheless, they are used to evaluate neuropathy in men with erectile dysfunction. The most common tests include: penile electromyelograms, bulbocavernosus reflex latency (Parys, Evans, & Parsons, 1988), dorsal nerve conduction velocity (Bradley, Linn, & Johnson, 1984), and the somatosensory evoked potential test (Padma-Nathan, 1988). The reader is referred to the discussion by Schiavi (1992) for a more detailed understanding of these tests.

MEDICAL TREATMENTS

In the last decade, new medical treatments for erectile dysfunction have developed rapidly, influencing the psychological approaches to managing erectile problems. Now therapists are challenged to understand the many factors fundamental to the structure and functioning of the male sexual system. Moreover, flexibility is required when combining the medical and psychological treatments for erectile dysfunction.

Three significant medical advances occurred in the treatment of erectile dysfunction during this decade: development of the intracavernosal injection (Linet & Ogring, 1996), the transuretheral suppository (Padma-Nathan et al., 1997), and the oral medication, Viagra (Goldstein et al., 1998). Medical treatments for erectile dysfunction currently include: penile implants, vacuum pumps, tourniquets, injections, transurethral suppositories, a prescription drug, herbs, homeopathic remedies, and, in rare instances, vascular surgery. Many of these treatments have been available for the last 20 years but were not discussed as openly as the new pill, Viagra. Each medical regimen is replete with contraindications and side effects. Most of them require the man and his partner to adjust to procedures or paraphernalia that could interrupt spontaneous sexual enjoyment. Others, such as herbal remedies, are not only questionable in terms of efficacy but may also have harmful side effects. Many men and their partners, however, have chosen to tolerate the discomforts and risks associated with these medical treatments in order to regain erectile functioning during sexual activity.

The following section examines the existing medical treatments for erectile dysfunction. It is possible that by the time of publication of this text, there will be more advances in this rapidly changing treatment arena.

Vacuum Pump

The vacuum pump, first released in 1982, is a noninvasive device used to facilitate an erection. Many FDA-approved vacuum devices are available by prescription. A vacuum system consists of three parts: a pump, a vacuum cylinder, and a tension ring. After applying a tourniquet or tension ring loosely around the base of the penis, the man or his partner inserts the penis into a clear plastic vacuum cylinder. The pump creates a vacuum by drawing air from the plastic cylinder, removing air from around the penis. The vacuum effect then draws blood into the corpora cavernosa of the penis through the penile arteries, temporarily trapping the blood in the now tumescent penis. The erection is maintained by tightening the tourniquet or tension ring around the base of the penis. The clear plastic cylinder is removed before sexual relations. After sexual relations, the tourniquet is removed. According to Trapp (1998), the overall success rate is about 90% regardless of etiology. The vacuum pump is considered safe for most men with the exception of those with a coagulation disorder or prior priapism. The most commonly reported side effects include hematoma, bruising, and discomfort (Turner, Althof, Levine, Kursh, Bodner, & Resnick, 1990). Because of the pressure of the tourniquet on the penile nerves and spermatic cord, ejaculation is sometimes difficult. In addition, some couples are distracted by the pump apparatus and find it sexually unappealing. The erection sustained from using the pump can be incomplete, giving the appearance of a "floppy" penis, according to some of our clients. This is a less than satisfactory outcome and explains why some do not like using the pump.

Venous Flow Controller

The Actis device, manufactured by Vivus, is a latex tourniquet that enhances erections by trapping blood in the erect penis. It is an adjustable loop that is placed around the base of the penis, allowing blood to enter the corpora cavernosa through the penile arteries and preventing the outflow of blood from the veins near the surface of the penis. It should not be used for more than 30 minutes at a time because of the risk of impaired circulation. Like the tourniquet used with the vacuum pump, the venous flow controller can make ejaculation difficult. Some men experience retrograde ejaculation, whereby the ejaculate is forced into the bladder rather than being expelled through the penile urethra. Although harmless, retrograde ejaculation is another unwanted side effect of the tourniquet.

Penile Implants

Penile implants were introduced in 1966 and have been used by increasing numbers of men with erectile dysfunction for over two decades. Because of the recent availability of other less invasive remedies, demand for the penile implant procedure decreased dramatically by the mid-1990s. A urologist who consults with the us, for example, reported that he performed over 200 operations a year prior to 1995 when Caverject (the injectable treatment; see below) was FDA approved. Since then he has performed only a few implant surgeries per year.

There are many versions of penile implants, but they fall into two general categories: a flexible rod type or an inflatable implant. In both procedures, flexible or inflatable tubes are inserted into the corpora cavernosa of the penis, enabling sufficient tumescence for sexual relations. The flexible implant is made of silicone and stainless steel or silver and can be manipulated into different positions for sexual relations, rest, or daily ordinary activities. The inflatable implant includes more working components than the flexible version. A pump is usually inserted into the scrotum and a reservoir of sterile liquid is infused from the abdomen where it is stored. When an erection is desired, the man pumps the fluid from the reservoir to the cylinders within the penis.

Penile implants are permanent and require a surgical procedure for insertion. The benefits of an implant need to be carefully weighed against the associated risks of invasive surgery, anesthesia, and infection (Govier et al., 1998; Rossi et al., 1997). In a small number of recipients, the pump fails and needs to be surgically replaced. According to Lewis and McLaren (1993), the repair rate is 5–15% in the first 5 years. Most penile prostheses, especially the inflatables, need to be replaced in 15 to 20 years (Mulcahy, 1998). Also, the authors have worked with clients who have been disappointed by the results of their penile implant. They complained that penetration was difficult, even with the implant inflated, because the penile glans remains flaccid, although the shaft was rigid.

Considering the surgical, mechanical, and financial issues involved in using a penile implant, this option should be carefully chosen only after thorough consideration of other options. In order to avoid revision surgery or other complications, only carefully selected and well-informed men should consider this option (Nukui, Okamoto, Nagata, Kurokawa, & Fukui, 1997). It is the responsibility of the therapist to review the advantages and risks associated with this choice as well as discussing the other medical treatments. For men who do not respond well to the other medical treatments, however, the penile implant remains a viable medical option.

Injection Therapy

Intracavernosal injections were first used for the treatment of erectile dysfunction in the mid-1980s after an accidental discovery that certain vasodilators produce erections when injected into the penis (Lue & Tanagno, 1987). The science of injection therapy was inexact at first, as various uncontrolled combinations of medications were used to promote smooth muscle relaxation and tumescence. Such medications were mixed in a "cocktail" tailored to the needs of each man by his treating urologist. The efficacy and safety of these pharmacological cocktails for intracavernosal therapy had not been studied systematically until Caverject was developed by Upjohn and finally approved by the FDA in 1995 (Linet & Ogring, 1996). This direct delivery approach involves injecting alprostadil (Caverject), a vasodilator, directly into the corpora cavernosa of the penis roughly 20 minutes prior to anticipated sex. Essentially, the injection promotes an erection that can last for an hour by increasing the blood flow into the penis. There is a significant dose-response relationship: Better erectile responses occur as the dose is increased (Linet & Ogring, 1996). Even high-dose injection therapy does not work for men with severe vascular disease. Each man requires an individualized regimen; most men using Caverject report successful erections once the proper dose is found. The recommended frequency of injection is three times per week and no more than once daily. Injection therapy promotes robust erections in over 90% of men and is considerably more reliable than the transuretheral pellet (Linet & Ogring, 1996).

Alprostadil (Caverject) is the most effective intracavernosal preparation with the least likelihood of side effects (Wilke et al., 1997). Various other substances can be used singly or in combination, such as papaverine, phentolamine, and prostoglandin. Some of these combinations can produce a priopic condition, a persistent, painful erection that does not detumesce and does not relate to sexual desire. Priapism is considered a medical emergency because prolonged engorgement of the penis without venous drainage can cause damage to the erectile tissue. In addition to priapism, other unpleasant side effects may occur with injection therapy. Although the needle is very small, some men report pain or burning from the medication and/or bruising, bleeding, or fibrosis at the injection site (Althof et al., 1987; Linet & Ogring, 1996). Needle use also necessitates safe-sex practices because the injection site is a point of entry for organisms and sexually transmitted viruses. Aside from the possible side effects is the less-than-ideal reality that the resulting erection is not dependent upon sexual desire. Once the decision is made to inject, an erection occurs until the drug effect dissipates. For this reason, injection therapy is considered less natural than oral sildenafil (Viagra).

Most men using Caverject are satisfied with their erections and the reported side effects are relatively minimal (Sundaram, 1997; Wilke et al., 1997). Intracavernosal injection is therefore a viable treatment option for long-term erectile dysfunction. The literature does report that some users discontinue treatment after an initial period of satisfaction (Sundaram et al., 1997). Perhaps these men or their partners discover that injecting the penis in order to have an erection is ultimately unsatisfying. Sexton, Benedict, and Jarrow (1998) believe that the reason for discontinuing treatment may be unrelated to the modality since compliance problems occur with other forms of treatment as well. Nonetheless, counseling should be encouraged so that the couple can discuss their reactions to the various forms of treatment, including injection therapy.

The Transurethral Suppository

In 1996, the first transurethral suppository was approved by the FDA for the treatment of erectile dysfunction. This product, manufactured by Vivus as the MUSE system (medicated urethral system for erection), is a tiny pellet that is inserted into the penile urethra, using a thin plastic applicator, approximately 15 minutes prior to desired sexual relations. The pellet contains alprostadil (a vasodilator), which dissolves within the urethra and is absorbed into the corpora cavernosa of the penis. Relaxation of the smooth muscles surrounding the corpora cavernosa occurs, promoting vasodilation of the penile veins and arteries. The resulting erection can last for an hour.

According to some studies (Costabile et al., 1998; Padma-Nathan et al., 1997; Williams et al., 1998) more than 50% of the men using the transurethral pellet in a dose-escalating regimen experienced satisfactory erections. These optimistic clinical studies were contrasted by others, which reported disappointing results, even at the highest doses (Engel & McVary, 1998; Fulgham et al., 1998; Porst, 1997; Werthman & Rajfer, 1997). In these instances, the erections were only partially rigid or there was no response whatsoever to the alprostadil. Another problem with the transurethral suppository is that it can be painful. One of the most commonly reported side effects was a burning sensation within the urethra after the pellet was inserted, although the incidence varied from 10–30% depending on the study (Hellstrom et al., 1996; Padma-Nathan et al., 1997; Porst, 1997; Werthman & Rajfer, 1997). In our practices, we have found that MUSE is reported by our patients to be less reliable than the injection method perhaps because it is unevenly absorbed by the penis. Even at the highest doses many men experience only a partially rigid erection which is insufficient for intercourse. Our experience is consistent with that of Fulgham and colleagues (1998): Only a small percentage of clients continued to use the transurethral pellet at home due to penile discomfort and limited efficacy.

Vascular Surgery

Usually, vascular surgery of the penis is a last resort for the treatment of erectile dysfunction due to vascular compromise. It is extremely difficult to repair tiny nerves, veins, and arteries that are impeding circulation within the penis, which is why surgical intervention for erectile dysfunction is considered controversial. Vascular surgery is considered only when a patient has failed to respond to the nonsurgical methods and is not prepared to undergo the rigors of a penile implant. Most of the studies of microvascularization report results that are less than encouraging (Sarramon, Bertrand, Malavand, & Rischmann, 1997). Although the surgery may improve blood flow to the penis, the man may not be able to sustain a spontaneous erection or he might need pharmacological therapy, such as the intracavernosal injection, in order to achieve an erection (Drawz, Kittner, Seiter, & Schnemichen, 1998; Manning et al., 1998). Generally, only a small percentage of men with vascular problems are candidates for the surgery. The selection criteria eliminate men over 50 and those with diabetes (Manning et al., 1998). Even properly selected candidates have a low rate of regaining the capacity for spontaneous erection (Manning et al., 1998). Nonetheless, this type of surgery is effective for some men.

Drug Therapy

Many oral drugs believed to affect sexual arousal have remained uncontrolled by the Food and Drug Administration (FDA). These nonprescription herbal and homeopathic remedies, such as ginsing, licorice, and teas made from hops are sold in pharmacies and health food stores. Another oral preparation, yohimbine, is made from a substance extracted from the bark of an African tree. One of the oldest known remedies for the treatment of sexual problems, yohimbine comes in many formulations: synthetic (Yocon, Yohimex, Aphrodyne), herbal (YBRON), homeopathic, and in combination formulas. Crenshaw and Goldberg (1996) discuss the many actions and uses of yohimbine. The FDA has not formally approved yohimbine for the treatment of erectile dysfunction per se. Nonetheless, many doctors prescribe it because there is a growing body of research suggesting that yohimbine *may* be helpful in the management of erectile dysfunction (Crenshaw & Goldberg, 1996; Ernst & Pittler, 1998). Others, however, have found little or no effect on sexual arousal (Morales et al., 1987; Teloken, Rhoden, Sogari, Dambros, & Souto, 1998). There is also evidence of side effects known to be associated with this substance such as agitation, elevated blood pressure, mania, depression, and anxiety (Guirguis, 1998). In many of the studies, the results do not approach statistical significance or the number of men in the sample is too small to generalize to the population at large. Because it is believed to be natural or homeopathic, many consumers are unaware of the serious side effects of yohimbine.

Sildenafil

Viagra is the only oral medication approved by the FDA for the treatment of erectile dysfunction (Goldstein et al., 1998). Released in 1998, it is intended for men who wish to regain erectile compentency but it is not an aphrodisiac and does not directly increase the sexual appetite. Sildenafil acts selectively to facilitate an erection (when the man is stimulated) without causing unwanted vasodilatation throughout the rest of the body. Typically, it is taken 30 to 60 minutes prior to sexual relations. In over 80% of the men studied, sexual performance improved once the correct dose was determined (Goldstein et al., 1998).

Sildenafil acts in conjunction with the presence of sexual desire. The brain sends electrical signals throughout the body by releasing neurotransmitters at the nerve endings of body organs. During sexual arousal, the brain alerts the penis to release the neurotransmitter nitric oxide which in turn produces a second chemical messenger within the penis called cyclic GNP, which causes the smooth muscles of the penis to relax, thereby promoting vasodilatation (and tumescence) (Goldstein et al., 1998). Men with erectile problems do not produce enough cyclic GNP. Sildenafil promotes the release of nitric oxide and inhibits the breakdown of cyclic GNP, making the penis more responsive to sexual stimulation. The result is a natural erection that occurs *only if the man desires sex*; sildenafil has no effect on the flaccid penis.

In rare instances, the chemicals in sildenafil that cause vasodilatation in the penis stray into other parts of the body and produce side effects such as flushing (Guirguis, 1998). Also, sildenafil can effect an enzyme in the retina of the eye, causing tinted blue vision; this is reported infrequently. The most common side effects of headache, flushing, and indigestion are mild, transient, and occur in less than 10% of the men studied (Goldstein et al., 1998; Padma-Nathan et al., 1998). However, sildenafil can interact dangerously with other vasodilators, causing excessive dilation of the blood vessels throughout the body and a drop in blood pressure. Sildenafil amplifies the impact of nitrate-based heart medications and the combined effect of the drugs can be fatal; therefore the two medications cannot be taken concurrently.

In 1999, Pfizer expanded its safety information in the labeling of Viagra by updating the known side effects based on postmarketing data. Several kinds of side effects were reported, and a warning issued regarding the possibility of serious cardiac disturbances, even sudden death, that have been reported to occur in a small percentage of men either during or after sexual activity. It is not possible to determine if the cardiac problems were directly related to Viagra use; some men may have had underlying cardiovascular disease that was aggravated by sexual activity following years of inactivity. Of course, men for whom sexual activity is inadvisable due to cardiovascular disease should not use treatments for erectile dysfunction, including Viagra. For this reason therapists need to require a complete medical work-up on men with whom they are discussing treatment that will increase sexual activity.

Although sildenafil works by enhancing sexual arousal, indirectly it can promote increased sexual desire by reducing the man's fear of erectile failure (Perelman, 1998). Free of anticipatory anxiety, he can once again experience sexual desire and fantasy and then proceed to the next stage of the sexual response cycle: sexual arousal. In addition, sildenafil use might indirectly enhance the relational aspects of sex by reducing or eliminating the hurtful pattern of sexual avoidance that arose as the couple began to anticipate failure, disappointment, anxiety, anger, rejection, etc. Climaxing is no longer rushed for fear of losing the erection.

So far, the use of sildenafil in men who do *not* have an erectile dysfunction of organic etiology has not been studied. It would seem, however, that there might be an unexpected positive effect as a further result of the popularity of Viagra. As previously emphasized, this requires a medical examination to rule out underlying conditions associated with erectile dysfunction, such as diabetes or heart disease. Perhaps because of the amount of publicity and/or because this treatment does not involve devices such as a pump, injection, or suppository, men are more inclined to try it. In our practices, it is not uncommon for the partner to encourage the man to consider Viagra.

ORAL DRUGS OF THE FUTURE

There are a number of oral medications for erectile problems currently under investigation by various drug companies. With the exception of sildenafil, the FDA has not yet approved the use of any oral erectogenic medications, although the manufacturers are currently conducting clinical trials.

Apomorphine

Unlike sildenafil, apomorphine (manufactured by Tap Pharmaceuticals) works centrally by exciting chemicals in the brain associated with sexual arousal. It stimulates the production of penile neurotransmitters that allow the smooth muscles and the blood vessels to dilate. The problem with this drug is that it causes nausea and vomiting, especially in higher doses. Tap Pharmaceuticals is working on a sublingual version that, while taken orally, dissolves more slowly, reducing the risk of nausea.

Phentolamine (Vasomax)

Manufactured by Zonagen, Vasomax is an oral version of the injectable drug phentolamine, previously used in conjunction with other drugs to treat erectile dysfunction. It works by preventing stress hormones from interfering with erections. Taken orally, however, it causes the blood vessels throughout the body to dilate, thereby reducing the blood pressure while improving erections. Therefore, the effects are not specific to the penis; men taking oral phentolamine are at risk for systemic side effects such as flushing or even fainting. One small study showed promising results with the use of oral phentolamine in cases of organic erectile dysfunction (Becker et al., 1998). Another study suggested that oral phentolamine, used in conjunction with intracavernosal injection, may have a beneficial effect in men for whom injection therapy alone fails (Kaplan, Reis, Kohn, Shabsigh, & Te, 1998). Further clinical research is needed before it is ready for presentation to the FDA.

Other Drugs

In addition to the two oral medications discussed above, there are numerous other treatments for erectile dysfunction currently in the stage of preliminary trials. These include injectable drug combinations (Quadmix and Trimix), transurethral suppositories (Alibra by Vivus), topical applications (Topiglan by MacroChem), and products using nitric oxide in conjunction with other compounds (NitRx by NitroMed). For more information, consult the following websites: www.viagra.com; www.vivus.com; www.nitromed.com; and www.macrochem.com.

Assessment and treatment of erectile dysfunction continue to change rapidly, although some of the treatment technology is still at a preliminary stage. The future treatment of erectile dysfunction is certain to blend the ever-changing medical discoveries and the less rapidly evolving psychological modalities. In order for marital/sex therapists to remain current in their approach to treating erectile problems, greater knowledge and comfort with the medical technologies is essential.

3

⌘ ⌘ ⌘ ⌘ ⌘

Psychological Aspects of Erectile Dysfunction

THE PURPOSE OF THIS CHAPTER IS TO IDENTIFY some of the psychological risk factors that contribute to an erectile problem. In everyday language, we tend to think in terms of finding *a cause* for a problem or a disorder. A risk factor is a condition, circumstance, or vulnerability within the individual or the couple that could predispose the male partner to an erectile dysfunction. Unfortunately, a single event or factor rarely causes mental health problems, and psychogenic sexual difficulties are no exception. They tend to be multicausal phenomena, involving a confluence of risk factors that contribute to the problem's manifestation.

Many of the contributors to Rosen and Leiblum's (1992b) text on the assessment and treatment of erectile disorders also argue for a multicausal framework in explaining erectile dysfunction. They found that two risk factors were evident in at least two-thirds of reported cases of erectile dysfunction. In fact, all the contributors writing from a psychological perspective argued for a biopsychosocial explanation. In other words, the dysfunction is seen as having biological, psychological, and social components. Some authors stressed one component more than another, but they all seemed to agree on the underlying premise of multicausality. Our intersystemic approach builds on this concept in proposing that the erectile dysfunction should be conceptualized in individual, interactional, and intergenerational dimensions.

Before discussing the various risk factors identified in the intersystemic framework, we should note the many historical explanations of erectile dysfunction. Kaplan (1974) offered an overview of these early psychoanalytic, system theory, and learning theory explanations and proffered her own psychosomatic theory.

The focus in this chapter is on identifying the psychological risk factors; in a later chapter, we will identify the medical risk factors. One of the historical debates in determining appropriate treatment for erectile dysfunction has concerned whether it is an organic or a psychological problem. Masters and Johnson (1970) believed it was primarily a psychological problem. Many physicians today believe it is primarily medical, and certainly the popularity of Viagra has given the medical model more power. The lay person assumes that if a pill solves the problem, it must have been medical in nature. No definitive studies distinguishing between organic and psychogenic causality in erectile dysfunction exist. Our experience suggests that, more often than not, there is an overlap of both components. Though the degree of organicity or psychogenic pathology varies with each individual, it is common for one factor, such as anxiety, to predispose the patient to an increased vulnerability to the effects of organic pathology.

We do know that some cases are primarily organic, some primarily psychogenic, and some involve a mixture of organic and psychological risk factors. Making a differential diagnosis for a disorder that has so many risk factors poses a considerable challenge. Those cases that defy classification are labeled idiopathic. These men may still be treated, but the treatment is not so systematic as it might otherwise be if the causes were well understood. To further complicate matters, identifying the risk factors becomes more difficult the older the man is at the time of seeking treatment. The previous chapter discussed age-related changes in physiology related to erectile functioning. As men age, the number of medical risk factors increases, and they become more vulnerable to the anxiety because their bodies are no longer as robust. When assessing a young man for an erectile problem, the chances are that it is psychogenically-based; when assessing an older man, the chances are that it is organically-based. It is valid for clinicians to assume that as men grow older, sexual responsivity is more susceptible to the influences of anxiety. For middle-aged men, the problem may be a mix of the two.

It is important not to overlook a whole class of risk factors due to one's training and biases. Mental health professionals are prone to look for psychological risk factors; physicians are prone to look for medical risk factors. We believe that every erectile dysfunction has a secondary if not a primary psychological risk factor, even when the problem had a medical origin. For example, suppose a man has had prostate surgery and suffered nerve damage. Before the surgery, he never had an erectile problem. After the surgery, his erectile ability returned slowly, but his erections were never as firm and as lasting as before surgery. It is clear the problem has a medical basis, but the erectile problem also triggers psychological responses that now contribute to the continuation of the problem. Every time the man attempts to function sexually, he is fearful, anxious, and apprehensive, and feels a sense of grief over the loss of something he had enjoyed in the past. These feelings interfere with his ability to attain and sustain the erection. The following example illustrates that though not every man with a psychogenic erectile dysfunction needs medical intervention, every man with an organic erectile dysfunction does need psychological intervention.

Harry,* age 52, entered therapy at the insistence of his wife. The couple had heard one of the authors give a presentation at a prostate cancer support group about the psychological and sexual effects of prostate cancer. One year had passed since Harry had undergone his prostate surgery to remove a small tumor. The physical trauma of the surgery had rendered him completely incapable of sustaining an erection during the first few months. He was beginning to regain some erectile ability, but his erections were inconsistent. He reacted by becoming upset, depressed, overly focused on getting the erection, and worried about his wife's reaction.

We began by dealing with his emotional reactions to the cancer, the surgery, and the subsequent erection problems. Their relationship showed rapid improvement. Understanding what had happened and why was reassuring. However, Harry's initial response to the sex therapy was disappointing. The couple could communicate sexually and satisfy each other without intercourse, but Harry still had trouble with erections. He was started on Caverject, but his doctor decided to switch him to Viagra. Many men who were using Caverject were switched to Viagra because it was believed to be safer, and men preferred taking a pill to injecting their penis. The Viagra did not work for him, and he went back to Caverject. Using Caverject helped to boost his confidence and decrease his anxiety. As a result, he was sometimes able to achieve a usable erection without using Caverject. It was clear that he still had a physical component to his problem, but the psychological component had improved to the point that he could acquire enough of an erection to enjoy penetration. What had happened was that his anxiety over being able to achieve an erection had been reduced via the therapy. Also, he felt he could interact sexually with his

---

*All names and identifying information of individuals mentioned in this book have been changed to protect their privacy.

wife without the need of an erection. The surgery had produced a residual problem which might never fully resolve. He might need to use Caverject or another type of medical intervention on an ongoing basis.

We will describe the model for this treatment in a later chapter on combining treatment approaches.

INDIVIDUAL PSYCHOLOGICAL RISK FACTORS

Performance Anxiety

Performance anxiety has probably received more attention than any other psychological symptom in the literature on erectile dysfunction. Perhaps this is because Masters and Johnson (1970) stressed this factor in their early work, which became so influential in the field of sex therapy. This anxiety stems from excessive concern over attaining and sustaining erections. The man worries and anticipates negative consequences, inadvertently removing himself emotionally from the pleasurable feelings associated with sex play and intercourse. He participates by "going through the motions"; he is unable to focus on his partner because he is totally and fearfully absorbed in himself as he performs. Masters and Johnson (1970) described the profound role that fear plays in inhibiting the erectile response, as did Kaplan (1974). Performance anxiety, however, is almost always secondary to a failure. A man who has been able to perform sexually is shocked to experience a failure, and he begins to worry that it could happen again. The next time he tries to have sex he anticipates failing, which creates performance anxiety that inhibits his ability to perform.

Although rare, we have seen men who had performance anxiety prior to a failure. These were men who had other risk factors and anticipated that they would not be satisfying sexual partners. One man, for example, was 47 and had limited dating experience. For many years he had felt attracted to young boys, but never acted on these impulses. Years of therapy had helped him lessen his attraction to boys and to begin to find that women could be attractive, but he still feared being sexual with women. He anticipated being criticized by any woman with whom he might attempt to have a relationship because this had been his experience with his mother, who had criticized him from the earliest years to the present. He felt fearful and incompetent going into the sexual situation. Although he had never attempted to have intercourse, he still anticipated he would have an erection problem. With considerable support and information about how erections occur, he was able to begin a sexual relationship with a woman.

Levine (1992) included performance anxiety in his theory of erectile dysfunction and placed this concept within a larger schema in which he stated there are three spheres of causality. The here-and-now sphere is performance anxiety that is anxiety directly related to the sexual situation. Antecedent life events such as an argument with a partner, or a smoldering level of resentment that causes discord but not obvious arguments, are the second sphere. In essence, the man experiences several anxiety-provoking events that then create a general state of anxiety and a gradual deterioration of coping skills. Thirdly, Levine describes developmental vulnerabilities within the family of origin, such as a lack of attachment and caring by a parent. As a result, this person may have inadequate coping or defense mechanisms and be fraught with personality defects that make it difficult to gain support and reassurance from others. Levine's ideas contribute to the individual and dyadic dimensions of the intersystemic framework with greater emphasis on individual factors.

Psychiatric Problems

In addition to performance anxiety, a number of psychiatric problems may affect erectile performance. These risk factors could range from major mental illnesses such as schizophrenia, to the more common disorders such as depression and anxiety, to the lesser recognized personality disorders. It would be impossible to catalogue all the ways in which psychiatric disorders can affect sexual functioning because of individual variabilities.

Major mental illnesses, such as schizophrenia and bipolar disorder, can create systemic personality disorganization. Thoughts and/or feelings are not well modulated, making it difficult to sustain feelings of sexual desire and focus behavior in order to achieve intercourse successfully. Men experiencing a major depression would have little interest in sex and possess little energy to organize themselves for a sexual interaction. A long-term mild depression such as dysthymia can also erode sexual interest and ability. These men learn to conserve their energy and generally experience high levels of self-doubt and guilt. Bipolar illness is more extreme and is considered to have an organic basis. Many of the medications used to treat bipolar illness may interfere with sexual desire and performance. Henry, for example, was a middle-aged professional with a long history of bipolar disorder. He had protracted bouts of severe depression followed by manic behavior during which he used drugs and acted out sexually. His psychological disorganization impeded the build-up of sexual desire, resulting in erection problems.

Depression is also associated with negative affect. Carey, Wincze, and Meisler (1993) reviewed several studies that showed that negative affect and anger tend to lower the level of sexual arousal. Contrary to popular belief, anger inhibits sexual feelings. This impact is usually obvious when the anger is directed toward the partner but less obvious if the source lies elsewhere.

Men who have anxiety disorders (generalized anxiety, phobias, and posttraumatic stress disorder) may be vulnerable to erectile problems because whatever its source, be it sexual or nonsexual, anxiety directly impedes relaxation. Our clinical experience suggests that as the level of anxiety increases, erectile abililty decreases. Morokoff, Baum, McKinnon, and Gillilland (1987) reported that a combination of chronic and acute stress is associated with impaired erectile ability. Chronic stressors might include work issues, conflict over parenting, financial concerns, or ongoing relationship conflicts. Acute stressors might be an argument with one's spouse or an unusually unpleasant event that happened at work. The source of the anxiety is irrelevant, and the level at which it begins to interfere with getting an erection appears to vary across individuals. Some men can tolerate a high level of anxiety without losing erectile ability, while others experience difficulty at a relatively low level.

One of our clients, Jim, had gone through a series of short-term relationships. In each case, the woman ended the relationship complaining about his general lack of respect for her. He was also beginning to drink more heavily than was his adult pattern. Jim realized he was doing something to drive women away and was resorting to alcohol to avoid thinking about the situation. He was also getting worried that he was becoming an alcoholic like his mother. He started to date one woman to whom he was not attracted but who was attracted to him. This relationship, he thought, would enable him to prove to himself that he could keep a woman interested in him. For the first time, he found that he could not sustain an erection.

Some types of personality disorders can be a risk factor predisposing a man to sexual arousal problems. The clearest example would be the obsessive-compulsive type. This individual is overly controlled emotionally and finds it very difficult to experience and express emotions. What is experienced is a great deal of underlying anxiety that he tries to ameliorate through his obsessional thoughts and/or compulsive behavior. Being sexual involves experiencing feelings and sexual sensation, giving up some measure of control and "going with the flow." They do not like to engage in an experience that is messy by its nature. These men tend to prefer a highly controlled sexual encounter and expect everything to go according to their needs or to completely meet the needs of their partners. A related psychiatric disorder is attention deficit disorder (ADD). Men with ADD find it difficult to stay focused, for they are forever mentally distracted. When they are particularly distractible, it may even be difficult for them to focus on their sexual feelings long enough to build much arousal. Since ADD is a continuum disorder, the degree of distractibility varies and so does the degree of difficulty focusing on sexual arousal. The man may be more vulnerable to erectile failure at times of heightened distractibility. Men with obsessive-compulsive disorder and ADD both find it difficult to focus on feelings, although the former is hyperfocused, and the latter is distracted.

To our knowledge, sexual fetishes have not been mentioned in the literature as a risk factor. Some men with fetishes are able to feel aroused only in the presence of their object of desire. They are "turned on" by the favored objects that must be introduced into the sexual interaction to gain full arousal. One man reported that he liked to have sex with his wife, but only if she wore bright red lipstick, a red scarf, and red high-heel shoes. Obviously, it was the fetish that turned him on—not his partner.

Men who are unsure about their sexual orientation may also find they have difficulty with desire and performance. These men sometimes live in a state of sexual confusion, wondering whether they are gay or not. If a man has not recognized or accepted that he is gay and is trying to relate to women, he will probably experience a lack of desire and feel ambivalent about having sex. If he is heterosexual but has fears that he is gay, he may associate various behaviors and desires with being gay. For example, as an adolescent, Bob had a one-time experience of engaging in mutual masturbation with a boy his age. He assumed this must be abnormal and that he was a latent homosexual. Too fearful to ask anyone about this behavior, he labored under this misconception for over 20 years! Whenever he was with his wife sexually, he wondered about the meaning of this experience and felt guilty and confused. Another client reported he could sometimes feel attracted to men and because he liked anal stimulation assumed he must have some "latent homosexuality." This client's underlying question was whether he might really be gay.

Not surprisingly, men with other psychogenic sexual dysfunctions are at risk for erectile difficulties. Masters and Johnson (1970) found that about 50% of the men who experienced an erectile problem were also premature ejaculators. Typically, when a man ejaculates prematurely, he becomes extremely concerned and tries to slow down. This attempt usually fails; he becomes more anxious over ejaculating too quickly, fails again, and the anxiety continues to mount. In effect, he is too preoccupied with his penis and whether it will fail him by ejaculating too soon. He has developed performance anxiety over his premature ejaculation. As this anxiety increases, the chances of it reaching a critical threshold increase such that he can no longer get or maintain an erection.

The same kind of process can occur when inhibited sexual desire (ISD) is the initial sexual dysfunction. Anxiety and worry are certain to inhibit desire. These men become preoccupied over why they don't feel more desire, and they try to force themselves to feel more desire, becoming anxious that they don't feel more turned on. But sexual desire cannot be forced. Instead, the man must be able to relax enough to enjoy sexual fantasy and the intimate interaction with the partner. Men with ISD do not feel turned on, do not become aroused, and then feel more anxious about it. As the anxiety builds, erectile performance becomes more and more likely to be impaired.

NONPSYCHIATRIC RISK FACTORS

A myriad of factors could be considered nonpsychiatric. These factors could be considered mental health issues, although not officially listed as psychiatric diagnoses, and others could be considered problems in living or those things that cause us personal distress. These are problems that are not officially considered psychiatric disorders as defined in *DSM-IV*. For example, a man may feel upset and anxious over the loss of a marriage, or divorce, or over the fact that one of his children is sick. Perhaps one of his parents recently died. These are psychological problems that are normative enough that they do not have official psychiatric labels. However, any number of life events may cause both a loss of desire or a loss of performance. One such typical event is when a man begins dating following the end of a long-term marriage. He may equate sex with a woman as being unfaithful or simply feel anxious about sex with a new partner.

Sexual Ignorance

Mosher (1979) was able to empirically demonstrate that sexual mythology, misinformation, and a lack of scientific information was common in American culture. While more recent studies have not been carried out, our clinical experience suggests that little improvement has occurred over the past 20 years. We have found that many men do not understand the most basic anatomy and physiology related to sexual functioning, nor do their partners. They don't know that sexual functioning changes naturally with the aging process. Men may also attach too much of their self-esteem to sexual performance, the standards for which were established during adolescence. The sexually misinformed male is certain to feel inadequate as he ages. Performance changes that should be anticipated as a natural consequence of aging, such as an increasing period after ejaculation when the penis is refractory to further stimulation, are instead cause for worry and anxiety, both of which are certain to distract him, removing him emotionally from his partner and the pleasure he might experience with sexual intimacy.

Ultimately, he may suffer from erectile problems primarily because he is misinformed about normal sexual performance. Moreover, the dreaded anxiety will cripple him at the thought of being sexual, interfering with desire as well as performance.

Sexual mythology and misinformation have been shown to be related to increased levels of sexual guilt and anxiety, both of which determinably affect erectile ability (Mosher, 1979). Guilt can wreak havoc with the sexual response. One of the most pernicious guilt-instilling mentalities is related to Puritanism and religious orthodoxy. This is not to say that religion always induces sexual guilt in the individual. It is more the way a particular religion is used within the family of origin, and how its tenets are understood and internalized by the individual that may have a destructive impact on the sexual response. The old idea that pleasure is bad or wicked, or that one will suffer negative consequences if one loses control is a part of the Puritan heritage. Some religions are more negative about sex than others. Catholicism contains many negative injunctions about sex, including masturbation. Most boys do masturbate, but not all masturbate without guilt. Associating guilt with getting an erection can have long-term implications that many Catholic men have been unable to escape. As boys, they believe they are committing a serious sin each time they masturbate. Eventually, they introject a negative feeling about themselves because they are unable to stop doing something they are told repeatedly is bad or wrong. Ultimately, they may equate all sexual pleasure with negativity because they cannot control or prevent themselves from doing something bad. This takes a toll on their self-esteem.

Men raised in Christian Science families are taught to suppress all negative feelings and view any problem as a fault in one's thinking and an indication of insufficient faith. These men intellectualize their problems and their relationships. They think about the world abstractly and see negative feelings as failure. In order to protect themselves from negative feelings and problems, they distance themselves from other people. Having an intimate relationship is difficult. One man with a Christian Science upbringing commented, "I can only have sex with my imagined partner, not with my real partner."

Negative Cognitions

Men with erectile problems carry a network of negative cognitions in their minds. They think about the potentially dismal outcome of sex both in the sexual situation itself and during the course of daily activities. Just prior to and during sex, they are flooded with thoughts of failure and humiliation that cause them to doubt themselves. The resulting performance anxiety, fear, and apprehension are further intensified by even more negative cognitions. As the cycle repeats itself, negative cognitions beget anxiety that begets more negative cognitions. These thoughts not only perpetuate the negative feeling but also interfere with his ability to attend to the positive erotic signals in the situation. He is too busy monitoring himself and comparing his current erectile state to where he thinks it should be. Of course, his performance does not match his expectations. He evaluates this discrepancy negatively and the cycle resurges.

Secrecy, Negative Attitudes, and Traumatization

Secrecy is a learned behavior often modeled within the family of origin. Sexual secrecy can take many forms, such as labeling the genitals with code words or never discussing them, or any aspect of sexuality, at all. Circumventing what should be a normal process of anatomic labeling sends a strong message to children that sex is unspeakable. In such families, it is the norm rather than the exception that reproduction, sexual intimacy, and masturbation are never discussed. To make matters worse, there is a strong, albeit silent, prohibition against sexual pleasure. It is no doubt that men raised in such families carry into their adult sexual lives the notion that sex is forbidden, and that pleasure from it is unmentionable, creating conflict and emotional inhibition. They have assimilated the implication that if it is unspeakable it must be bad, or the more destructive message that it if it feels good it must be bad. Masturbation, oral sex, certain sexual positions, even orgasms may be viewed negatively by these men. Even if they participate in such activities, they communicate a message nonverbally that they are not enjoying their own or their partner's sexual pleasure.

Some families have sex-related secrets, such as miscarriages, infidelity, children born out of wedlock, and incest. The boy who grows up in a family with such a secret will soon learn not to discuss anything in this area. He will begin to internalize the family's guilt and anxiety over the secret. He will learn the process of keeping secrets and will be inclined to repeat the pattern in his own life. Silence is a powerful and destructive learning tool, particularly if it provides a barrier to intimacy between partners. The child introjects what he experiences within his family of origin; by adulthood these patterns are ingrained with him and predictable. Unless he has disrupted this indoctrination by taking in other views (say, through self-reflection and/or psychotherapy), it is unlikely that he will achieve any more intimacy than he experienced within his own family of origin.

Men can also be the victims of incest. Although far rarer than female victims, male victims experience similar traumatization. These men tend to equate their adult sexual experiences with what happened during the incest; sex becomes connected with fear, trauma, violation, and betrayal. In order for some acts of incest to occur, the boy would need an erection or would often get an erection from sexual acts not requiring penetration. In addition, he experiences guilt and shame over having become aroused in the process. Erections begin to represent the incest, and he tries to suppress erectile responses in order to avoid reliving the incest.

Fear of Aging and Loss of Health

One of the authors once treated a man who called for an emergency session because of his erectile problem. He had been married for about 10 years and had just experienced his first erectile failure. He was in a state of panic, fearing that he had lost his sexual ability. When asked about the nature of the problem and its duration, he reported that it had begun "last Tuesday" and had persisted every day since then. Prior to that time, he had never had a problem. The prior Tuesday was his 40th birthday. This fact was a definite clue and, when asked what significance his birthday had, he recalled his father telling him he should enjoy sex because "when men reach 40, they lose it." Perceptions about aging and what is "normal" sexual behavior have a significant effect on sexual functioning. It is not uncommon for men to believe they have aged beyond their sexual years and simply give up. For this patient, the biological panic struck on his 40th birthday; for others, anxiety sets in as soon as they notice subtle changes in erectile stamina. Such perceptions are clearly based on sexual ignorance born of misinformation and sexual mythology.

Perceptions of health, be they real or imagined, can also be important risk factors. A man might imagine something is terribly wrong with himself and become preoccupied and anxious with that thought. He may also have a medical disorder, the significance of which he exacerbates by obsessing about it. He may believe that he will die prematurely or be doomed to bad health for the remainder of his years. In the worst case, he may fear that he will die or that his partner will die. Fear about one's health may arise spontaneously, or the seeds may have been planted in childhood as a consequence of an event or belief arising in the family of origin. For example, men whose fathers died at an early age often experience an "anniversary reaction": They imagine they will die or become ill at about the same age.

The same may be true for men whose mothers died prematurely. They will fear the premature death of a spouse or partner. A man who has experienced loss, illness, and death in his family of origin may fear that his partner will leave him; his actions toward her then begin to reflect his fear of abandonment rather than his love. This fear may be obvious to the man, or it may manifest indirectly. One man who had experienced the long-term illness and death of a loved one was unable to consummate his marriage for three years because he feared that his wife would die. In this instance, he was unaware of the forces behind his inability to become intimate.

Divorce

Some divorced or divorcing men take on a tremendous burden of guilt and self-recrimination for the marriage not working and believe they have failed themselves, their family of origin, their spouses, and their children. By the time the divorce is complete, their self-esteem may be shattered as they endure all the stresses associated with a fragmented family and increased financial worries. In some cases, it has also been many years since they have dated; they are feeling awkward attempting to do so now and may have ambivalent feelings about being sexual with a new person. The combination of all the internal and external stressors can trigger an erection failure. These men are simply too fragmented and vulnerable to the effects of their anxiety and depression to participate in an exchange of intimacy with another person.

One of our clients, Michael, was typical of this pattern. Michael had married his high school sweetheart when he was in his early twenties. After 12 years of marriage, he decided to divorce his wife. A man with a shy disposition, Michael was predisposed to feeling guilty and responsible. He forced himself to date occasionally in order to feel that he was normal. When the relationship reached the point when sexual contact was desired by both, he always had an erection problem. He viewed having sex as making another commitment and feared ruining another relationship.

INTERACTIONAL (DYADIC) RISK FACTORS

Systems Perspective

The couple is a dynamic and interlocking system with its own rules and regulating mechanisms. One partner's behavior always influences the other; a difficulty in one affects the other. It is not useful to consider the individual without considering the context of the intimate relationship. Our work grew out of the framework of systems/family therapy and has been further refined in the development of the authors' own theoretical framework—the intersystemic view described in the first chapter. The second component of this theory is the interactional or dyadic level of explanation and treatment. This section will explore some of the dyadic risk factors associated with an erectile dysfunction.

A systems approach to viewing sexual problems has received little attention in the literature on sex therapy with the exceptions of Schnarch, 1991, 1998; Weeks, 1995; Weeks and Hof, 1987; and Woody, 1992. Although Masters and Johnson (1970) stated that there is no such thing as an "uninvolved" partner, they did not have what would currently be considered a comprehensive approach to treatment of the couple *system*. Kaplan's (1974) approach utilizes psychodynamic and behavioral components in identifying several general "dyadic causes" for sexual dysfunction, though none are mentioned in her chapter on erectile dysfunction, but then she proposes the concept of "bypassing" couples' problems in order to treat the sexual dysfunction. In other words, she believes it is possible to treat the sexual relationship without attending to the emotional problems of the couple. From an intersystemic perspective, this approach does not make sense. Moreover, Kaplan's actual method of treatment is to push aside couples' nonsexual problems. The couple is simply told to put aside their emotional concerns and carry out the exercises provided to treat their sexual problem. Our experience demonstrates that for most couples struggling with a sexual dysfunction, this is not only too difficult an assignment, but it is also an ill-advised one: All too often, ignored or denied emotional issues are central to the sexual dysfunction.

Verhulst and Heiman (1979) were among the first to propose that sexual dysfunctions be viewed from a systems perspective. They suggested four categories (sets of risk factors) that should be examined in understanding sexual dysfunctions: territorial interactions, rank-order interactions, attachment interactions, and exploratory/sensual interactions. *Territorial interactions* concern issues of power and control and personal ownership of one's body. *Rank-order interactions* include those behaviors of power, control, dominance, submissiveness, and self-esteem that determine status and control. *Attachment interactions* relate to the dynamic of love and intimacy. *Exploratory and sensual interactions* involve how the couple communicate and explore sensual and sexual interactions with each other. Verhulst and Heiman's template can be applied to a range of sexual dysfunctions. Later in this chapter, we will discuss how problems of attachment in the couple's interaction may effect erectile ability.

Levine (1992) proposed a model that is consistent with a systems perspective. He described the concept of "sexual equilibrium" or the balance between two partner's sexual characteristics. Each partner, he proposes, brings six components to the sexual situation: gender identity, sexual orientation, intention, level of desire, ease of arousal, and preferred means of having an orgasm. The fit between the components brought by each partner determines the nature of their sexual interaction. Should the fit be poor, such as in the case where the man's partner is never interested, and he is always interested in intercourse, or she just wants to have sex in a mechanical way and he always wants variety, may lead to conflict that disrupts erectile ability.

Leiblum and Rosen (1991) proposed one of the most extensive sets of couple-oriented risk factors. They devoted an entire chapter to the role the couple plays in the cause and treatment of erectile problems and also identified four core issues that could influence erectile ability. Clearly, this work is consistent with our assumption that interactional (dyadic) factors play a major role in the etiology of erectile dysfunction. Leiblum and Rosen's dyadic risk factors include:

- status and dominance
- intimacy and trust
- sexual chemistry and desire
- sexual scripts

Men are socialized to assume *status and dominance*, Leiblum and Rosen point out. When a man experiences himself as dominant, he feels a sense of potency that helps him give up some measure of control over himself during a sexual encounter, which allows him to relax and lose himself in pleasurable erotic feelings. There is also recent scientific evidence that supports Leiblum and Rosen's finding that feelings of power are associated with higher testosterone and cortisol levels (Crenshaw & Goldberg, 1996). Should his status or dominance be threatened by a loss of self-esteem through depression, job loss, or sexual difficulties, he begins to feel that he is "one-down" in relationship to his partner. Should he also be married to a partner who is competitive or whom he perceives as dominant, emotional conflict can ensue, triggering an erectile problem. Of course, the question is what does he unconsciously derive from being in this type of relationship. He is setting up a relationship in which he feels one-down. These feelings of loss of potency may also be the direct result of an erectile failure, which sets the vicious cycle in motion.

Leiblum and Rosen next address the *differences in intimacy needs* of men and women. Men are socialized to be "strong," which is equated with not expressing emotion or vulnerability; in contrast, women are socialized to value emotional intimacy. These two sets of needs come into conflict whenever the woman begins to make requests or demands for more intimacy, thereby disturbing the man's need to maintain some emotional detachment. The man will withdraw further if he is uncomfortable with the change in dynamics. He does not want to be vulnerable, and he does not know how to be expressive, particularly when he is required to assume an emotional role. Predictably, the woman reacts to his withdrawal by becoming critical. He then feels like he is the target of hostility and withdraws even more. He may even begin to believe that he cannot trust her *not* to hurt him if he were to decide to come closer to her in the future. This pattern of interaction was probably first identified by Fogarty (1976). He called it the pursuer-distancer pattern. Men tend to distance emotionally; women tend to pursue emotionally. When the sexual encounter symbolizes an emotional interaction, the man may have difficulty engaging and performing. The only way he may be able to insulate himself emotionally from the experience is to have a problem that shifts the focus away from emotion and onto "mechanics."

Sexual attraction and chemistry remain scientific mysteries. Leiblum and Rosen point out that some men form relationships with women to whom they feel no sexual attraction. They may like these women and find them to be compatible partners but report they just don't feel "turned on" by them. Typically, these couples appear to have a high degree of marital satisfaction, although they report low levels of sexual compatibility. Their relationship seems more like compatible roommates or even siblings instead of lovers.

Maryann and Bob were typical of this type of couple. They met at a running marathon and had been dating for four months. They were a young and athletic couple who liked to exercise together, but shared few other activities. Though they had initially found each other attractive, the feelings of sexual chemistry rapidly dissipated. They began to have sex infrequently, and then Bob developed an erectile problem. Their therapist initially remarked that in therapy they appeared to be like a brother and sister trying to find some way to be sexual with each other. In cases like this, both partners may have unconscious conflicts about being sexual and choose to remain in a relationship that will continue in spite of the lack of passion and sex.

Next, Leiblum and Rosen cite *sexual scripts*, a sociological concept referring to how sexual behavior is organized in a relationship. Each individual brings his or her own blueprint of how one should behave sexually in relation to another: which behaviors are acceptable, with whom, under what circumstances, and for what purposes. Each partner's sexual script was developed during childhood in the context of the family of origin. The script is refined during adolescence and the adult years, primarily through dating and other close relationships. When the partners' scripts are too incompatible, the couple will not be satisfied with how sex occurs. The most problematic scripts are those in which sex must be patterned so that it is restrictive, repetitive, and mechanical.

Doug, for example, had a sexual script whereby his partners had to assume a totally passive role in order for him to feel, and get, aroused. He, and he alone, would direct the couple's behavior during sex. If things went according to his script, he was pleased and could get and keep an erection. If his partner deviated from the script, however, he would react angrily and irrationally, thinking how demanding and controlling the woman was being, and then lose his erection.

In addition to the factors identified by Leiblum and Rosen, we have observed several other relationship risk factors for erectile dysfunction in our clinical practice.

Sexual Difficulties

We presented statistics of the clinical picture in which an individual experiences several sexual difficulties instead of just one. From a statistical perspective alone, it is unlikely that a couple would experience only one sexual problem. Our clinical experience supports empirical data in terms of multiple sexual dysfunctions (Masters & Johnson, 1970). For instance, a number of the men presenting with an erectile dysfunction were first premature ejaculators. The same outcome is likely for those men who have difficulty ejaculating, the delayed ejaculators, men who can thrust coitally for an indefinite period of time and not reach orgasm. Typically, they are overly concerned about their partner's satisfaction and anxious about their own performance. In other presentations of delayed ejaculation, the man is simply not aroused enough by his partner or by coitus; he may suffer from a form of inhibited sexual desire (hypoactive desire) (Apfelbaum, 1989). Regardless of the cause of the delayed ejaculation, these men eventually begin to feel anxious before and during sex, often criticizing themselves and worrying about their partner's reaction. Consequently, they try to force themselves mentally to ejaculate instead of enjoying the natural progression of events. These men try to will themselves to ejaculate with the aid of active thrusting. At the same time, they fear they will not ejaculate, and that their partner will think they do not find them attractive or that the experience is taking too long. Forcing ejaculation is certain to increase performance anxiety and trigger an erectile problem.

Inhibited Sexual Desire

Men with erectile dysfunctions sometimes have partners who also experience sexual problems. Commonly, these women suffer from inhibited sexual desire, vaginismus (painful intercourse), or they may not be able to have an orgasm. The man begins to sense the woman's anxiety, and in some cases her avoidance of sex, and he begins to view sex as a task, and his task is to help her climax or find some way to make sex more comfortable or enjoyable.

The absence of desire and incompatible levels of desire are common phenomena in relationships. The frequency of sex varies tremendously from couple to couple, and clinicians agree that a wide range of frequency is normal. Some men expect their partners to have the same level of sexual desire they possess. When a large discrepancy exists, and the partners are unable to accept such a difference and negotiate something that works, then anger, resentment, and sexual rejection may follow. The problem generally increases over time, the negative feelings increase, sexual avoidance may creep in, and an erectile dysfunction may emerge.

Lack of sexual desire has been identified as one of the most common problems in men and women. Inhibited desire or hypoactive desire is an inability to experience sexual desire in spite of wanting to feel interested. It is a complex disorder, requiring careful assessment and an integrative approach to treatment. Weeks (1995) has covered this topic extensively elsewhere. A man who has inhibited sexual desire may be disinterested or even sexually aversive or phobic. This disorder is always accompanied by anxiety over not feeling more desire. If the partner's level of desire is higher, the anxiety is compounded: He is now worried that he must feel more desire in order to "hold his own" with his partner.

Conversely, it may be the woman who has a lack of desire and the man who has a high level of desire. Eventually, he begins to feel sexually rejected and angry that his partner cannot will herself to become aroused. He may wonder what she thinks is wrong with him, or he might begin to find her less sexually attractive because she keeps rejecting him in his perception. In this situation, when sex does take place, it is usually mechanical, patterned, rushed, and devoid of much feeling. The man feels like he is imposing himself on his partner. He will begin to lose desire for her and may unconsciously collude with her to protect the relationship by making himself incapable of having intercourse.

Relationship Difficulties

This class of risk factors covers an extremely broad spectrum of problems, some of the more common of which will be described below. The link between these difficulties and sexual dysfunction still needs to be established empirically. Research has demonstrated that the amount of sexual intimacy is correlated with relationship satisfaction (Birchler & Webb, 1977; Blumstein & Schwartz, 1983; Sprecher & McKinney, 1993). In addition, frequent and satisfying sexual interactions have been correlated with more affection, cohesion, and positive verbal statements (Russell, 1990). However, the specific impact of relationship (nonsexual) difficulties on sexual functioning has not been documented.

Communication, Problem-Solving, and Conflict Resolution

Typical couple problems that lead to sexual dysfunction are poor communication, ineffective problem-solving of daily life concerns, and anger and conflict mismanagement. Communication problems may contribute to couple discord in a variety of ways. Partners may not feel they are connecting because they talk at different levels (Weeks & Hof, 1995). One partner might be cognitively oriented and the other emotionally focused. They may both be low on self-disclosure, leaving each wondering what the other person is really feeling and who he or she is. They may have a number of deficits in how they communicate which leads to numerous miscommunications and misunderstandings (Gottman, 1994). Gottman and others have summarized many studies that show ineffective communication contributes to lowered relationship satisfaction, which in turn may produce less sexual interest and satisfaction. Couples who communicate poorly are also likely to have difficulty communicating sexually.

Couples who are unable to solve the problems of daily life will experience higher and higher levels of frustration as these problems accumulate. They will often comment about how nothing ever gets decided or talked about. They appear to work at cross-purposes with each other, increasing the level of tension. When ineffective problem-solving has been the modus operandi for a period of time, small issues become major issues because they symbolize all the past failures and the fact that the underlying inability is still operative. These relationships are filled with tension, and the partners are easily set off by small problems because nothing has ever been resolved. Underlying anger and resentment suppress sexual desire and may, in some instances, also produce an erectile problem.

Couples who lack conflict resolution skills will not be able to work through the myriad of differences that are inevitable in an intimate relationship. Many couples also develop or inherit a number of bad or destructive fighting habits such as name-calling, bringing up the past, and being unwilling to compromise because each partner insists he or she is right and the other is wrong. This deficit does not allow the couple to work through anger and, in fact, has the effect of escalating the anger. As the number of unresolved conflicts builds, so do the anger and resentment between partners. They become less and less sexually attractive to one another, and sex may even become one of the "weapons" used to punish the partner. Erectile dysfunction could be an unconscious means of withholding something the man knows his partner wants.

Addictions

An addiction in one or both partners may lead to gross relationship dissatisfaction and alienation. The addicted partner is, in effect, already coupled with his or her drug of choice. The drug will always take priority and is the central focus of that person's existence. A sexual addiction is especially troublesome because the partner typically finds it very difficult to view it as a disease. The sex addict is driven to view pornography, others, or have sex with multiple partners, including prostitutes. This behavior is typically judged in moral terms and equated with having an affair or being rejected in favor of a perversity. Partners are unaware that the addict is filled with a sense of desperation, depression, and shame (Turner, 1995). The sex addict may be highly functional when he is engaging in his addictive behavior but finds he is unable to respond to his partner out of guilt and a lack of desire.

Depression

Depression in one partner is a couple's issue. Couples tend to deal with depression in a way that only exacerbates it and creates additional problems within the marriage (Howard & Weeks, 1995). Marital dissatisfaction may even be the major contributor to the depression. In spite of the emphasis that psychiatry now places on the biological basis of behavior, depression is often the result of a relationship that isn't working. The combination of a distressed relation and a psychological depression (which may include symptoms of anxiety) predispose the man to having an erection problem.

Affairs

Extramarital affairs are another source of distress, anger, and anxiety. An affair is one of the most stressful events that can happen in a marriage, for it shatters trust and loyalty and triggers tremendous feelings of anger, betrayal, rejection, confusion, shock, and denial. The question of whether or not to continue the relationship is almost always one of the major issues. Although some couples become hypersexual when an affair is revealed or discovered, most experience a significant disruption in their sexual lives. Trust is basic to having a sexual relationship. The absence of trust after an affair has been discovered or revealed tends to depress sexual activity and causes the partners to feel uncomfortable around each other. Each one is thinking about what happened in the affair partner's sexual relationship.

Life-Cycle Changes

Life-cycle changes are inherently stressful for couples. The introduction of a child into the relationship, coming into middle age, children leaving, and retirement each necessitates significant changes in rules, roles, expectations, self-image, and self-identity. We have observed that some men develop erectile difficulties when the couple is trying to conceive. They feel ambivalent about being a father but rather than express this feeling directly, they act it out unconsciously. Many men have erectile troubles when there is a fertility problem and the couple must have sex at prescribed times (Mahlstedt, 1987). The man may also fear that he is the one with the fertility problem and construe this as a lack of virility or manliness.

Fears of Intimacy

Weeks (1995) has written about the underlying fears of intimacy in relationship that create and maintain distance between partners. These fears are usually unconscious and often rooted in the family of origin (Bowen, 1976). In order to maintain the needed distance, partners use tactics such as fighting, avoiding each other, overworking, overfocusing on children, and developing sexual problems that defy resolution. Fear of intimacy is typically a bilateral issue. Fearful partners have a way of finding each other. One seeks out a partner who desires the same level of intimacy, although in many cases this fact is verbally denied with great vigor. Partners may carry the same fear(s) of intimacy or they may carry complementary fear(s). Six fears of intimacy are common in our experience: fears of dependency, expressing feelings, anger, losing control/being controlled, exposure, and rejection/abandonment.

Some partners fear *dependency* on another person because they equate it with weakness, submissiveness, or disempowerment. One client commented that if he ever showed women he cared about them, he would consider himself "a nothing."

Fear of *expressing feelings* often stems from an underlying fear of losing control, of opening the floodgates and being swept away emotionally. Partners who learned to turn off feelings in early life as a defense mechanism will have an equally difficult time feeling pleasure. All feelings become muted and the unconscious contract with the partner is to *avoid* feelings.

Fear of anger is manifested in two ways—either as the fear of getting angry and losing control or of being the recipient of a partner's uncontrollable and hurtful anger. Such people obviously avoid conflict and minimize any angry feelings that do manage to surface. Partners locked into this pattern may avoid each other in order to avoid conflict. Underneath all this suppression and denial is a great deal of resentment and anger.

Partners who were reared in families with a controlling parent may fear *losing control or being controlled*. This fear is specifically related to one's self-definition or the degree of autonomy a person feels. Individuals who fear losing control or being controlled cannot tolerate taking directions, let alone being told what to do or how to "be." Their first reaction is to say no and feel angry for a reason they cannot identify. They may experience any type of sexual initiation as a form of control. Some partners feel controlled to the point that they believe the other person is trying to proscribe their innermost reactions. This type of fear has much deeper roots and is difficult to treat.

Partners who *fear exposure* believe they are incompetent, incapable, unintelligent, unworthy, and unlovable. Their self-esteem is generally low and affects both relationship and work arenas. They protect themselves by not letting anyone get too close and not letting anyone look within them. On the surface they may appear well adjusted and quite competent, but inside they feel they have fooled everyone into thinking they are one kind of person, when, in fact, they are the opposite. They think that if their partner knew who they *really* were, his or her love would quickly evaporate. Sexually, they try to make sex look good and feel right, but they hold themselves back and simply perform the motions.

Partners who were emotionally or physically *rejected or abandoned* as children, often carry this fear into adulthood. They believe that one of these catastrophes will surely happen if they allow themselves to love or get too attached to another person. It happened before in a so-called loving relationship, so it can happen again. Not only will they not allow themselves to get too close, but, they will also unconsciously set up partners to keep their distance. For example, men who have this fear may sabotage the relationship by setting up the other person so that they feel justified in rejecting them before they are rejected. An erection problem can be used in this way. The man may not be able to perform, senses his partner's anger/disappointment over the problem, and then rejects her saying she simply does not love him enough to be patient with the problem.

Intergenerational Factors

Sexual Messages

This category of risk factors has been overlooked in the literature. Hof and Berman (1986) and Berman and Hof (1987) were the first to develop a genogram in order to assess intergenerational factors and sexual functioning. The sexual genogram is used to uncover the connections between adult sexual functioning and the implicit and explicit sexual messages and patterns that occurred in the family of origin: What messages about masculinity and femininity, and sex were modeled? In all too many families sex is a taboo topic, implying that something must be *really* bad about it.

The dynamics in the family may also play an important role in how sexual identity is formed. In the family of origin of one of our clients, for example, the parents were overtly sexual around their children. They would perform sexual acts, such as intercourse, in front of their children and then criticize them for noticing and looking on with confusion, disgust, and disappointment. The parents encouraged everyone in the family to be enmeshed—to think, feel, behave, and believe like the parents. Our client commented that if she were sexual she might be "just like my parents." The husband in this couple also came from an enmeshed family where the push toward cohesion was more emotional then sexual. However, he eventually realized that to be sexual with his wife was a move toward autonomy that violated his family's need for loyalty.

Enmeshment

Enmeshed families present another interesting dynamic. They do not want children to grow up and become independent. Being sexual with another person in a particular context such as a marriage is a form of growing up. Some men from enmeshed families appear to be sexually shy and incompetent. They may report "not knowing what to do." At a deeper level, they are afraid the sexual connection will further remove them from the enmeshed family system.

Alex, for example, was 23 when he entered therapy for his erection problem. He had been dating since high school and was popular, but he had never asserted himself sexually with women. When a woman took the lead and he tried to perform intercourse, he would feel he did not know what to do, become very anxious, and lose his erection. Alex's father had referred Alex to us because he had sought treatment from a therapist for the same problem. Both father and son were overanxious individuals from a highly enmeshed family. Alex unconsciously recognized that any long-term relationship he formed would be a threat to the family's enmeshment. Helping him separate from his family of origin was instrumental in his becoming sexually entitled.

Incest

The most obvious type of intergenerational problem is incest, either overt or covert. In overt incest, a particular sexual behavior occurs. In its covert form, the interaction, though not sexual, still crosses sexual boundaries. Asking a boy all the details about his date, including a blow-by-blow account of his sexual contact, would constitute covert incest. One recently married client approached sex with intense fear. His mother, who was psychotic and living at home much of his childhood, attempted to form an enmeshed and sexual relationship with her son. He not only feared losing himself as a person in his marriage, but he also feared being consumed sexually. His erectile dysfunction disappeared after months of work on the overt incest and the family enmeshment and pathology.

Cultural Factors

Finally, negative cultural messages concerning sex may pose a risk to the extent that these messages are accepted as true. Men who have not had the benefit of proper education are likely to internalize these messages without question. Zilbergeld (1978) discussed the fantasy model of sex that is so common in American culture. In this model, the man purports to be a sexual superman with a penis that is "two feet long, hard as steel, and goes all night." Men who believe they must be sexual supermen will fail to meet their own unrealistic expectations. They will also assume that other men have this superhuman quality. Additionally, they assume that women want this type of man, and that they are being compared to all other partners. The pressure to meet an impossible standard may lead the man to drop out of the game by avoiding sex or become extremely performance-oriented.

The risk factors we have discussed in this chapter are the most common and constitute those with which we have considerable experience. It is probably impossible to list every risk factor because men have different vulnerabilities and the psyche is too complex to reduce to just a short list of common risks. Once again, we caution the reader to consider the concept of multicausality. In our experience, it is rare for a single risk factor to produce a problem. In general, a problem requires the confluence of several risk factors. In the next chapter, we will describe assessment methods for investigating these risk factors.

4

⌘ ⌘ ⌘ ⌘ ⌘

Assessment of Psychological Risk Factors

THE ETIOLOGY OF A SEXUAL DYSFUNCTION IS multicausal, often involving an overlap of organic and psychogenic factors. As noted, three major areas of psychogenic risk factors contribute to the development and maintenance of an erectile dysfunction:

1. vulnerabilities within the individual,
2. factors arising from the family of origin, and
3. relationship issues.

The intersystemic model described by Weeks (1994) provides a comprehensive framework for the assessment of these psychogenic risk factors. These three foci shape the evaluation although questions do not necessarily follow a sequence or order. Flexibility is a key feature for organizing information about the individual, the individuals as partners, and their relationship as a system.

INITIAL TELEPHONE INTERVIEW

The assessment phase of therapy begins with the initial telephone call requesting help with the sexual problem. During this call, a cursory appraisal can be made in approximately ten minutes. The therapist begins to gather data about the nature of the dysfunction and its impact on the couple's relationship, noting which partner is making the telephone call and why the call was made at this particular time. The therapist also inquires about the referral process. How was the referral for psychotherapy made, and by whom? Is the referring person a physician, friend, or is the client self referred? What does the client(s) want from the therapy?

Referral information also tells the therapist something about the couple's expectations of the therapy.

- What does the client know about therapy for the treatment of the erectile dysfunction?
- Does he/she believe the problem can be "cured" quickly by the therapist?
- How did he/she learn about the particular therapist? What is known about and expected of the therapist?
- If there is a partner, does the couple expect to receive treatment or is the individual designated as the patient?
- How does each partner feel about talking to a therapist about his or her sexual problem?
- Is each willing to attend regularly scheduled therapy sessions?
- Is the expectation of therapy reality-based? Do they realize that the treatment is not magical but involves a working relationship between the therapist and both partners?

In the first telephone contact, the therapist must be sensitive to the feelings of the client when discussing sexual material. Embarrassment and shame about the situation often inhibit the client, making it difficult to accurately describe the problem. It is important to take control of the conversation by asking questions about the sexual problem in a direct manner. Clarify the information presented in an empathic fashion. Reassure the client that it is usually difficult for most individuals to discuss sexual information on the telephone with an unknown therapist. This normalization serves to reduce embarrassment and promote efficient use of the telephone conversation. Explain that it is necessary to know something about the sexual problem but that a greater amount of information will be gathered in the first session. The conversation should be brief, ranging from 5 to 15 minutes. The material covered should be limited to the presenting problem, the relationship, and scheduling of the first meeting.

By the end of the initial telephone interview, the therapist has a basic cursory understanding of the onset, persistence and recurrence of the erectile dysfunction. Also, the couple's attempts to resolve the problem are typically discussed, providing an opportunity for an initial assessment of the couple's coping style and ability to work together. When the client describes measures that have failed to correct the problem, inquire about the couple's relationship in general by asking in a nonintrusive manner about how they are getting along. In what ways has the erectile dysfunction affected their relationship? Ask about the degree of stress they have experienced as a couple since the onset of the sexual problem. This kind of empathically guided discussion provides an initial assessment of the clinical picture while the beginning stage of the therapeutic alliance is established.

THE INITIAL SESSION

There are three main goals of the initial session:

- Continue building the therapeutic relationship, which began in the first telephone contact.
- Firmly establish a systemic rather than individual context for the therapy.
- Accurately assess the sexual problem.

Establishing the Therapeutic Relationship

Once in the office, the process of assessment continues while the relationship between therapist and clients gradually develops. In the initial interview, the therapist strives to nurture the important processes of joining (Minuchin, 1974) and empathic understanding (Rogers, 1951). The literature is replete with references about the importance of providing a safe, supportive environment during the initial interview (Marziali, 1988; Odell & Quinn, 1998). These processes are particularly critical when treating sexual dysfunctions because of the embarrassment and hopelessness typically experienced by clients. The therapist must remain keenly aware that reassurance and support are necessary while inquiring about the origin and maintenance of the sexual dysfunction.

The therapeutic relationship that develops when treating an erectile dysfunction requires sensitivity and patience. Unlike many therapy situations, the main reason for treatment is extremely private and personal. Most individuals have difficulty discussing sexual feelings and behaviors with their intimate partner; it is even more taxing to talk to a therapist that they just met.

Initially, expect the clients to control the level of risk; tell them to share only what is comfortable. Trust in the therapist and in the process of therapy develops slowly. Eventually, the working alliance will enable the clients to trust that they are on the "same page" with their therapist (Pinsof & Catherall, 1986). It cannot be overemphasized that an environment of safety and positive regard is to be provided at all times. Safety is a critical factor when treating an erectile dysfunction. The individuals need to feel as though they are taken seriously. Use humor sensitively and judiciously. It is entirely possible for the vulnerable client to feel a lack of empathy, even when it is not intended. It is critical that *both* clients trust the therapist. The partner needs to feel that her concerns (usually doubts about her self-worth and appeal) are not overlooked. In addition, there may be times during the course of therapy when each will need a private session.

The couple should be assured that the therapist is reachable by telephone if they have a brief question or concern. It is typical for sex therapy clients to need occasional clarification of an assignment and/or reassurance because the treatment may elicit fears and vulnerabilities about their relationship. Thus, the therapeutic relationship involves a high degree of discourse between therapist and each client during the assessment as well as treatment phases.

In most situations the therapist will be working with a male patient and his female partner. Regardless of the gender or sexual orientation of the couple, however, the therapist must be aware of the dynamics that can occur when a therapist is working with a heterosexual couple. Openly discuss the feelings of the clients about working with a male or female therapist. Be aware of perceived triangulation and encourage discussion if a client is feeling left out. For example, a man with an erectile dysfunction feels embarrassed at the outset, discussing a problem that cuts to the core of his masculine identity. He could feel either overempowered or more insecure discussing his "failure" in the presence of two women. On the other hand, the female client, feeling insecure and vulnerable herself, could easily feel competitive or threatened by the presence of a female therapist. There are numerous possibilities of emotional reactions to the gender of the therapist. Anticipating the vulnerabilities of each client and encouraging open discussion of these feelings will help to reinforce the therapeutic alliance.

The need for appropriate dress and demeanor by the therapist is a given in any therapeutic context, but in sexual counseling the concerns are amplified. The therapist *must never* engage in behaviors that might be misconstrued as flirtatious. Also, if the therapist notices jealousy in the same-sex client or seductiveness in the opposite-sex partner, these behaviors need to be addressed and interrupted *immediately*. There is fertile ground for vulnerability and sensitivity when dealing with a sexual dysfunction.

Therapeutic Questions

Individuals and couples experiencing an erectile dysfunction often report a range of feelings that need to be addressed early in the initial conversations and throughout the course of therapy. Most notably, they experience a sense of embarrassment related to talking about private sexual behaviors. Typically, there is a feeling of failure because the man is not able to perform sexual acts that were once so pleasurable for him and his partner. Often the couple experiences a loss of hope about their situation. The best way to facilitate discussion about such feelings is to use open-ended questions or statements that promote a flow of affective and cognitive material. Particularly in the early stages of therapy, clients will feel understood and supported if they are helped to discuss their reactions to the erectile dysfunction (Shields, Sprenkle, & Constantine, 1991).

Open-ended questions foster empathy and positive regard, elements that are essential to the development of the working alliance between therapist and clients (Rogers, 1951). For decades the psychological literature has underscored the importance of open-ended questions in the clinical interview as an effective way to learn about the client while minimizing the risk of therapist bias (Frolich & Bishop, 1977; Hackney & Nye, 1973). The client is asked questions that *cannot* be answered with "yes" or "no" responses. Also, the therapist avoids asking "why," as the answer to that question typically closes off discussion. Instead one might ask "How does this make you feel?"

The following vignette illustrates the value of the open-ended statement or question. One of the authors noticed some discomfort on the part of the male client when he joked about the drug, Viagra, at the beginning of a conjoint meeting. This was the third session for this couple, who were in their sixties. The man was experiencing an erectile dysfunction of mixed etiology. Using a series of open-ended questions, the man was encouraged to say more about his "joke." The therapist asked, "What about Viagra?" The man described the recent news about the drug and was encouraged by another open-ended statement, "Looks like you have been thinking about this drug lately." He talked about his interest in possibly taking the drug. He was again encouraged, "Tell us more about your idea." His partner was invited to join in. "Is this news to you?" Later she was asked, "And how do you feel about Marty's idea?" Predictably, the open-ended statements facilitated discussion about the couple's worries, concerns, and reactions to his gradual decline in erectile capacity. In addition, they felt hopeful because options for future consideration were discussed.

Often, when couples finally seek treatment for an erectile problem, they feel sad and hopeless about correcting the situation because all of their problem-solving efforts did not work. Knowing these feelings often underlie their discussion, the therapist can make it a priority to ask about their feelings related to the sexual problem. The couple, typically, will want the therapist to know all of the "facts," however, we find it more useful to expose the underlying feelings first. The following are examples of open-ended statements or questions:

To the man
You have described the problems you are having with erections. What do you feel now, talking about it with me?

When you notice you are losing your erection, what concerns or worries do you have?

Tell me about your worries about your partner.

It seems you have lost hope about correcting the problem.

What embarrasses you the most?

To the woman
Do you feel the same as your partner?

What thoughts do you have when you notice he is struggling sexually?

How does it make you feel when he loses his erection?

Subsequently, the open-ended question is used when asking for specific information about the mechanics of the erectile dysfunction and other issues experienced in the couple's sexual relationship (Dozier, Hicks, Cornille, & Peterson, 1998; Tomm 1988). The therapist asks the couple:

How would you describe the sexual problem?

How long have you had difficulty with erections?

When do you lose your erection during lovemaking?

It is beneficial to collect information from each partner, noting areas of agreement or disagreement. This format also provides the opportunity to observe how the couple manages conflict and solves problems. Although the questions are potentially nonthreatening, it is important to pace inquiries about sensitive material in accordance with the tolerance level of each

partner. When asking direct questions about sexual practices, pause periodically to "check in" by asking how each partner is feeling.

Open-ended questioning also helps the couple see the interlocking or
reciprocal patterns that cause them to feel stuck or restricted in the ways in
which they react to each other by exposing the more automatic or reflexive
patterns that the couple has accommodated to over time. These questions
are useful in establishing a systemic reframe for the problem. Examples
include:

To the man
How do you approach your partner when you attempt to have sexual rela-
    tions?
What do you do to let her know you are interested?
In what way does she indicate she is interested?
When you begin to lose your erection, what do you do or say?

To the woman
How do you express interest in sex?
When you notice he is losing his erection, what do you do?
What do you say to him then?

While the therapist does not directly challenge the couple with questions, the suggestion is implied that certain patterns of problem-solving
actually create erectile problems. The couple begins to recognize their particular pattern of cause and effect and the reciprocal nature of their interactions.

As the therapeutic alliance is strengthened and the couple experiences
trust in the process of therapy, the therapist increases the risk level by
challenging the couple to create their own solutions to the erectile problem:

To the man
Have you discussed your feelings about the sexual problem with your
    partner?
If you tell her how you are feeling when you lose your erection, how do
    you suppose she would respond?

To the woman
How would you help him if he talked to you when he loses his erection?

The level of trust between therapist and clients and stage of therapy
dictate the range of freedom used in selecting therapeutic questions. If the
therapist is too tenacious or confrontative, trust in the process of therapy

will decrease. When working with couples experiencing an erectile dysfunction, the possibility of hopelessness is ever-present, requiring wisdom and sensitivity in selecting the risk level of questions.

There is a considerable overlap between assessment and treatment as early as the initial interview when the therapist begins to create a supportive environment that provides relief and fosters hope that the problem can be addressed. Ostensibly, the purpose of the interview is to collect information. In reality, treatment begins as the therapist joins with the couple to make sense of the situation.

The Systemic Context

Reframing is used (1) to change the cognitive and/or perceptual meaning of a symptom from something that is negative to something that is positive, and (2) to change the meaning by viewing the symptom in a relationship context instead of in strictly individual terms (Weeks, 1995). With psychogenic erectile problems, it is essential to think about and discuss the situation from a perspective of the couple rather than the individual. The symptom exists within the framework of the *relationship*. The reframe, therefore, is more than a technique. It is a method of conceptualizing and addressing the sexual problem without pathologizing the individual or artificially removing him from the context in which he exists. The reframe, an essential component of the systemic framework (Haley, 1976; Watzlawick, 1978), is a part of the repertoire of the couple or marriage therapist.

For example, it is not uncommon for the woman to state that the erectile dysfunction is *his* problem and that she cannot understand why her participation is necessary. The therapist responds by providing a context for the symptom, explaining that her help is necessary to determine the factors that might trigger the problem and engaging her further by explaining that she is "needed" to "help" with assignments that will be performed at home. In addition, the therapist asks how she feels about their sexual relationship and includes her in all discussions.

Using the therapeutic reframe, the therapist helps the couple to make sense of their situation and engenders the sense that they are working toward a common goal. The erectile dysfunction is described in nonpejorative language and feelings of hopelessness and embarrassment are discussed openly and supportively. A clear message is conveyed that the couple can be helped to correct the erectile problem by understanding the conditions that precipitate and maintain it. Essentially, the therapist controls the structure of the session by providing the context within which the erectile problem is understood and discussed.

The therapist elicits information from the couple and emphasizes certain aspects of this information, thereby teaching the couple to think about the problem differently. Though this new way of thinking about the problem guides the therapeutic work, it is also important initially not to stray too far from the client's perception of the erectile dysfunction, as this may create a breach in the therapeutic alliance. The partners are helped to view the meaning of the symptom more favorably through repeated, carefully timed questions and comments. For instance, a man with an erectile dysfunction might be commended for "preserving" his relationship by not "pressuring" his partner for coitus. Another way of reframing the erectile dysfunction is to say, "It makes sense to not pressure yourself to act sexual if you are feeling angry" or, "It makes sense that your penis stops you from having sexual relations when you are feeling anxiety." Another more global reframe is, "Somehow you knew that conditions were not favorable for sex" or, "It is understandable that you didn't want to push things when you were so worried about your relationship."

Addressing the couple, the therapist might say, "The two of you have been too angry or mistrustful to have sex." For the woman, the reframe could be: "It is a relief to know that an erection is not the ultimate sign of desire for you."

Instead of blaming the man because *he* is seen as the one with the problem, the reframe depolarizes the situation by addressing the function of the sexual symptom within the relationship. This contextualizes the problem and thereby helps partners understand the erectile dysfunction as an expression of the struggle within the relationship. As early as the first session the reframe helps to convey a broader understanding that the symptom does not magically appear but that there are relational patterns that trigger and sustain the recurrence of the erectile dysfunction. Anticipatory anxiety, power struggles, and congealed resentment can often be restated as "struggles," "worries," or "concerns" about the relationship.

Accurately Assessing the Sexual Problem

Ask the couple to describe their reasons for seeking therapy at this time instead of last month or a year ago. Their answers will yield information about the time frame for the development and persistence of the problem(s). Pay particular attention to the description of the events that preceded the initial telephone call. Consider the following questions:

- Was there a turning point in the relationship that was related to the sexual dysfunction?
- Which partner is most distressed by the sexual symptom?

- Who took charge of setting up the initial appointment with the therapist?
- What does this tell us about the couple and their pattern of relating?
- Is this typical of the way in which they resolve problems?

Take note of which partner first tells the story. Then ask about the other partner's account of the situation, being mindful to provide a balance whenever possible between the speakers. Avoid getting "pulled in" to one account of the story by asking both partners about areas of agreement or how they might view the situation differently. Next ask about what measures, if any, they have taken on their own to help their situation. Note those strategies that worked for the couple as well as those that failed. Assume that the partners are feeling helpless because they have not been able to "fix" the problem on their own. Therapy for the treatment of an erectile dysfunction is always a last resort and, more often than not, long overdue.

To interrupt feelings of hopelessness, it is useful to ask about areas of strength in their relationship, particularly toward the end of the first session. For example, the therapist asks each partner:

- What do you like best about [partner's name]?
- What attracted you to [name] when you first met?
- What joint activities do you enjoy the most?
- What is working well in your relationship?

These kinds of questions help to stimulate a modicum of hope by reminding the couple of the positive features of their relationship. One technique that often helps to distract the couple temporarily from their hopelessness is to ask them to tell the story about how and when they met. They are likely to leave the session on a more positive note if the session is ended with this discussion.

Once clients begin to discuss the sexual problem, determine if the man is describing an erectile dysfunction or perhaps a lack of sexual desire for his partner. Ask specific questions that help him to operationally describe the sexual problem using behavioral language. For example:

- Do you lose your erection before or during sexual relations?
- Does the level of tumescence or rigidity vary during sex?
- In what ways have your erections changed? For instance, do they lack tumescence completely or is there a partial erection?

- Do you lose your erection before or during lovemaking?
- Are you unable to perform certain previously enjoyable acts such as intercourse?
- When did the problem begin?
- In what situations does it occur and how often?

At the initial session a thorough clinical assessment is conducted based on the diagnostic criteria of erectile dysfunction identified in the *DSM-IV* (APA, 1994). The concise criteria serve as a standard for determining if an erectile dysfunction exists. In order to fulfill the diagnostic criteria in the *DSM-IV*, the erectile dysfunction must be "chronic." The terms for chronicity used in the *DSM-IV* are "persistent" and "recurrent." Does the problem occur in all situations or only at specific times or places? If the man has more than one sexual partner, does he have erectile problems with each sexual encounter, or is the incidence less frequent?

Begin to determine the extent to which the erectile dysfunction is of organic, psychogenic, or mixed etiology. Answers to two important questions about nocturnal erections and masturbation can give you reliable indicators.

1. Ask the client if he awakens from sleep with an erection, how frequently this happens, and how firm these erections tend to be. If, upon awakening, the erection is either absent or lacks tumescence, the etiology is more likely to be organic.
2. Ask if he has erectile problems when masturbating. An affirmative answer suggests that the etiology is more likely to be primarily organic.

Gather data about any organic or medical factors that might negatively impact erectile capacity, such as vascular and cardiac disease, diabetes, and hypertension. (The latter two notoriously cause erectile problems.) Inquire about all medications taken, length of time the client has been taking the medication, and the dose. Do not assume that he or his partner knows the action or effects of the drug. For example, diuretics and antihypertensive drugs are used to treat hypertension. Although these have very different actions, each may impair erectile function. Also, inquire about any psychiatric condition or anxiety.

Answers to all these questions give the therapist an initial perspective about the duration of the erectile dysfunction and whether it is situational or global, recurrent or persistent. Also, the therapist begins to form an impression of the extent to which relational and organic factors are contributing to the erectile dysfunction.

In the first session, it is not uncommon to introduce the notion that sexual problems are related to what was learned in the family of origin about sex. This intergenerational assessment can be approached through questions about the marriage(s) of the client's parents. Often clients offer information about family values related to sexuality. The astute therapist will welcome this opportunity to ask a few pertinent questions about the family of origin of both partners, although the majority of time is spent on relational issues. Later in the assessment process, the sexual genogram (Berman & Hof, 1987) is used to gather intergenerational data.

It might appear that the goals for the first session are ambitious. In our experience, it is the rule, rather than the exception, that the therapist has obtained a clear understanding of the situation from an individual and relational perspective by the end of the initial session. Moreover, the way in which the couple views the problem has been reframed in a more positive, relational context. A working relationship has been established and the couple is often eager to attend the next session.

SUBSEQUENT SESSIONS

There is no universal reaction to an erectile dysfunction, although feelings of anxiety, inferiority, and vulnerability are common in both partners. After the initial interview, the therapist begins to understand the erectile problem and more immediate factors that provoke it. This preliminary information is shared with the couple while the therapist continues to make sense of the situation. A helpful blueprint for the early assessment is to consider the following:

- immediate response of each partner in the sexual situation
- worries about lack of desirability within each partner
- deeper feelings of inferiority predating the relationship that were triggered by the sexual problem
- nonsexual relationship issues that are magnified by the sexual problems

In the early assessment, it is assumed that there is an overlap of influences from these four areas. Typically, however, more attention is given to the behavioral description of "what happens" in the sexual situation and feelings that are experienced by each partner in response to the erectile dysfunction (the first two items in the blueprint).

In the immediate sexual situation, anxiety experienced by the man is related to his sexual performance and feelings of inferiority. Because he worries that he will not be able to attain or maintain his erection, his erotic thoughts and feelings are short-circuited. Thus, he "removes" himself by becoming preoccupied with his performance rather than his partner. The sexual "performance anxiety" he feels tends to be contagious causing the partner to react without considering the source of his problem. The following is an example of a therapy session in which the initial session is processed:

THERAPIST: Describe what happens when you begin to have sexual relations. Tell the physical details as you would describe a movie, starting at the beginning. For example, who usually initiates and how does it look?

RICK: Usually, I am the one who gets things going. I start by lightly kissing Rachel and if she seems interested, I proceed.

THERAPIST: Is this the way you see it, Rachel?

RACHEL: Yes, although sometimes I initiate too, usually in the same way.

THERAPIST: What happens next?

RACHEL: I know he is really feeling sexy when he begins to touch me all over and starts to remove my clothing. This usually gets me interested too.

RICK: Yes, she's right!

THERAPIST: When this kind of caressing happens, are you sexually aroused, Rick? Do you notice that you have an erection?

RICK: Oh yes.

RACHEL: [Giggles]

THERAPIST: I know it is embarrassing to talk about such intimate information, but it is necessary for us to understand many of these details. You are doing a great job! Please continue. Rachel, do you notice that Rick has an erection?

RACHEL: Yes. Usually I begin to touch him all over, especially in that area.

THERAPIST: You touch his penis.

RACHEL: Yes.

THERAPIST: What happens next?

RICK: Well, sometimes I enjoy the way I feel when she is touching me and my erection remains firm. When I have trouble, though, I notice that my erection begins to go away. This can happen even before we try to have intercourse.

THERAPIST: When you begin to lose your erection, what are you thinking?

RICK: I am thinking that I am going to lose it again and that Rachel is going to be disappointed with me.

THERAPIST: When you notice that Rick is having trouble with his erection, what thoughts do you experience?

RACHEL: I think about whether or not it is going to happen again.

THERAPIST: [To both] And how do you feel then?

RICK: Terrible, I actually feel scared.

RACHEL: I begin to feel sweaty and nervous.

In a heterosexual relationship, the woman typically assumes the blame for his erectile problem, fearing that he does not find her physically attractive or desirable. The mixture of situational anxiety superimposed on other feelings within each partner will undoubtedly complicate the couple's response to an erectile dysfunction. On the surface, each appears merely anxious but at a deeper level each might be experiencing feelings of great magnitude indirectly related to the situation. This is fertile ground for projection of incompletely understood feelings onto the partner. At best, the situation can become quite complex. Until these reactions are uncovered in psychotherapy, they are certain to insidiously generate sexual anxiety or avoidance in both partners.

Following the early assessment, the focus changes to the deeper individual and relational issues that may contribute to the erectile dysfunction.

ASSESSING RISK FACTORS

Individual Risk Factors

Every individual brings his or her early beliefs, values, and preferences regarding sexuality to an intimate sexual relationship. In addition, the psychological characteristics of each partner, personality traits, strengths, and vulnerabilities add to the mix, creating a couple system that acts and reacts continuously. It is necessary to be aware of conditions existing within each individual that require attention when assessing and treating a sexual dysfunction. Often present are psychological risk factors that have predisposed the individual to be vulnerable to experiencing a sexual dysfunction.

The nonrelational or individual psychological risk factors to be considered include negative cognitions, body-image concerns, performance anxiety, sexual ignorance, life-cycle stressors, sexual identity issues, fear of intimacy, and psychiatric factors. These factors affect sexual functioning by making the man more vulnerable to the influences of anxiety. Moreover, the impact of these factors on the couple's sexual experience can be profound. It is useful, therefore, to assess the extent to which the *individual* is inhibited by his or her psychological issues while simultaneously monitoring the relational response.

Cognitions

The man with an erectile dysfunction creates cognitions that are negative and often irrational. Typically, he falsely believes that his problem cannot be corrected and therefore fails to seek treatment until the sexual situation creates a crisis in the relationship. Believing that the situation is hopeless, he comes to *feel* hopeless instead of optimistic. He thinks that his penis should work in all situations, regardless of his desire or interest. Often, he maintains overzealous standards of performance clearly based on misinformation. Further exacerbating the situation, the man generalizes his negative cognitions about sexual ability well beyond the sexual realm, causing him to believe that he is a failure. Naturally, it is essential to assess how and what he thinks about his erectile dysfunction, and the impact of these cognitions on his feelings and behavior.

Body Image

It is not uncommon to learn that a man with an erectile dysfunction often feels embarrassed about the appearance of his body, and that this factor plays a significant role in inhibiting the sexual response. The individual may go to great lengths to conceal his fears or to avoid sexual intimacy altogether. This can be frustrating to the partner who desires sex. Body-image anxiety can interrupt sexual enjoyment by inhibiting the natural communication of sexual preferences. Since anxiety is often contagious, the woman might also become uncomfortable with sex without realizing that she is reacting to her partner. Embarrassment or discomfort with one's physical appearance is typically described by women. Body-image discomfort is different in men only in that they often worry about penis size and performance rather than more generalized concerns about weight and beauty. Assessment therefore addresses personal perceptions about what is considered normal in terms of body image and physical attractiveness.

Performance Anxiety

Sexual performance anxiety is another common concern of the man experiencing erectile problems. He tends to worry and even obsess about the size and stamina of his penis, diverting his focus from his partner's arousal. He worries that his penis will not continue to work and that his partner will be unfulfilled. He might catastrophize that his partner will find someone else more sexually desirable. If his cognitions are distorted enough by anxiety, he might obsess about his sexual orientation. Eventually, his partner also becomes anxious and joins in the obsessional focus on his penis.

In order to understand the degree of anxiety the man experiences, ask about his thoughts and feelings prior to and during sexual relations. Determine the extent to which anxiety inhibits his sexual response during masturbation. Help him to describe the physical components of his anxiety by using Wolpe's (1958) subjective unit of discomfort scale (SUDS). This involves assigning a numerical value to the anxiety (1–10, with 10 being the highest level) at various points in the sexual response and describing how his body feels at that time. For example, at a level 1 or 2, men typically report thinking "I am going to lose my erection" or "She will become upset with me. At level 5 it is not uncommon to experience a rapid heart rate, sweating, and a knot in the stomach. Help him link his cognitions to each level of anxiety.

Sexual Ignorance

Sexual ignorance often fuels erectile dysfunctioning, particularly if the man is worried about penis size. He fears he is not normal because he is not large enough to please his partner. He also believes misinformation about performance, subscribing to the myth that men should be capable of coital thrusting for indefinite periods of time (Zilbergeld, 1992b). He does not know that penile thrusting alone is an ineffective method of providing stimulation to his female partner. In fact, because of his concern about his own performance, he is likely to avoid asking his partner about her preferences as noted in chapter 1, thereby distancing himself when he should be experiencing the greatest degree of closeness. Eventually, his partner incorrectly interprets his anxiety as disinterest in her, or worse, she fears he finds her unattractive.

Ask about his sexual knowledge. What does he think will please his partner? Ascertain his comprehension of female sexual anatomy and physiology. Determine if his view of "normal" sexual functioning is contributing to her sexual problems. In what ways is he failing to live up to his own expectations of sexual performance? *What he thinks* and *how he feels* are interrelated and it is essential that the therapist help him to see this connection through open-ended questioning. For example:

To the man
So you believe she needs you to be erect for the duration of lovemaking?
Are there ways in which you can touch her that give her pleasure?

When you think you have failed, how do you feel about yourself?

It must make you disappointed that you cannot pleasure her without using your penis.

To the woman

Do you know what kinds of touch are stimulating for you?

Do you show your partner how to touch you during lovemaking?

Do you need him to use his penis to give you an orgasm?

What do you say to him when he loses his erection?

Life-Cycle Factors

The assessment must also be sensitive to life-cycle factors that could adversely affect erectile functioning. One example of such a transition is from the married-without-children stage to that of becoming parents. Sometimes the man feels overlooked or even jealous because the baby demands so much of the mother's attention. Naturally, he understands that the focus of attention shifts from the couple with the birth of the baby but this does not always translate at an affective level. In addition, the man often does not wish to "burden" his partner with requests for sex in the first months of the baby's life. Another transition occurs at mid-life, when men often begin to notice subtle but predictable consequences of aging. Some men fear the loss of health and stamina as they get older. Others notice changes in sexual functioning, such as the increasing refractory period, and begin to worry that they are losing their sexual stamina. This is especially prominent in men who are sexually misinformed about normative changes in the sexual response. These men tend to adhere to cognitions and beliefs that are rigid and unrealistic about sexual performance. Another example is the crisis that occurs when men undergo the rigors of divorce, suffering from the loss of a partner and the stress involved in the separation and the process of starting over.

Assessment questions concerning life-cycle stages, transitions, and periods of crisis, which the therapist ponders, include:

- Did the erectile dysfunction first occur when the client was undergoing a period of transitional stress?
- Is it possible that the precipitating factors are no longer operative but that the dysfunction is persisting in an encapsulated way?
- What are the client's beliefs about life-cycle transitions? Is he aware of normative physiological changes in the sexual response as he ages?
- What are his expectations of sexual performance now and in the future?

- Is he able to articulate his concerns, or does he tend to internalize them and ruminate over them?

Sexual Orientation Issues

Sexual orientation influences one's gender preferences, sexual behavioral repertoire, and fantasies. Although these issues do not usually appear as the presenting problem for which therapy is sought, they can emerge during therapy because they are so closely related to sexual desire and arousal. For instance, a man with a predominantly homoerotic arousal pattern will have difficulty becoming and staying aroused by a heterosexual partner. This issue might not have been discussed by the couple prior to therapy. Assessment, therefore, includes determining if the individual is comfortable with sexual fantasies, images, thoughts, and feelings related to his or her own sexual desires. Therapists need to investigate:

- Is he able to develop and sustain sexual fantasies during lovemaking or masturbation?

- Does he have feel guilt or anxiety because the fantasies are ego-dystonic?

- Is he sexually attracted to his partner, or has he chosen someone who fits the family expectation while forsaking his own preferences?

- Does he need to fantasize about homosexual relations in order to become aroused in heterosexual encounters?

Fear of Intimacy

Fear of intimacy is an individual risk factor although it may have a relational consequence. For example, a man who experiences discomfort in intimate situations will enter a sexual scenario with a moderate degree of anxiety at the outset. This anxiety is about *his* fear of getting too close emotionally or being afraid to trust in his partner. He is fearful of abandonment or criticism. Of course, the genesis of such fears *predates* the current relationship. He is most likely unaware of the causes however, and might think that it is having sex with his partner that makes him anxious. Typically, this type of man describes a succession of relationships in which there was a premature ending or perhaps a history in which he experienced an erectile dysfunction with more than one partner.

Taking a detailed sex history will allow the therapist to track the client's intimate relationships and sometimes glean information about intimacy patterns within his family. LoPiccolo and Heiman (1978) offer an excellent example of a comprehensive sexual assessment in which specific historical data and current sexual learnings and practices are examined.

Psychiatric Factors

The last set of individual risk factors are a result of psychological problems such as depression, personality disorders, psychoses, addictions, and the presence of other sexual dysfunctions or paraphilias. Although these factors are discussed in previous sections, it is important to stress that psychiatric problems that profoundly affect interpersonal relationships *must* be addressed and treated prior to conducting psychotherapy for the sexual dysfunction. The clinician will detect the obvious presence of these profound problems, recommending referrals when appropriate.

The presence of less obvious yet severe psychiatric risk factors can confound the treatment if they are not detected early. Sometimes, the erectile dysfunction is the presenting problem, but may be a reflection of low sexual desire, paraphilias, or mild depression. The symptom represents the lack of a sexual appetite, *not* the loss of functioning. For example, a man with a paraphilia or fetish will have a low appetite for sexual relations because the preferred object or behavior is not a part of the sexual situation. Although it is not a common manifestation, our experience shows a surprising number of individuals who engage secretly in behaviors such as cross-dressing, fetishistic activities, and exhibitionism. It is essential to determine which came first, the other less obvious psychiatric problem or the erectile dysfunction.

Interactional Risk Factors

Risk factors affecting the couple's relationship are certain to have an impact on the sexual relationship. These include negative emotions toward the partner, such as anger or resentment, stemming from either more immediate relational problems or of longstanding discord. It is not uncommon to hear that an individual is not "interested" in the partner when, in fact, he or she is experiencing smoldering resentment. When considering the interactional situation, it is critical to determine the way in which it is affecting the sexual response: That is, does he actually have an erectile dysfunction or is he suffering from a lack of desire for his partner?

As noted previously, the sexual response is conceptualized as a cycle with three phases: desire, arousal, and orgasm (Kaplan, 1979). Desire has to be continued throughout sex for the response to be maintained (Schnarch, 1998). Often, the sexual response is inhibited at the desire stage if the couple is not getting along. This is especially true for women. When this occurs, the formation of erotic fantasies and desire for the partner is short-circuited by anger or resentment. Although some feuding couples have great sex, it is not the norm. While it is possible for some couples to enjoy sexual intimacy while feeling angry or resentful, eventually the effects of the negative emotions will interfere with sexual desire, arousal, and orgasm.

Typically, men report the presence of sexual desire for their partner even if they are feeling somewhat angry. This is particularly true of younger men probably because of the powerful force of circulating testosterone. As men grow older, the sexual response is more vulnerable to the effects of anxiety (Crenshaw & Goldberg, 1996). Even in the presence of sexual desire, men become more vulnerable at the arousal phase of the sexual response cycle. Therefore, while the man might feel like having sex and be able to sustain an erection at the beginning of lovemaking, he is more likely to lose the erection if he is not comfortable. Thus, the response cycle is inhibited at the second stage, that of arousal.

Cognitions

Two sets of cognitions need to be assessed when working with the couple struggling with an erectile problem. The first is the set of thoughts *the man* ponders moments before the erectile failure. These negative cognitions alone might be responsible because they can produce anxiety that interferes with the sexual response. Anxiety and sexual arousal are incompatible and competing responses. Each seeks expression within the individual and only one can prevail: Typically, the thoughts that immediately affect erections are about performance anxiety. *Will I lose my erection? Is it going to happen again? What will she think of me? I am such a failure.* It is impossible to sustain a steady natural expression of sexual arousal when the man is thinking self-defeating thoughts.

The man's *partner's* negative thoughts about him might also be responsible for the inhibition of sexual arousal in him. In the presence of low, steady levels of resentment, mistrust, anger, defensiveness, etc., sexual enjoyment is inhibited without his awareness of the cause. The woman's concealed resentment may build over time and erupt, perhaps without warning, when he wants to be sexual. In this state of conflict, he experiences desire but cannot become aroused because he is actually on guard. He attempts to become close or vulnerable when his autonomic nervous system is warning him to protect himself.

Max and Mora are a case in point. After ten years of marriage, this couple in their mid-thirties came for therapy because they had been avoiding sexual relations. For a six-month period prior to their total cessation of sexual contact, he had experienced an erectile failure during lovemaking. Penetration was impossible. Each was convinced that the erectile dysfunction had a medical cause, although Max could masturbate to orgasm, with a firm erection, when alone. After several sessions, it became apparent that he was resentful of Mora's controlling nature and felt helpless to get her to change, despite attempts to express his feelings. Couple therapy included sensate focus exercises as well as ongoing discussion of his anger and resentment.

The assessment should differentiate between the sets of cognitions that immediately precipitate the erectile dysfunction and those related to the man's partner. Therapeutic questions will implicitly convey the point to the couple that his anxiety is coming from two sources. If he is able to articulate the thoughts that feed the erectile dysfunction, he may feel less helpless as he understands the power of his own thinking as well as some of the underlying dynamics related to his partner. He may make the connection between thinking and behavior. He can choose not to force himself to be sexual until he has discussed his resentment with his partner. The partner will be involved in the process of understanding and changing the couple's interactional patterns. If the therapeutic alliance is strong, the therapist can challenge the man's cognitions and responses by utilizing questions that can also serve to mobilize the couple's problem-solving skills:

To the man
What do you think just prior to losing your erection?

Do you tell her how you are feeling at these times?

What do you say?

How does she respond?

What would you like her to do when you are having difficulty?

What do you believe your body is telling you when your penis will not stay
   erect?

To the woman
You stated you have not been getting along. What is that about?

Have you talked about the way you have been feeling?

What have you shared about the problems you have been having?

Do you think the erectile problem is related to how you have been arguing
   lately?

What makes you want to have sex when you are feeling so upset?

Do you think he should be able to sustain an erection under these circumstances?

This type of therapeutic questioning gently leads the man and his partner to understand that it is unreasonable to expect to be intimate when he is not feeling safe. They are led to this conclusion, even as they are empowered to challenge their own assumptions and expectations. They are helped to see why some of their problem-solving has not worked in the past. The couple learns new ways to conceptualize their difficulties and make the necessary adjustments. Moreover, they are able to identify some of the hidden cognitions and feelings that have been driving their interactional patterns.

As mentioned previously, a man who experiences an erectile dysfunction might be compensating for a sexual dysfunction in his partner. Alternatively, he could be experiencing less arousal because of her lack of interest in having sex with him. In either scenario, he is maintaining an interpersonal distance that is intended to protect the couple system. Although the presenting problem will direct the assessment to the male, the assessment should be based on a systemic perspective. Determine if she enjoys sexual desire, arousal, and orgasm. Inquire about the effect of his erectile dysfunction on her sexual response. Do not assume that her inhibitions, if present, were precipitated by him.

Sexual Desire

In assessing an erectile dysfunction, the therapist focuses on the arousal phase of the sexual response cycle. It is also beneficial to determine the level of sexual desire of each partner, as desire precedes arousal and is a necessary component for maintaining sexual excitement. The therapist therefore determines if one partner has more sexual desire than the other. This discussion can be introduced by talking about chemistry or appetite. These words tend to normalize the notion that individuals have different interest levels in sex over the course of the relationship. Ask about sexual *frequency* as well as level of sexual *interest* because frequency is not always a true indicator of desire. Some couples need help discriminating between the two. Discern if the current pattern is normal for the couple or a departure from the status quo. It is possible that the partner with less sexual desire might develop anticipatory anxiety or even avoid sexual relations. The situation creates pressure as this partner either anticipates disappointing the other or feels forced to engage in sexual relations when not in the mood. If the man has less sexual desire than his partner the anticipatory anxiety potentially could interfere with erectile functioning.

Another possibility is that the man who has lost all sexual desire for his partner becomes anxious whenever she approaches him for sex. He anticipates that it will be difficult for him to generate desire and therefore his arousal will be diminished, directly affecting his erection. If it is awkward to assess the factors responsible for his precipitous lack of desire in the conjoint session, it is always prudent to change the format. Introduce the idea of an individual session for each partner to have the opportunity to discuss those concerns that cannot easily be addressed in the presence of the other. Prior to the individual sessions suggest that the issues discussed need to be explored at a later time in the conjoint format. While the therapist does not want to restrict what is discussed in these sessions, he or she does also not want to become a cohort in collusion if a secret is revealed. During the individual sessions, the likelihood of affairs or other secrets can be assessed.

In this Internet era, we have noticed a trend in monogamous couples in which the man prefers to watch pornographic videotapes or Internet pornography over having sex with his partner. Many of these men settle into a stable pattern of masturbating two to three times per week in the absence of the partner. Typically these men are conflict-avoidant and greatly prefer retreating into the world of fantasy over confronting their partner about their lack of desire or anxieties about sex. Needless to say, this practice eventually affects the intimacy levels in the relationship.

Commitment and Conflict Management

Finally, couples with ineffective conflict management styles and low levels of commitment will have difficulty resolving a sexual concern even with the help of a therapist. Sometimes the signs of difficulty in either or both of these areas are obvious, such as canceled appointments or lateness, resistance to suggestions, failure to engage in a therapeutic alliance, chronic blaming, or reports of physical abuse. In such instances, it must be determined if the couple is unsuited to sex therapy or conjoint therapy in general. Often, individual concurrent therapy is more appropriate.

A couple in their late forties, married for 18 years, arrived for sex therapy with multiple problems. The woman described what we would call primary inhibited sexual desire and said that she had no interest in sex and that she avoided it most of the time. She told us that this condition was lifelong. He entered the marriage knowing this was a problem for her, and complained about her lack of desire throughout the marriage. For this couple, sex occurred infrequently and only when he persuaded her. In his mid-forties, he developed an erectile dysfunction of mixed etiology, due to lifelong diabetes, and used Caverject, MUSE, or Viagra to potentiate his erections. He pressed for intercourse often, to no avail, and finally created a crisis by issuing an ultimatum: that she have sex with him or he would leave the marriage. She suspected that he was having an affair, but he denied this, even in a private session. His intention was to prove that she was the cause of his unhappiness. She agreed to address her intimacy issues and had sex with him after several months of therapy. Soon thereafter, he left the marriage. Sometime later, she discovered that he was, in fact, having an affair. He blamed her for his lack of commitment to their marriage. We referred each to a therapist for individual sessions.

The evaluation that a couple is ready for sex therapy needs to be made quickly. The therapist does not want to increase the hopelessness experienced by the couple by conveying a message that they are too dysfunctional to treat. At the same time, it would be poor judgment to proceed with psychotherapy for the sexual dysfunction if the couple is not committed or prepared for the work involved. It is plausible that such couples can return for sex therapy when their relationship is on more stable ground or when their individual issues are under control. The therapist can reframe the therapeutic goals in a nonpejorative way in order to promote the couple's cooperation.

Intergenerational Factors

Another place to seek information about people's sexuality is to look within the family system. It is common to find themes of sexual secrecy, ignorance, and traumatization in many families, particularly in the histories of individuals with sexual dysfunctions. As noted previously, sexual scripting (Gagnon, Rosen, & Leiblum, 1982) is learned in the family and determines what is, and is not, the blueprint for decoding sexual information into categories of "normal" or "appropriate." Cultural, ethnic, and religious messages about sex influence every family's script. Sex roles, attitudes, beliefs, and cognitions are built upon the belief system of the family of origin. When the family script is rigid or based on misinformation, it is difficult or impossible for the individual to develop natural sexual responses or to enjoy sex that is free from the effects of guilt and anxiety. This task is easily accomplished by using the sexual genogram (Berman & Hof, 1987) as well as the sexual assessment and history interview (LoPiccolo & Heiman, 1978). These practical tools provide balance by assessing the sexual responses of each partner.

It is useful to ask about how sex education occurred within the families of each partner. Questions for the therapist to ponder include:

- Was sexuality discussed, if at all?
- What family members imparted information about normative milestones, such as menstruation, masturbation, and reproduction?
- What cultural and religious beliefs or myths influenced the family's teachings about sexuality?
- How much learning about sex occurred outside of the home?
- What rules regarding sex were operative in the family and how were these rules expressed?

- What were the family beliefs about "normal" or "abnormal" sexual behaviors?

One cannot underestimate the power of secrecy in transmitting messages regarding sexuality within the family of origin. Without the use of language, one learns that sexuality is unspeakable, dangerous, and forbidden. Moreover, not talking about the body or sexuality makes it difficult or impossible to express and clarify conflict. This creates vulnerability within the child, predisposing him or her to sexual anxiety, guilt, or conflict. If prevented from talking about it, the child concludes that there is something "bad" about one's body. Adults cannot easily exorcise the "demons" generated by sexual secrecy, as such messages tend to be pernicious, and the damage not exposed until later in life.

The parental relationship is often a part of the bigger picture affecting the person with an erectile dysfunction. We learn how to interact in an intimate relationship, in part, by observing our parent's relationship. Some behaviors in adult intimate relationships are habitual and reflect the climate of the parental relationship. At times, the therapist needs to help the couple recognize that they are behaving in a way that is not useful in the current relationship even though this pattern was learned in the family. Questions for the therapist to consider include:

- Was the parental relationship conflicted by power struggles, fear, and resentment?
- How did his/her parents regard each other?
- Was intimacy or affection demonstrated?
- What beliefs does he/she hold about their intimate relationship?
- In what ways is he or she like or unlike the same gender parent?
- What does he or she wish he had done differently?

The use of open-ended questions can reveal the intergenerational factors that might be contributing, albeit covertly, to the erectile dysfunction. Also, it is essential to inquire about sexual trauma during the assessment. Covert incest (Adams, 1991) as well as obvious sexual trauma need to be addressed. Clients will disclose this material eventually, provided the clinician is comfortable with this area, patient, and persistent. When a client denies sexual trauma, return to the subject periodically until you are able to confirm or disconfirm the therapeutic hypotheses. It is not surprising how many individuals with sexual dysfunctions are survivors of rape, molestation, or covert incest during childhood or adolescence (Maltz, 1988; Talmadge & Wallace, 1991). Assessment should investigate themes of inappropriate closeness or "special" relationships between adult and child that transgress intergenerational boundaries.

We have worked with several couples in which one or both partners were victims of childhood or adolescent sexual abuse, and the incest was revealed for the first time to the partner in the conjoint session. Often, this type of information emerges as trust in the therapy grows. Because such information is unexpected, it can divert the therapy from addressing the problems that brought the couple to therapy. Nonetheless, the sexual abuse must be addressed before proceeding with sex therapy.

The sexual genogram described by DiMaria, Weeks, and Hof (1999), is a practical tool for the assessment of intergenerational factors influencing sexual attitudes and behaviors. Superimposed on the genogram format are the messages or sexual scripts learned within the families of origin and carried through the generations of each partner. Myths, legacies, secrets, and conflicts are explored. Couples often report that prior to the therapy, they had not shared the information they revealed in the session, at least to the extent that it is discussed in therapy. Each partner develops an understanding of the influences on the other that predated the relationship. Empathy for the other replaces resentment and blaming as the varying pieces of information are given their proper perspective. The couple is helped to separate the areas of conflict that originate in the families of origin from those within the relationship. Habitual processes, such as projection, are interrupted and replaced with reality-based information about how the sexual problem developed. The partners can also learn to recognize ways in which their responses have exacerbated the problem and regain control over their reactions to each other.

The beauty of the sexual genogram is that it can be used by the couple at home to collect information and to facilitate discourse. The couple is given the assignment to spend a predetermined amount of time between sessions learning about the other rather than focusing on fixing various problems. They are encouraged to be creative with their note-taking in an effort to discern and decode the contextual sexual messages. In session, the genogram information is further discussed and clarified with the help of the therapist. Throughout the course of therapy, the material is re-introduced when necessary. Sexual genogram work is another example of how the process of assessment interrupts habitual patterns of communication by offering partners more constructive ways to work together. Change begins as each piece of the puzzle is put in its position.

5

✥ ✥ ✥ ✥ ✥

Sex Therapy with Couples:
Basic Principles and Strategies

IN THIS CHAPTER, WE HOPE TO FILL A GAP missing in the literature. Masters and Johnson (1970), Kaplan (1974), Leiblum and Rosen (1991), and Wincze and Carey (1991) described the treatment of erectile dysfunction in terms of various techniques formalized in a treatment protocol. With the exception of Schnarch (1991, 1998), sex therapists have stressed techniques of treatment. Schnarch's work goes to the opposite end of the continuum and stresses a particular theory that should guide the clinician, much like the early work of Murray Bowen. The work we do is guided by a number of principles and strategies. These range from dealing with the client's belief about the erectile problem, to determining how the problem is framed, to formulating the case from the intersystemic perspective, to working with the affect surrounding the problem, to developing homework assignments and gaining the client-system's compliance. These issues have been overlooked in the literature because they were seen as generic, the assumption being any well-trained therapist should automatically know these principles. Yet, the students we have trained do not know these principles, especially as they are applied to treating erectile dysfunction.

In the prior chapter, we discussed the first phone call from the perspective of assessment. For conceptual clarity, we now present how the first phone call is used to establish the therapeutic alliance and actually begin the treatment process.

THE INITIAL PHONE CALL

The first step in treating erectile dysfunction is to ensure that both partners appear for treatment. In couple therapy, the female partner most often calls for an appointment, but in these cases where the complaint is erectile dysfunction, it is usually the male who calls to make the appointment for himself. He assumes that he is the one with the problem and that he should be the one who should seek individual treatment. Unless he has done some reading about the problem or has been told by a referring professional that the treatment involves the partner, he will not understand the need to discuss this matter with her. Therapy begins with the initial phone call. As noted, this call is the therapist's first opportunity to connect with the patient and to begin setting the stage for treatment. The difficulty in getting the patient *and* his partner started in treatment and keeping them in treatment cannot be underestimated. Our experience over many years is that men will postpone treatment, often for many years. In many instances, the urologist will make a referral and send a report (with the patient's permission), and the patient will never call. This pattern is the rule rather than the exception. Studies also support our clinical experience. Segraves, Schoenberg, Zarins, Knopf, and Camic (1981) found that only 62% of the patients referred within their hospital made an appointment. Of those who began treatment, 43% ended therapy prematurely. Another study also found that the majority of men evaluated and referred for treatment of an erectile problem had not followed up for treatment as of two to three years later (Tiefer & Melman, 1987).

During the initial phone call, it is important to spend some time with the man discussing a few aspects of treatment. Besides addressing the usual concerns such as fees, appointment-setting, insurance, and nature of problem(s), the therapist needs to make two important points: (1) that most erectile problems can be resolved with the right combination of treatments, and (2) that he will need to bring his partner. Prior to making this point, however, the therapist needs to state that just talking about an erectile problem will not make it disappear or get better. Men are very skeptical that talking about any problem will make it disappear or get better. They are especially skeptical that they can talk themselves into having an erection or that talking to someone else about it will help. In short, they almost always begin treatment with an abundance of skepticism and pessimism. The therapist must emphasize that in order to improve the problem, he will need to follow a program of treatment that involves doing things at home. Without doing the homework part of the treatment, he should not expect improvement. This statement makes sense to men at some level because they tend to believe they have to "do something" to make things better. Obviously, in order to do something, they will need a partner with whom to do it.

At this stage, as the therapist talks about the need for the partner to be involved, the therapist does not want to imply that the partner is a part of the problem but, rather, part of the solution. The therapist could suggest that the partner is another useful source of information by pointing out that he may not be fully aware of everything that is happening. In addition, the partner will need to participate in various homework exercises and therefore must be able and willing to participate and must understand her part in the exercises. Of course, the client is usually concerned about how to elicit his partner's cooperation and how to explain to her what he is told to do in therapy. Understandably, the client usually prefers that the therapist does this job rather than take it on himself. In most cases, the effort to elicit the cooperation of the partner works. When it fails, the therapist may suggest that the partner call him or her directly to talk about her involvement, and the therapist could then repeat what was already suggested and try to ascertain her reservations. In those cases in which partners absolutely refuse to participate or help, there is a much deeper relationship problem at issue, often accompanied by hostility in the partner; or the partner has a sexual problem such as lack of sexual desire, and they do not want to confront her problem or upset the equilibrium in the relationship. The therapist might have to work with the patient without his partner to the extent that such work is possible. It is unlikely the erectile problem can be effectively treated in this context, but the therapist can help the man understand his problem and his relationship more fully. Sometimes the partner is impressed by the changes, and she agrees to participate in sessions focused on their relationship, which may eventually make it possible for the couple to begin sex therapy. Sometimes the sexual problem is symbolic of the relationship's dissolution, and sex therapy is no longer relevant.

Skepticism and Pessimism: Origins and Modifications

Patients often approach therapy with a sense of skepticism and pessimism. They cannot believe that talking about a problem could possibly lead to improvement. Many patients have a belief that things just *are* what they *are*, especially in the realm of behavioral change. Interestingly, when asked about the genesis of their belief about the impossibility of change they will not usually know, but an investigation of family history often reveals dysfunctional behavior in a parent or parents that persisted over decades. What was modeled for the child was that *people do not change*. The family members' personalities and all of the accompanying psychopathology were persistent and stable. Moreover, men presenting with erectile dysfunction have usually been dealing with it unsuccessfully for years. They have tried to remedy the problem on their own, hoped that it would go away, and found that the harder they tried to make "it" work, the worse things got. Eventually, they begin to think they are beyond help. Given this mind-set, it is a wonder that men seek help at all. Obviously, if they come for treatment it means that their distress, or that of their partner, outweighs their pessimism.

In an earlier volume, we argued that instilling hope is an essential component or principle of treatment (Weeks & Hof, 1995). This principle seems even more salient in the treatment of erectile dysfunction. The therapist communicates hope in two ways. First, the therapist's attitude needs to be genuinely optimistic. The therapy can begin on a positive note with the therapist praising the couple for their strength in getting help, how much they must care about themselves, and for the fact that they value their relationship. The therapist can also honestly state that with currently available treatments, most erectile problems can be significantly improved. The therapist should describe a course of treatment that involves weekly sessions over a period of 10 to 15 weeks. The number of sessions and the number of months of treatment may be extended if medical intervention is needed. (We will discuss this matter further in the chapter on combining treatment). The program of treatment might focus solely on sex therapy or might also include medical treatment. After this discussion, the therapist might ask whether they feel any better about the outcome of therapy, and if not, why not? Unless the issue of skepticism and pessimism is confronted in the initial session, the couple may not return for treatment.

A related issue is that of commitment. A high level of commitment is probably one of the best predictors of success in couple's therapy. The therapist may wish to focus on the evidence of commitment as a way of praising them for seeking help. Additionally, it has proven useful to discuss the need for a commitment to the therapeutic process if they are to achieve their goals (Weeks & Treat, 1992). Fostering commitment and compliance are addressed later in this chapter.

CONTRAINDICATORS OF SEX THERAPY

The other task is to determine whether the couple will be appropriate for sex therapy. For the sake of argument, assume the man does not have an organic basis for his problem, and there are several psychological risk factors involving disinterest or opposition in one partner. The most appropriate course of treatment would be sex therapy, if the circumstances would allow for it. For example, the man has no interest in sex therapy; he is, in fact, antitherapy but came to the session at the insistence of his partner. Unless the therapist can break through his resistance, his only other option would be medical. This option could be discussed and the feelings his partner has about his rejection of any psychological help processed. She could then "make her case" in favor of sessions with the therapist to deal with other aspects of their relationship.

A second situation is when the partner has no interest in sex therapy. She basically sees the problem as being his and wants him to see a physician or a therapist to correct his problem. The therapist can explain that her participation is essential, that homework assignments involving both partners are integral to the therapy. This strategy works when the partner's opposition has arisen due to ignorance of what therapy requires. Once the therapy begins, the issues addressed can be expanded to include relationship concerns. If the partner still refuses, the man can be referred for medical help, but the outcome of such a referral is problematic.

If a partner is unwilling to help her mate, it is probably because of marital discord, or because she does not want him to overcome his erection problem. The partner is attempting to sabotage the treatment before it begins and will continue to do so throughout his efforts to solve his problem. This client is well advised to continue working with the therapist to "help integrate the medical treatment into the relationship." In this way, the client will have a way to process why his sexual and/or marital relationship isn't improving in spite of taking a drug that makes an erection possible.

The following case illustrates this point. Rich and Barbara had been involved with each other for several years. They were both professionals and both had been married twice. They were in their late forties when they met. In the beginning of their relationship, both were drinking excessively. Over time, Rich decided to seek treatment for his problem, joined AA, and began individual therapy. Within a couple of years he was sober; Barbara maintained her pattern of drinking. In addition to the alcohol problem, Rich had an erectile problem from early in the relationship. Whenever he had difficulty, Barbara would feel sexually rejected and criticize him for not being attracted enough to her. She felt that if he were truly attracted to her, he would not have a problem. Of course, Rich just tried harder, thinking that would solve his problem and help him avoid her criticism. He sought treatment for his erectile problem, but Barbara was reluctant to come with him because she said it was too painful, and it was his problem anyway. She continued to drink, which disturbed him, and he began to question whether he wanted to be in the relationship. However, his self-esteem was so low that he felt he could not leave anyone who would "put up with him." Therefore, he was desperate to correct his erectile problem. Obviously, doing behavioral sex therapy was not an option because she refused to participate. Rich was referred to a urologist and prescribed Viagra. He quickly found the Viagra helped him gain an erection, but then Barbara complained about other aspects of his sexuality. She told him that his penis was too small, and that he could not sexually please her in spite of having an erection. She also criticized his lack of skill and technique, lack of expressed desire and affection, and the fact that he had become an AA convert. Barbara realized that in order to keep Rich *and* continue to drink she would have to diminish his self-esteem both sexually and generally. The focus of the therapy shifted to help him understand Barbara's role in maintaining the status quo and explore his options for the future.

The third situation is when the partners recognize the erectile problem, want to improve their sex life, but are not ready as a couple to proceed with the sex therapy. There are several situations that all but preclude being able to start a course of sex therapy. These couples are in need of couple and/or individual therapy before they can begin the work on the erectile dysfunction. Some couples may be able to "bypass" their other difficulties, but our experience has shown this is usually not the case. It is also our belief that restoring sexual functioning in a relationship that isn't working is misguided. We try to help the couple understand why they need to do other work before tackling the sexual problem. For those who insist on proceeding, we will attempt a course of sex therapy but add that if the therapy doesn't prove effective within three to four weeks' time, they must begin work on the individual/couples issues.

In another case, Steve, 55, and Margo, 52, were engaged in a long-term affair and were considering marriage following a protracted divorce on Steve's part. The affair had gone on for about 15 years, during which time Steve tolerated a marriage to an extremely narcissistic wife. He initially entered therapy in order to work on his marriage, but his wife refused to participate. The therapy was designed to help him see that he was stuck in a relationship that had no hope of improving. After about two years of therapy, Steve decided to end the marriage. During this period, Margo, who had never been married, was beginning to insist that he divorce and marry her immediately. Her insistence sparked a number of arguments between them, with Steve threatening to leave the relationship if she did not "back off." The more he asked her to back off, the more she insisted on an immediate resolution to the situation. As the conflict between them escalated, Steve began to have problems getting and keeping an erection. He could not ask Margo to participate in therapy for this problem because he was ambivalent about whether the relationship should proceed. Steve obtained a prescription for Viagra, but rarely used it because he was losing his desire for Margo and began to think that being sexual with her would give her the upper hand regarding whether the relationship would proceed.

Following are eight contraindications to proceeding directly with couple/sex therapy for an erectile problem:

1. *When there is significant psychopathology in the client or his partner.* Serious psychopathology in the client makes sex therapy highly problematic; in addition, an erectile problem may be secondary to his psychiatric problem. Likewise, if the partner has a serious mental disorder, they will be unable to do the couple therapy and homework. The therapist should evaluate for an Axis I disorder and recommend individual treatment prior to attempting couple and sex therapy.

2. *When there is significant pathology in the couple's relationship.* A couple who is locked in a power struggle characterized by hostility and anger, where the partners cannot agree or work together, is not amenable to sex therapy. The couple issues would be an impossible obstacle in working together cooperatively.

3. *When the client or his partner is unwilling to participate in sex therapy.* The client or his partner may be unwilling to engage in therapy. The man with the erection problem may be present only at the insistence of his partner. He may not wish to participate in any kind of psychotherapeutic process. The same may be true of his partner.

4. *When both partners are narcissistically vulnerable and trade projections.* Narcissistically vulnerable individuals are extremely sensitive and react with hostility to almost every statement made by the other and is interpreted as critical. They also fail to see the other person for who they are because they have created a projective image of the other. This image consists of disowned parts of themselves, which are projected onto the other person. These partners do not see anything alike. They would not be able to agree to doing homework or to carrying it out.

5. *When one or both partners are having an affair.* Affairs create emotional havoc for a couple and must be dealt with first. Treating the affair takes priority over all other issues. Couples are not able to make progress until this issue has been partially resolved.

6. *When one or both partners are in an active addiction.* Addictions require priority in treatment as well. The addictive behavior is the central focus of the addict's life. Changing other aspects of an individual or a couple when there is an addiction is extremely difficult. Couples with

addictions should be referred for appropriate treatment as individuals, while concurrent work is done to maintain the relationship during its restructuring.

7. *When the couple is more distressed by other relational issues.* The couple may present with a variety of issues and have different levels of personal distress about each of these. In general, it is best to sequence the therapy so that sexual issues are treated last. In other words, the couple's relationship needs to be fairly healthy in order for the sex therapy to go well.

8. *When one or both partners are not committed to the relationship.* Having a sexual relationship is usually indicative of a committed couple. A couple on the verge of a divorce or in which one partner is not committed but just biding time will not respond to sex therapy. This couple needs to resolve the issue of commitment prior to working on a problem, which, by its nature, signifies commitment.

The next case illustrates several contraindications to being able to work with the couple. Derrick, 43, was an artist and teacher who traveled extensively. He had experienced erection problems from adolescence. As a teenager, he felt unattractive and awkward, and could not imagine why any girl would like him. He was so anxious and clumsy during his first few sexual encounters that each girl was openly critical toward him. Derrick probably elicited such criticism because he expected it, as it was consistent with all the criticism he experienced in his family.

His early failures, coupled with a depressive, anxious, and perfectionist personality, contributed to many subsequent failures in his marriage. His erectile ability would wax and wane unpredictably. He would always blame himself for the difficulty and for any problems in his marriage. Although Derrick and his wife had one teenaged child, his wife was pushing hard for a second child before "time ran out." Derrick was not sure he wanted to start parenthood over again. He also felt that his wife had been a much better mother than wife. In addition, Derrick had formed a relationship with a student in Europe and had been having an affair for about three years for several weeks out of the year. Though Derrick complained that he could not get enough attention from his wife, he began to realize that these problems were basically his, and he chose individual therapy rather than couple therapy.

Derrick's situation demonstrates the need for individual therapy prior to attempting to do sex or couple therapy. He understood the need to work on himself but did not want to deprive his wife of sex and also wanted to be able to function with his European partner. The available treatment at that time was Caverject, which he began using successfully. It gave him more confidence as a sexual partner, and he began to feel that he could leave the marriage if he chose. This knowledge paradoxically freed him to redouble his efforts to work on himself and the marriage.

Favorable Conditions

Couple and sex therapy is probably the treatment of choice under the following conditions:

1. The client is experiencing performance anxiety. As we have already shown, this particular type of anxiety maintains the erectile dysfunction, but high levels of general anxiety from other sources also make one a good candidate for sex therapy.
2. Both partners are relatively free of psychiatric problems that interfere with couple therapy.
3. Sometimes partners do have a relatively good basis of sex knowledge and are engaging in behaviors that should produce an erection; that is, stimulation of sufficient duration and intensity and proper technique under the right conditions.
4. The client is unable to free himself of obsessive negative sexual cognitions that lead him to observe and judge his behavior and distract him from sensory and erotic feelings.
5. The client has been carrying a sexual secret or has been the victim of physical or sexual abuse. A therapeutic approach is the treatment of choice for these types of problems.
6. The client or partner is experiencing a real or imagined loss of health. This anticipated loss produces fear, anxiety, and other negative feelings that can inhibit an erectile responsiveness.
7. Couples who do not understand the physiological changes resulting from aging can impose the same sexual expectations as when they were in their early years.
8. The man is going through a divorce or significant life stress. Major stressors increase anxiety. Divorce is unique because of the adjustment involved in beginning sexual relationships with new partners.
9. The couple has a high level of sex-related guilt and negative sexual attitudes based on religious beliefs. Guilt and a lack of internalized permission to experience sexual enjoyment and pleasure can inhibit sexual functioning.

10. Territorial, rank-order, power and control, and attachment difficulties exist in the couple.

11. The couple's sexual script has not been effectively negotiated. The partners may desire different sexual behaviors with regard to level of desire, ease of arousal, and means of having an orgasm.

12. The partners are compatible but lack sexual chemistry. They simply do not feel sexually attracted to each other.

13. The erectile dysfunction is embedded in a variety of other sexual difficulties. The erectile dysfunction may be related to another problem such as premature ejaculation or lack of desire in self or other.

14. There is discord in other areas of the relationship, such as ineffective communication and problem-solving, anger and conflict mismanagement, depression, and life-cycle changes.

15. The erectile dysfunction is a physical manifestation of an intimacy problem. The problem is a way of stabilizing the equilibrium in the relationship around intimacy. Sex therapy is indicated for couples who have fears of dependency, expressing feelings (both positive and negative), losing control or being controlled, feeling exposed, and rejection and abandonment.

16. The partners have internalized negative parental messages about sex and are still enmeshed in their family of origin. These partners need the dysfunction in order to remain tied to the family of origin. Assuming adult responsibilities and sexual roles would be a threat to the entire family.

If none of these 16 factors, with the exception of performance anxiety (which will almost always be present as a secondary problem), is present, the erectile dysfunction is most likely organic. In organic cases, the couple should participate in the sex therapy as an *adjunctive therapy* to facilitate the medical treatment. The following case demonstrates one in which some of the above-mentioned factors were present, and sex therapy was indicated. However, this case proved to be extremely difficult, and the husband did not improve until he was willing to try Viagra.

Shirley and Mark were a couple in their mid-thirties when they began treatment. They had both been married once before; they had one child from this marriage. In spite of the fact that both were professionals, they were very naïve sexually. Neither had had sex until he/she was married, and sex was unpleasant (at best) for both of them in their first marriage.

Although they got along nicely in all other areas of their relationship, sex was a chronic source of disappointment.

Shirley was extremely inhibited, which prevented her from initiating sex and reinforced her passive role during sex. Mark commented it was like making love to a doll. She was also anorgasmic during intercourse, but not otherwise. Unfortunately, Mark's measure of success as a lover was based on whether she climaxed, so he always felt incompetent as a lover. Neither partner could talk about their sexual needs, nor were they ever clear about what they wanted in their own minds. At the beginning of therapy, Mark also reported premature ejaculation, which was corrected, but the performance anxiety that grew out of this problem was motivated by his other issues and turned into an erection problem. Since this couple had many sexual difficulties, the therapy was sequenced to deal with the problems in an overlapping way. The couple's communication improved; they both became more aware of their sexual needs; and Shirley's inhibitions lessened, and she became orgasmic. Unfortunately, Mark's erectile problem proved to be difficult to treat. The couple tried all the usual exercises described in this text, but he still could not consistently maintain stable erections. Mark also had a generally anxious and perfectionist personality. He was in a career that was very competitive and demanding and work issues often took priority in his life. He refused to seek a psychiatric consultation for his anxiety, although he understood that it could be a contributing factor to his erection problem, because he believed that taking medication was a sign of weakness.

The couple had a pattern of participating in therapy for a few months, quitting, coming back, and then repeating the pattern. The entire course of therapy lasted about five years. When Caverject became available, it was suggested to the couple but Mark refused, saying he could not stick himself with a needle. In fact, he was rejecting the treatment because he felt that taking it would confirm his feelings of inadequacy. He read about Viagra when it became available and realized that many men had his problem. He had been told this fact many times but nevertheless interpreted his problem as a unique sign of personal weakness. The therapist once again normalized his problem as one that was very common and stated that "all the new drug did was to give the system a boost." For some reason framing the problem this way was more acceptable and together with what he had been reading allowed him to give Viagra a try. How well the Viagra worked instantly impressed him. Once he had experienced consistent erections during a few lovemaking sessions, he decided to try intercourse without it. At this point his confidence was up, his performance anxiety down, and his erections were working. He believed he could now use the Viagra as his safety net if he needed it.

REFRAMING THE PROBLEM IN THE INITIAL SESSION

As we suggested earlier, when men present for treatment with an erection problem with their partner, they usually think it is just their problem. In many cases, the problem is a result of unfortunate interaction between the partners that exacerbates performance anxiety and thereby worsens his problem. Additionally, the problem may truly be rooted in deeper pathology in the couple's relationship. In order to fully elicit the cooperation of both partners, the therapist must find a way of framing the problem that is acceptable to both and serves to define the problem in a systemic fashion. This process is known as reframing and is one of the most widely used strategies in marital therapy (Weeks & Hof, 1995).

Reframing is a gradual process done with the couple—not to the couple. A reframe cannot simply be imposed, no matter how compelling it is to the clinician. The therapist must slowly and carefully elicit information in a way that helps the couple accept the new frame that is gradually coming into focus. Sometimes the partners will spontaneously make the reframe before the therapist makes the observation. The process is somewhat like putting together a jigsaw puzzle: all the pieces are on the table, and we know when they are placed together properly an image will be formed. As the pieces are rearranged in various ways, different images begin to emerge. When the therapist elicits various pieces of information and highlights them, he or she is actually suggesting a particular image. When enough bits of information have been elicited, the image the therapist is trying to help them form becomes more and more apparent to them. Reframing is a general strategy that allows the therapist to create a new context for the problem—in the case of erectile dysfunction, a context that is sexual and relational. The reframe becomes the foundation for the treatment.

Erectile dysfunction may require two reframes. The first is to contextualize the problem. As we pointed out in chapter 1, it is rare to encounter a couple who has just a single sexual dysfunction or difficulty. The erectile problem almost always exists in the context of both recognized and unrecognized relational difficulties. The second reframe is needed when the erectile dysfunction serves some deeper function for the couple such as diverting attention from his partner's lack of sexual desire.

During the first three to four sessions, the therapist is usually able to create a new framework for the sexual difficulties. Each partner's sexual problems can be discussed in order to show it is probably not just the man who has a single problem. Hopefully, they will begin to understand their sexual dynamics better. Sexual difficulties can be identified and reframed simply through questioning the couple. An open-ended question can be posed such as, "Are there any other sexual difficulties either of you have experienced?" However, open-ended questions sometimes elicit "look good" responses and must be followed with more specific questions. Both partners should be asked a number of questions. The therapist is implicitly suggesting that the partner may have her own difficulties and be a part of the overall picture. He is not the exclusive focus of the session. As information is gathered, the therapist may ask how one person's behavior affects the other. Some of these questions include:

To both partners
Do you both have adequate sexual desire?

How often would you like to have some kind of sexual interaction?

Do you find there is a discrepancy in your levels of sexual desire? If so, how do you manage it?

What is your theory about his erectile problem?

How has this problem affected your sexual relationship?

How do you each feel when this problem occurs?

Can you think of any ways this problem has been good?

To the man
Do you sometimes ejaculate sooner than you would like?

Is ejaculating too soon a problem for you?

About how long does it take for you to ejaculate after penetration?

Have you had difficulty reaching ejaculation in the past?

How would you like to see your partner's lovemaking improve?

How do you think your partner feels about this problem?

To the woman
Have you had difficulty reaching an orgasm with oral or manual stimulation?

Have you had difficulty reaching an orgasm during intercourse?

Has a difficulty with orgasm interfered with your sexual relationship?

Have you experienced pain or discomfort with intercourse?

Has penetration been a problem due to lack of lubrication or tightness?

Besides the erection, how would you like to see your partner's lovemaking improve?

How do you think your partner feels about this problem?

Can you think of any benefits to having this problem?

As the interview unfolds, the clinician is constantly observing the way the partners provide information and relate to each other. They may appear calm and cooperative or volatile and overreact emotionally to each other. Their style of relating with each other and the clinician is like a snapshot of the problems that may exist in their relationship. The clinician may follow up on these observations with questions that either make explicit the relational problems or suggest that these issues need further exploration. At this point, the therapist remains on the alert for signs of factors (discussed earlier) that are contraindications for doing sex therapy.

The therapist then uses his or her observations and the information gathered regarding the relationship to create the second reframe, which moves the couple beyond the sexual context in which the erectile dysfunction is embedded. This second reframe may have two parts. One part is to describe how the partner's reactions to the erectile problem may contribute to its continuation. For example, if the partner becomes angry and blaming when the problem occurs, the man will feel greater pressure and anxiety. If she says that she has never encountered this problem in any other relationship, he may feel threatened that she will leave, or that he is not as good as other men. Sometimes a woman will insist that this is the man's problem and that he must fix it before attempting to have sex with her again. Statements such as these further demoralize the patient and increase his fear of failure and rejection and his performance anxiety. Most partners grappling with this problem will inadvertently make statements that exacerbate it. The woman may not realize the extent to which her comments intensify the man's fears.

Another reframe would be needed when the erectile dysfunction serves some deeper function for the couple. However, the therapist should not move too quickly in making this reframe. In order to move to this reframe, the therapist must have a solid working relationship with the couple because it is designed to help the couple see that the erectile dysfunction serves a more covert function in the relationship. For example, the symptom (erectile problem) may mask the partner's sexual difficulties. A woman who lacks desire may indirectly communicate this to her partner, and he may respond by developing an erectile problem. Her problem remains unstated and unseen so she does not have to confront the issue. His symptom may be expressing his lack of sexual attraction in the relationship, his attraction to someone else, a fear of intimacy, or any other relational risk factor previously described. Because the couple has colluded in ignoring or denying the real problem, they will not be immediately receptive to this reframe. They would rather keep the focus on (1) the erectile problem, and (2) on one partner only. They are, in fact, unconsciously cooperating with each other in defining the problem in this way. This collusion is why the therapist must have a strong relationship in place before attempting to help the couple face the deeper issues of the problem.

THE CASE FORMULATION

A case formulation is a way of organizing information based on a theoretical approach that guides treatment. The format presented below is based on the intersystemic approach stressing a multileveled or comprehensive view of the client-system. The intersystemic approach is unique in that it combines the individual, interactional (dyadic), and intergenerational (family of origin) perspectives in evaluation and treatment. Using this format, the therapist collects various types of information, interprets the data using different constructs, and formulates a treatment plan with various goals and change strategies. In addition, the therapist considers the prognosis for treatment and examines his or her strengths and weaknesses in dealing with the case. Systems therapists have often overlooked the last point, viewing countertransference as a concept that belongs to the individual therapies and has no place in systems thinking. For example, a therapist who is uncomfortable talking about sex or asking very detailed and personal sexual questions will have difficulty treating a patient with an erectile problem, or any sexual problem for that matter. A detailed explanation of the intersystemic approach to case formulation can be found in *Couples in Treatment: Techniques and Approaches for Effective Practice* (Weeks & Treat, 1992).

The components of a case formulation include a preliminary assessment of the couple, an intersystemic assessment, and a treatment plan.

Preliminary Assessment

Initial impressions and reactions. These are formulated into systemic hypotheses about the couple, which will be confirmed or disconfirmed throughout the course of treatment.

Presenting problem(s). Give a concrete description, including the who, where, what, and how of it. What is each partner's view of the problem? How is the problem maintained in the system?

History of the problem. This is a brief summary of the preceding point over time. Solutions attempted by the couple (including previous therapy): What has the couple tried to do to solve the problem? If they had prior therapy, what worked and didn't work? How have their attempts to solve the problem made it worst?

Changes sought by the clients(s). What do they wish to change? What outcomes do they expect from therapy?

Recent significant changes in their lives. What life stressors or life-cycle changes have occurred? These might include new job, relocation, death, marital conflict/separation, divorce, child leaving home, illness, career change, etc.

Intersystemic Assessment

The individual. This involves a detailed psychological assessment of the intrapsychic components of each partner (i.e., cognitive distortions, irrational thinking, and ego-defense mechanisms such as denial, projection, beliefs, outlook, and personal narratives). Also include *DSM-IV* diagnoses on all three axes.

The couple. The interactional system of the dyad is assessed and evaluated. This includes emotional contracts, styles of communication, linear attributional strategies (debilitation, justification, vilification, and rationalization), and conflict-resolution skills.

The intergenerational system. Each couple brings certain family-of-origin issues that tend to be enacted within the relationship. These patterns are usually repeated because they are beyond the individuals' awareness. Couples therapy not only exposes these intergenerational issues but also serves to interrupt them, giving choice to the couple about how they wish to interact. Common issues include anniversary reactions (e.g., dates of deaths), scripts (e.g., how each partner is to behave), boundaries (e.g., how much emotional space they give each other), cutoffs (e.g., whether one partner is cutoff from a family member), triangles (e.g., are two people overly close to the exclusion of a third), and closeness-distance difference (i.e., does one person desire more closeness than another). Intergenerational assessment has been thoroughly described in DeMaria, Weeks, and Hof, 1999.

The Treatment Plan

The treatment plan includes a refinement of the hypothesis originally generated about the couple. It is usually one simple statement that captures their central dynamic, such as "each partner has difficulty being emotionally close" or "this couple can only relate through conflict." The treatment plan includes the goals for therapy, which goals or changes are to take place first, and the strategies for accomplishing each change (i.e., principles, techniques, implementation strategies).

With regard to sex therapy, three areas are addressed: treatment goals, prioritizing, and implementation. Treatment goals include improved erectile functioning, increased level of sexual satisfaction, and improved overall functioning for the couple. In dynamic and analytic therapy, the symptom per se is rarely treated because it is believed to represent a much deeper historically-based problem. In systems approaches, the point of departure for the treatment is the symptom, which remains a clear focal point in treatment. It is the symptom that brings the couple to treatment, and unless the symptom remains in focus, the couple may lose motivation and discontinue treatment. Hence, one of the goals of treatment is to treat the symptom and improve erectile functioning. However, a working erection does not mean a couple will have a working relationship, sexual and/or otherwise.

A second goal of therapy is to increase the level of sexual satisfaction and enjoyment, regardless of penile functioning. Studies have clearly indicated that in those cases where erectile functioning does not improve, sex therapy could improve the perceived quality of the sexual relationship (Heiman & Meston, 1997). In all cases of sex therapy, the goal is not necessarily to enhance performance but to enhance the pleasure and enjoyment derived from being together in a sensual and sexual interaction.

The third treatment goal, improving the overall level of functioning for the couple, has been viewed as a secondary gain or effect but not as an intent of sex therapy. Put simply, sex therapy has been concerned with just sexual problems (e.g., Kaplan, 1994). Sex therapy and couple therapy have been two distinct professional, academic, and clinical domains. In 1987, Weeks and Hof published the first textbook aimed at the integration of these two fields. Subsequently, Schnarch (1991, 1998) and Woody (1992) published texts that were intended to contextualize the sexual relationship within the couple/family system. Each field has begun to incorporate elements of the other, but a well-integrated approach is still lacking in today's texts on erectile dysfunction (Rosen & Leiblum, 1992b, 1999; Wincze & Carey, 1991) and in the practice of sex and couple therapy in general. Because we do not believe the sexual difficulty can be separated from the rest of the relationship, we treat the couple's reactions to the problem, what each might have contributed to the problem, and the couple's relationship. Some might say we are fundamentally couple therapists practicing sex therapy. We prefer to think of ourselves as treating the whole person and the relationship as a system, not just the symptom.

The second issue addressed in regard to the case formulation is deciding on the priority of the problems to be treated. This involves developing a flow chart for treatment. Some problems will take priority because of the level of distress for the couple. For example, let's assume we have a couple in which the man experiences both premature ejaculation and an erection problem, and he wants to resolves both problems. As we mentioned earlier, this is a common example. Masters and Johnson (1970) stated that about half of the men they treated with an erectile problem were also premature ejaculators. The clinician must decide which problem to treat first, or if they can be treated concurrently. The following principles guide our thinking about which problems are treated first in a couple:

1. Lack of desire takes priority over all other problems, except general problems that make doing sex therapy impossible.
2. Treat the erectile problem before premature ejaculation or retarded ejaculation.
3. Once progress has been made on the erectile problem, some overlapping treatment can occur for the premature ejaculation.
4. The partner may be treated for vaginismus and inorgasmia concurrently up to the point of penetration exercises. Then, the man must have achieved erectile stability in order to continue with this treatment.
5. If couple problems are presented and do not impede progress in the sex therapy, the sessions can be split, spending time on both sets of issues.

These general principles will allow the therapist to develop an individualized flow chart for each couple. In a typical case, the sequence usually involves treating the following set of problems:

1. erectile dysfunction and general issues in the couple, such as communication
2. premature ejaculation once some progress has been made on the erectile dysfunction
3. partner's lack of orgasm
4. the overall sexual relationship
5. deeper issues uncovered during therapy such as old hurts, fears of intimacy

A common problem is to see a lack of sexual desire in the man who has an erectile dysfunction. He might be seeking treatment for his partner's sake or because he does not want to see himself as dysfunctional. In this case, we would treat his lack of desire before attempting to work on the erection problem. If a couple insists on working on the erection problem in spite of other clearly defined difficulties, then the therapist can attempt to do so, after explaining that if this attempt fails, it will indicate that the other work must be done first. Sometimes the choices are not clear, and one course of treatment might be attempted and fail. Failure is a diagnostic indicator that something has been missed or the wrong problem is being treated. Helping the couple frame failure in this way also helps obviate premature termination and gets them to accept another direction. In short, the therapist might agree to try it the couple's way first, and if the treatment does not work, then to try it the way the therapist initially suggested.

Another common pattern is a man with an erectile dysfunction and a woman who is inorgasmic; these two problems can be treated at the same time. Each partner can begin specific homework exercises (these will be described in greater detail later); and toward the middle of therapy, when the woman has completed her exercises up to the point of penetration sex, she may have to wait for her partner to regain erectile functioning.

Many couples present with the pattern of male erectile dysfunction and female inhibited sexual desire. If she is averse to doing the exercises with him, it is obvious that she will have to be treated first. This particular combination requires a good deal of clinical sensitivity. She should not be forced into anything that she is not ready to do, for to do so would only serve to exacerbate her lack of desire. The degree of her lack of desire and the degree to which she wants to help her partner must be carefully assessed.

In prioritizing the existing problems, the therapist will also need to plan how to treat issues in the relationship. Two of the most common relationship problems seen in cases involving erectile dysfunctioning are a lack of communication across the board and unresolved issues around anger and conflict. These issues are a clear hindrance, if not an actual barrier, to doing work around the sexual problem. It is the therapist's responsibility to suggest which issues are to be managed first. If the couple refuses to address their interpersonal issues, sex therapy can proceed with the understanding that if they can do the work, fine, but if not, they will need to back up and address the relationship problems or try to integrate this work with the sex therapy.

The final issue related to the case formulation is how the treatment plan is implemented. The plan should be logical and coherent and make sense to the couple. The therapist should freely answer questions and ask to be challenged about parts that aren't clear. Sharing this information facilitates clients informed consent, shows the couple that the therapist has a plan, which, in turn, is inspiring, and enables the couple to be involved in planning how they will be treated. These factors are all essential in promoting compliance with treatment. Dropout rates in psychological and medical therapies are substantial because patients are not given any sense of responsibility for their treatment. To accomplish this task, the therapist must join with the couple in a collaborative relationship (more will be said about this later in this chapter).

Lowering Fear and Anxiety

The man who has an erectile dysfunction will inevitably experience both fear and anxiety over the problem. The fear is that he will not be able to get an erection and perform according to his expectation. He may also fear his partner's disappointment, rejection, or even ridicule. He begins to monitor himself closely in order to see whether he is going to function "properly." A one-time failure to achieve an erection can trigger this fear, and multiple failures serve to increase the fear. Unlike fear, which has a specific object, the anxiety over the problem is more pervasive and triggered by multiple stimuli, for example, having intercourse, anticipating having intercourse, partner removing clothes, etc.

The first step in helping the patient deal with his performance anxiety is to help him become aware of his feelings and understand them. He may realize he is feeling anxious but not understand the relationship between his anxiety and erectile difficulty. Asking the patient to describe past feelings and to anticipate the feelings he might have in future sexual interactions develops this awareness. He needs to recognize that he is watching himself very closely to see what happens. Masters and Johnson (1970) called this "spectatoring," though Viktor Frankl (1952) was actually the first to observe and label this phenomenon ("hyperreflection") in sex therapy. In fact, Frankl (1991) was practicing sex therapy long before Masters and Johnson began their work in the field of human sexuality. According to Frankl, hyperreflection leads to hyperintentionality, which means trying to will something to happen. These two behaviors are experientially linked and form a vicious circle. The man experiencing an erectile problem begins to watch himself, feels doubt that he will be able to function, and then tries to force the erection to occur. What is normally a natural and transparent process is experienced with great attention and self-apprehension. The normal process of getting an erection is transparent in the sense that what should normally happen is noted without apprehension. The man can passively note what is happening to his penis, without it becoming the object of great concern.

Once this cycle of spectatoring/hyperreflection and hyperintentionality has been described to the man, and it is clear that he understands the intrapsychic dynamic that is causing him so much trouble, it is then necessary to find ways to interrupt it. Perhaps the simplest technique is to suggest stopping the troublesome thoughts. Some men are able to suppress these thoughts once they understand how destructive they are to their sexual functioning. However, the method that we suggest is more active and useful to the overall therapeutic process. We talk about the purpose of sex not as that of achieving any given goal, but to experience pleasurable sensations and the enjoyment of physical intimacy. Sex is not a thinking-oriented activity (like, say, chess), but a feeling-oriented activity (like dancing or getting a massage). The man needs to stop thinking so much and literally come to his senses. He needs to focus on the pleasant physical and emotional sensations that emanate from the sexual interaction. He might be instructed as follows:

> You don't need to worry about what your penis is doing. It is going to do whatever it is going to do and you can't force it to do anything. You've learned that the harder you try to force an erection, the more likely you won't be able to get one or to keep it if you do get one. From now on, focus on the pleasurable physical and emotional sensations you feel when you are together with your partner. You might try asking yourself over and over again, "What feels good at this moment?" and "What would I like to do or have done to me to keep things feeling good?" Focus on positive things, such as enjoying the pleasure you are helping your partner feel, and the pleasure she is helping you feel.

The final strategy used to lower fear and anxiety is to structure the therapeutic exercises so that these feelings are gradually desensitized. This principle will be described in the next section.

Small Steps and Homework

One of the hallmarks of sex therapy is homework. The treatment of many sexual difficulties involves the process of systematic desensitization—a well-known behaviorally-oriented strategy that has received more empirical support in the research literature on sex therapy for erectile dysfunction than any other treatment (Heiman & Meston, 1997). The behavior to be desensitized must occur in the sexual context in as natural a setting as possible. This requires that the couple follow various homework prescriptions. In general, treatment follows a standard protocol first identified by Masters and Johnson (1970). Each week, the therapist provides an individualized homework assignment for the couple that helps the man learn to experience some aspect of his sexuality in a safe and relatively anxiety-free environment. The basic principle underlying these exercises is to provide small incremental steps that help the man achieve success in an anxiety-free context. As he builds on his successes, he gains confidence and competence, thereby lowering his anxiety.

Homework is a way of extending the therapy beyond the therapist's office. One hour of therapy per week is insufficient for resolving problems, especially when patients need to undergo a gradual relearning process. In general, when treating an erectile dysfunction we will prescribe three experiences for the intervening week. One experience might be above the couple's expectations, another about what they expected, and one below their expectations. By suggesting that they will experience variability in the exercises, they will, hopefully, not be disappointed if the next exercise they do doesn't exceed the last. On the other hand, if none of the exercises work, then they can move back to ones that are safer and simpler. When exercises don't work, they provide invaluable diagnostic information. For example, the therapist might have suggested the couple do a genital stimulation exercise without the man focusing (spectatoring or hyperreflecting) on whether he is getting an erection. Unfortunately, he finds he just can't stop thinking about the erection occurring during the exercise. The therapist will then want to back up to a prior step or create another step that might be easier for him to do. Rarely does therapy follow a linear progression. The couple may move forward quickly for several weeks and then get stuck or regress. Whatever the case, the therapist should reassure the couple that their progress is "normal" and they may, at times, have to back up a step or two.

Having pointed out that homework is an integral part of being in sex therapy, the therapist then has a responsibility to give homework at the end of each session and follow up on it at the beginning of the next session. Defining homework as essential but not following up on assignments will undermine the therapist's credibility and negate the value of homework.

What has been overlooked in the literature on psychotherapy in general is the issue of how to give homework. The two most active proponents of assigning homework in therapy have been marriage and family therapists and behavioral clinicians, but the descriptions of the assignments have been more extensive than the description of *when* and *how* the homework is prescribed.

A homework assignment includes four structural elements: scheduling, duration, frequency, and place. The first element is *scheduling* time to do the homework assignment. Couples lead busy lives and, in addition, may have hidden reasons for *not* doing the assignment. We usually ask whether the partners foresee any problem in being able to do the exercise three times during the week. If they don't, then we simply ask when they might get together for the exercise. They may need the aid of the therapist to schedule times to do exercises or set aside time at home to make time on their calendars. In some cases, couples disagree over times or say they are just too busy. Clearly, this represents resistance to doing the homework and needs to be processed prior to leaving the office. For this reason, the therapist might need to allow extra time when making the first assignment in order to determine the couple's level of compliance and process any resistance. The issue of scheduling is the most problematic of the elements because it is a measure of resistance. Once the couple agrees to do assignments, the other elements are easier to handle.

Regarding the second element of *duration*, or how long the assignment should last, the therapist sets time parameters to ensure that the exercises will not last too long. Initial exercises may need to be shorter than those that follow. The couple should also be consulted regarding how much time and energy they believe they can devote to the homework. Most sex therapy assignments are prescribed for between 20–30 minutes.

We generally recommend a *frequency* of two or three exercises per week. Men with erectile dysfunction place a great deal of pressure on themselves every time they have sex. If they haven't attempted sex in a while, they tend to place even more pressure on themselves. They view each homework experience as an opportunity to succeed or fail. The therapist should point out that success or failure for any given experience is not the salient issue, but that it is the overall direction of the experiences that is important. Explaining this to the couple usually helps to reduce some of the pressure the man is feeling, which, in turn, may enable him to function better. The only exception to assigning homework three times per week is with the treatment of premature ejaculation, which requires more frequent homework in order to make rapid progress. We encourage the couple to do as many exercises as they can during the week.

The final element of *place* will vary for each couple. Though the bedroom provides greater privacy, and is associated with sexual activity, it is also the place where they have experienced some unpleasant sexual encounters. Some men describe feeling more relaxed doing some of the sensual exercises in another room, because it is easier to separate his enjoyment from the expectation and demands for sex that he associates with the bedroom. Ultimately, it is the couple's choice. The therapist's role is to facilitate making the choice that feels the safest and helps to lower fear and anxiety most effectively.

Giving homework to patients without attending to whether they will comply is a waste of both the therapist's and the couples' time. In many areas of medicine and psychology, patient compliance is known to be poor (Teifer & Melman, 1987). Patients frequently do not fill prescriptions or take the full course of medicine prescribed. Psychotherapy patients often forget, ignore, deny, or distort their homework assignments. Three factors have been identified that can help to promote greater compliance in psychotherapy (Strong & Claiborn, 1982). The first is *choice*: Patients are more likely to do a task when they believe they have some choice in the formulation of the task. For example, the therapist gives a general outline of the task and then elicits input from the couple in designing the final assignment. Getting their input allows partners to express their preferences regarding what is to be done, and it is also therapeutically useful for other reasons, such as determining the pace. They may also be given choices regarding the structural elements just discussed; they can choose when, how frequently, for how long, and where the exercise is to be done.

The therapist also has to make a choice in what to call the homework. For some patients, the concept of homework makes sense immediately. For example, schoolteachers, professors, and professionals can relate to this concept as a way to learn something new. On the other hand, the patient who equates homework with school failure may have a negative reaction to the word. Considering the couple's background and experiences usually provides some clues about what to call this aspect of treatment. Some common terms are *assignment, chore, experience, exercise, task*, and even *experiment*. Experiment can be appealing because it does not imply a predetermined outcome.

Depersonalization is the second factor that can be used to increase compliance. Patients do not like to be pressured, especially when a therapist is directing them to do something. We have found it helpful to avoid phrasing such as "This is what I want you to do." At the beginning of therapy, the therapist explains the need for homework and that there are standard assignments that will be tailored for them in order give them the best results. Basically, the therapist wants the couple to attribute the need to do the homework to the *program of treatment*, not the therapist's request or requirement. Positioning the homework in this way also helps eliminate power struggles between the therapist and the couple. Partners who are oppositional or reactive usually do not like to be told what to do and easily feel controlled by others; they need to be directed *very indirectly*.

The third factor, the *use of implicit vs. explicit directions*, is less applicable in the treatment of erectile dysfunction because specific homework assignments do need to be explicitly described and carried out. However, greater compliance is gained with implicit directions. This finding can be applied in our context of treating erectile dysfunction by specifically prescribing the behavioral activity itself and then adding suggestions implying that a variety of feelings and reactions might occur. Specifically, the therapist might say, "Notice the sensations that occur in your penis when it is touched. You might notice that at times you don't feel much; at other times, the sensation might be annoying or unpleasant; and sometimes you feel a rush of pleasure. Take note of what is going on between you and your partner when you feel these different sensations."

Integrating Behavioral, Cognitive, and Affective Facets of the Problem

Every problem has facets to it—behavioral, cognitive, and affective. In treating an erectile dysfunction, the clinician needs to keep a focus on all three. Largely, sex therapy has been a behaviorally oriented approach. Treating erectile dysfunction behaviorally with techniques such as sensate focus and systematic desensitization is the norm (Heiman & Meston, 1997). What has often been overlooked is any emphasis on the cognitive and affective facets. The cognitions that may have contributed to the development and perpetuation of the problem are not investigated. We assume the man with erectile dysfunction is spectatoring, but do not ask about his specific thoughts or negative cognitions. This technique will be described in the next chapter. The least emphasized facet of treatment is a direct exploration of the feelings the patient experiences at various points in the therapy. Therapists talk about performance anxiety, but they generally do not spend time asking the patient to describe what this experience is like. It would appear that we want the patient to *report* the feeling, but not really talk about it. We have seen this pattern in therapists we supervise time after time and suspect it is because of the strong behavioral emphasis within the field of sex therapy.

Patients' feelings require validation or normalization. They often believe no other person could feel what they are feeling and/or understand their experience. Those of us who have listened to hundreds of patients describe these kinds of experiences know all too well what is normal and expected. The patient needs to hear that it is normal to feel the anxiety, worry, fear, disappointment, apprehension, self-doubt, confusion, sadness, and lowered self-esteem with which he is plagued. He needs a safe and accepting environment in which to share these feelings with his partner and someone who understands. Many men have shared few of their feelings about anything with their partners and are now confronted with a problem that triggers very strong negative feelings. Partners can be very supportive and understanding about these feelings, but *only if they are shared*. Moreover, hiding these feelings may give the woman the impression that he does not care what happens, and he is not concerned about her during the sexual interaction. As he begins to talk about his fear of letting her down, she will be able to support him and reassure him that although disappointed, she understands and will do what she can to be helpful.

The domain of feelings is also highly significant in relation to the homework that is assigned throughout treatment. As we mentioned earlier, couples may resist doing the homework. Every time an assignment is given, the therapist should ask the partners how they feel about it. This question demonstrates both concern for the clients and elicits information about potential resistance.

Subsequent assignments are calibrated in relation to the level of anxiety experienced during the preceding assignment and the actual outcome. Any anxious feelings should be discussed before the couple leaves the office and, if necessary, the homework adjusted. For example, the therapist may attempt to move rapidly from sensate focus-I level to sensate focus-II. Too rapid a transition may result in tremendous anxiety in the couple, indicating that a slower pace and less intrusive assignments are needed.

Implementation and Process

Over the years, the senior author has treated many couples who had failed to improve in previous therapies they had sought for sexual dysfunctions. Some of these couples received treatment from therapists who were not qualified to treat sexual problems. A qualified therapist is one who has some professional credentials in the field, some knowledge of sex therapy, and has treated others. When asked about their prior therapy, they would describe trying some of the standard treatment techniques used to treat an erectile problem but in their cases without success. The question that emerged was, "Why would treatment work with a therapist who did the same things that had failed to work with the other therapist?" We believe the answer lies in attention to *implementation and process*. It is similar to surgery. For example, any number of surgeons may know how to perform a particular operation, but some clearly achieve better outcomes. Those who have the best outcomes are usually those who have had the most experience with a given type of surgery. Experience does not change the technique per se—it changes *how the technique is implemented*. Sex therapy texts are filled with a variety of techniques, but rarely is the process of providing the techniques mentioned. An exception to this deficiency is the text by Wincze and Carey (1991).

Process is an important focus in any approach to therapy, for it refers to the "how" of the therapy, how the techniques are utilized, and encompasses issues surrounding the therapeutic relationship. When couples come for treatment who have already tried therapy and not improved, questions arise concerning what the new therapist will do. First, it is useful to know what was done in the prior therapy. If the prior therapy involved using a program that should have been effective and will be used by the new therapist, how is this fact to be explained to the couple? The explanation we offer is that the first therapist may not have had enough experience to properly implement the techniques. As the therapy proceeds and assignments are made, we ask whether the first therapist explained things in the same way and adequately laid out the homework. Tim and Gigi had been referred by his urologist. They had seen another therapist for his erectile dysfunction, but no progress had occurred.

THERAPIST: Tell me what you did with Dr. Smith to help with the erection problem.

HUSBAND: He told me I needed to relax and things would work just find. I tried relaxing, but I guess I couldn't. I couldn't help but think about my penis. I've had this problem so long, I don't think anything will work.

WIFE: Dr. Smith kept encouraging us to keep trying and relax. I thought he was a nice man but I didn't have much confidence in him. I would ask him questions about this problem, and he didn't seem to know the answers.

THERAPIST: Did he give you specific homework to do?

HUSBAND AND WIFE: No.

HUSBAND: He told us to do relaxing things together and not to give up. We talked a lot about other things like my family and my health and our relationship. We felt better seeing him, but the problem didn't get any better.

We have observed several common process mistakes, some of which were discussed earlier in this chapter. At the beginning of treatment, it is important to identify the problem clearly, explain its nature to the couple, and position the presenting problem in the context of other sexual and nonsexual issues currently active in the relationship.

The most important process principle for therapists to bear in mind is to make explicit to the couple what is taking place in the treatment and why. Sometimes therapists just tell patients what to do, assuming that they will blindly follow their instructions. Today's patients are more educated and sophisticated. As the therapy proceeds from one step to another, the therapist should remind the couple of the principles being used and their purpose. For example, in treating erectile dysfunction a major goal is to reduce performance anxiety by setting up homework in a very slow and gradual way, starting with sensual assignments and moving to sexual assignments. Every exercise should be carefully based on sound principles of treatment. A cookbook approach may work for some patients but will fail with many others.

Couples usually have high expectations. They want an instant cure for the erection problem without understanding that they can only achieve this goal *gradually*. They do not know how to measure success. The therapist needs to describe what will probably happen and what will likely not happen during an exercise. As soon as penile stimulation begins, for example, men assume they should get an erection. The therapist needs to caution that this is neither a goal nor an expectation. In fact, the therapist can explain that feeling pleasurable sensations without an erection would be the best thing that could happen at this point. When partners discuss an exercise they have completed, the therapist needs to let them know whether they are moving on the right track and at a pace that is reasonable.

The therapist must keep checking with the couple about the pacing of the therapy, which problems are to be treated, and the sequencing of those problems. The couple is a dynamic system that is always changing. The treatment plan is a road map, but it is not the road. Every road has turns not shown on the map, unexpected obstacles, and potholes. A driver who pays attention to the process of driving will adjust to these realities. A therapist who pays attention to the process of the couple will adjust to the dynamics of the system. Effective implementation of therapy based on attunement to process requires knowledge, honed judgment, practical skill, experience, and an ability to listen carefully and resonate with the couple's needs. The following case illustrates how the therapy may need to be modified to meet the needs of the clients:

Marge and Harry had been married for three years and had not consummated their marriage. In fact, they had never successfully had intercourse. They were both professionals who married in their late 30s and were feeling the need to become pregnant due to Marge's age. This couple had a medical background, each one in a different area of medicine. In spite of their medical sophistication, they had many sexual difficulties. Of course, treatment started with Harry's inability to achieve an erection and how this was distressing them because they wanted to be pregnant. Harry's history revealed that he had never had intercourse in spite of his popularity in his youth. He also reported that during masturbation he always ejaculated within just a few strokes. The first assignment attempted was a sensate focus-I exercise. This exercise was prescribed to get some sense about where the couple could begin their work. They were unable to try even this exercise. It turned out that they were both overly optimistic and far more upset about their sexual relationship than they had reported. Each one had a strong need to appear "normal." Therefore, they both minimized the extent to which the problem upset them, and how each one had their own sexual fears. Their response to the first exercise helped to obtain history that showed Harry had been a victim of incest. Marge knew about this fact, but neither one had ever discussed it. The incest he experienced had led him to be sexually phobic. He had kept this fact carefully concealed by unconsciously developing an erectile dysfunction. The therapist explained that he would need to work on the issue of his incest prior to proceeding with the sex therapy.

Harry was then seen for an extended period for help with the incest. During the first few weeks, he came to sessions individually. Then, we began to alternate couple and individual sessions. When the couple sessions resumed, we worked on the couple becoming more physically connected by having them do touching exercises that were much less advanced than sensate focus-I. They were successful in doing these smaller exercises.

Of course, it was clear Marge must somehow be a part of this problem. She revealed that she had never had much sexual desire and married Harry because he was such a good companion. She had grown up in a family where there was covert incest that contributed to her lack of desire. Individual sessions were then held with her to process this material. While this therapy was taking place, both partners were beginning to wonder whether they could or would ever be able to have a child due to their problems and their ages. Not to have children was a very depressing prospect for both of them. Part of the therapy was to revisit this issue frequently and for the therapist to provide as much support and hope as possible.

Once the individual issues were largely resolved, which took about two years, the couple was ready to advance in their sex therapy. Harry's phobic reaction to sex had subsided, and he was able to approach the exercises with less apprehension. Marge's desire was higher than it had ever been but still not what they both agreed it should be. We continued the standard program of working on his erectile dysfunction and improving desire for both of them. In the following six months, Harry made great improvement to the point of being able to have intercourse. They were both delighted with this progress and feeling they must get pregnant as soon as possible. During the next year, we worked on Harry's premature ejaculation and kept focused on the issue of desire and sexual intimacy in the relationship. Unfortunately, Marge did not become pregnant as quickly as they had hoped so she began to see an infertility specialist. Because of her age, and only her age, she was accepted as a patient. They had only been having intercourse for three months when she began her medical treatment. Obviously, this treatment was a setback for Harry who now felt more pressure to perform, and Marge felt more pressure to get pregnant. The therapy shifted to help them deal with their "infertility." Over and over, the therapist repeated that three months, four months, etc., was a short period of time, but he nonetheless understood how they felt and the pressure they were under. A few months after beginning the infertility treatment, Marge became pregnant and eventually had a healthy girl. These types of complex multiyear cases demonstrate the need for the therapist to be flexible, develop a systematic program of treatment, and let the therapy evolve naturally in a way consistent with our basic principles.

This chapter has reviewed the basic principles and strategies used in treating couples who have erectile problems. We believe that these principles and strategies constitute the foundation of sex therapy. Although techniques are important, they will not work unless there is adherence to the principles. Understanding the principles informs and guides the therapist every step along the way. It allows the therapist to individualize the therapy, making it not only the best fit for the couple but cost-effective as well. The next chapter continues the focus on the process in its discussion of the major techniques used in working with couples who have erectile dysfunctions.

6

⌘ ⌘ ⌘ ⌘ ⌘

Sex Therapy with Couples: Basic Techniques

THIS CHAPTER PROVIDES A DESCRIPTION of the most common techniques used in treating erectile dysfunction. Beginning with the publication of Masters and Johnson's (1970) volume on sex therapy, the treatment of sexual dysfunction has been characterized by the use of specific treatment protocols. These fairly standard treatment techniques, which are well known among sex therapists, are often used in a way that is much too mechanical by the therapists we have supervised. The reader is cautioned against the cookbook application of the techniques. Instead, the treatment should be informed and guided by principles that allow for the flexible and individualized design and application of the techniques.

Unlike much of the earlier work in sex therapy that focuses just on the techniques, we have stressed the importance of treating the couple-as-a-whole. Treatment of the man's erectile dysfunction involves the participation of the partner. Our description will include how to work with the partner in implementing these sex therapy techniques. In Chapter 9, we will deal with some of the broader issues couples present, such as communication problems, conflict, and anger.

PSYCHOEDUCATIONAL INFORMATION

Educating the couple has been recognized as an important component of sex therapy for many years (LoPiccolo & Heiman, 1978). Although most

118

couples tend to think of themselves as fairly sophisticated in what they know about sex, the fact is that most are poorly informed. Moreover, partners typically do not communicate the knowledge they do possess because of discomfort with the topic. The most common mistake any therapist can make is to assume that couples know anything about sex or can talk comfortably about what is desired during lovemaking.

This mistake is especially easy to make when the couple has a background similar to that of the therapist. When the therapist has a strong sense of identification with the couple based on perceived similarity, which is certainly advantageous, it is easy to assume that the couple knows, understands, and can communicate what the therapist knows. In addition, well-educated couples are often assumed to know more than they actually do. Treating physicians and other mental health professionals can be especially challenging in this regard!

We have found that as we describe a course of treatment, clients will strongly proclaim that they have already tried what is being proposed, and it failed. Patients assume that if they tried it and it failed, there is no need to do the same things again. The therapist will need to spend time explaining how difficult it is to self-treat and that the therapist will be able use the same techniques with much more success. The therapist may wish to examine some of the details of what they tried in order to show the couple how they went amiss. Of course, the therapist must appear understanding, not judgmental or blaming, of the difficulty in treating oneself for a complex and difficult problem.

Once the couple accepts that their attempts to treat the problem have failed because of the difficulties related to self-treatment, they will be more willing to accept the direction of the therapist. The therapist wants to make a case for the importance of the couple gaining an understanding of the sexual problem. Most couples accept the notion that they can better inform themselves about their specific problem as well as their overall sexual relationship. They appreciate the fact that the therapist begins treatment by seeking to understand why the erectile problem started and how it continues to interfere with pleasurable sexual functioning. Couples want to be treated respectfully and with the attitude that their understanding and participation in the process is important. They do not want to be "done to" but "worked with." Couples who are well informed are much easier to treat because they understand how their sexual problem got started and what is involved in overcoming it.

BIBLIOTHERAPY

During the last 20 years, many excellent texts have been written for the lay person on sexual problems, sexuality, and relationships. We cannot mention all the superb resources that are now available, but we list a few at the end of this chapter that we believe cover some of the basic areas about which most couples are ill informed. Some of these texts are written primarily for women, others primarily for men. We often tell couples that they are both to read whatever text is suggested (men need to understand women, and vice versa) and to underline as they go along.

We also ask that they spend time talking about the material in the books as a way to facilitate sexual communication and better understand their sexuality. The goal of the reading is more than acquisition of knowledge. We want the couple to use the knowledge for self-understanding and to promote more openness and self-disclosure in the relationship. This process is further encouraged in the sessions by asking about the week's reading and what they found was pertinent to their relationship. Getting couples to discuss sex is difficult, especially when there is a lot of worry and anxiety about sexual performance. They will need encouragement, coaching, and practice in the sessions before they will be able to do much at home. The therapist might spend a considerable part of the therapy hour just having them talk about what they have read and personalizing the material. The couple learns through modeling in the office the behaviors that they will eventually enact on their own. To set this up, the therapist might say, "As you read the book last week, what struck you as pertinent to the two of you? Would you like to spend some time in the session talking about those things with my help and input?" Couples may find the session is a safe place to discuss some of this material, knowing the therapist can intervene if problematic feelings emerge.

We have found the books listed on pages 142–143 to be a necessary component of the many therapeutic approaches in treating erectile dysfunctions. They are a valuable adjunct to cognitive techniques and behavioral interventions. However, reading about techniques used to treat erectile dysfunction can create one common downside for the couple. Typically, the techniques are presented as a series of exercises that gradually increase the scope of participation toward a specific goal. Unfortunately, many men look ahead at the next exercise or the final exercise. They worry that they will not be able to "perform" adequately, and that they will become a treatment failure. Often, they manage to convince their partner that they will be unable to do the exercises. In fact, many men report doing a particular exercise with great success until they start to think about the fact that in a week or two, they will be asked to do a more advanced exercise. Not surprisingly, anxiety is triggered.

The patient and his partner should be warned about this tendency and instructed to think only about the current experience. Encourage the woman's support by reassuring the partners that they will never be asked to move on to the next exercise until they both are both ready. Women usually worry that the man is feeling too much pressure from them and feel personally responsible for having caused this pressure. Men worry that their problem is a burden to their partner, and they are forcing them into therapy (doing exercises) which is for his benefit only. Explain that they are not on an arbitrary treatment schedule, and that the therapist will design whatever exercise they need next in order to move ahead.

DISPELLING SEXUAL MYTHS

We live in a culture filled with a number of myths about sex. Most men learn about these myths at an early age, and they are never challenged. The mechanism that allows myths to develop is well understood. When a person has a lack of information about sex, he or she searches for an explanation. When sound information is absent, whatever data can be found, however inaccurate, are sufficient. This information is internalized and causes the person to experience sexual guilt and anxiety.

A myth that has not been pointed out, which interferes with the process of doing sex therapy, is what Zilbergeld (1978) called the myth of naturalism. This myth connotes the fact that we expect sex to be a natural and spontaneous act arising out of instinctive sexual knowledge. In therapy, couples may insist that the goal should be to help them have sex naturally and spontaneously. This idea is counterproductive though, particularly beyond the first couple of years in a relationship. Usually, couples discover that they need to *schedule* sex and that it is anything but natural. Instead, sexual behavior is learned through the knowledge we acquire as we mature and, in some cases, through modeling. Unfortunately, many men have reported that they learned most of what they know about sex from "letters to Penthouse" and pornographic movies. Once partners accept the idea that sexual behavior is learned, they can also accept the fact that some of what they learned was faulty, and needs to be *un*learned. This acceptance facilitates getting the couple to think in different ways, and, in turn, behave differently. The therapist and educational material suggested by the therapist become new sources of sexually correct information.

Elimination of Negative Thoughts, Accentuation of Positive Thoughts

Cognitive work may need to be done to counter negative attitudes. This involves careful examination of each negative cognition as well as thought substitution with more positive material. Besides the cognitive work, which is ahistorical, the therapist should ask where the ideas originated. In many cases, they have a religious foundation and are a core part of the person's religious belief system. Consequently, if the therapist disputes one of these negative attitudes, the man or couple may feel as if his/their religious beliefs are being challenged. These attitudes should be handled carefully by attending to their source and what the attitude represents to the individual. A combination of bibliotherapy and cognitive intervention helps to alter these ideas. In the following example the therapist attempts to change an attitude, which is necessary for treatment to continue.

THERAPIST: Next week I want your wife to stimulate your penis just for the purpose of providing you with sexual sensation and pleasure. Don't worry about getting an erection. In fact, it is better if you don't. Given the problem you have, you probably won't, and I certainly don't expect you to at this point.

JOHN: I'm going to have to think about this.

THERAPIST: What do you mean?

JOHN: I'm not sure this is okay. I'm a Catholic. This sounds a lot like masturbation, and then there's the idea of doing this just for pleasure.

THERAPIST: I understand your concern as a practicing Catholic. First, I have consulted with priests and they have assured me this is okay as long as it is for therapeutic purposes. I can give you the names of some priests, or you can ask you own priest about this matter. Second, I want to be respectful of your religion by not asking you to do anything that violates your sense of morality. I would like to hear more about your beliefs and where they came from—was it the Church, your family, or ideas you just picked up other places?

JOHN: Well, this whole thing about pleasure was drilled into us by the nuns, and my family was very strict.

THERAPIST: Did these teachings make sense to you?

JOHN: No, but I've always saluted, said "Yes, Sir," and done what was expected.

THERAPIST: Are you open to examining these beliefs and perhaps changing some of them?

JOHN: I think that would be a good idea, but I'm going to be a tough nut to crack. You've got your work cut out for you.

Through a combination of reading material, which was initially somewhat offensive to John, and cognitive work, he was able to rethink some of his sexually negative attitudes. In turn, we were able to proceed with the exercises and with the couple's sexual interaction, without the burden of guilt that John had experienced up to this point.

In many instances, these techniques are sufficient to nudge the person in examining his/her value system and making appropriate changes over time. In some cases, however, we have recommended that the couple have a consultation with a pastoral counselor or their minister, priest, rabbi, etc. in order to gain a different perspective. Great caution must be exercised in making this referral, especially if the referral's particular position is unknown to the therapist.

Besides eliminating the negative thoughts and beliefs, the therapist also wants to foster positive sexual thoughts and attitudes. Several techniques have proven useful in our practice. Some partners simply do not have a positive sexual self-image or, for that matter, a sexual image of self at all. We suggest they develop what we call a "sexual bill of rights." This proclamation should include what they believe they are entitled to sexually. It may include how they see themselves, how they are allowed to feel, how they are allowed to behave, and what they are allowed to ask of their partner. Each partner can write a statement and share it with the other. Once each partner has something they think appropriate, they can mentally rehearse it daily for a few weeks until the idea becomes incorporated in their thinking. The partner may read what they have written daily or go over it mentally.

Another technique to promote positive sexual thinking involves writing down as many positive thoughts as possible about oneself, one's partner, and the relationship (Weeks, 1987). Positive messages from the family of origin are also sought. Ideally, each partner writes five to ten positive thoughts for each category and then reads the list one time per day. This technique has been helpful in creating more sexual desire. In one case, Jim developed the following positive thoughts:

Self
I am attractive.
I can be/have been a good lover in the past.
I am sensitive to what my wife wants.
I know how to sexually please my wife.
I like it when my wife wants me and has an orgasm.
I have a sexy chest.
I really want to make my wife sexually happy because it makes me happy.

Partner
My wife has a great figure.
She is in great shape, and I notice other men looking at her.
My wife is always turned on.

My wife wants to make love to me and please me.

My wife loves oral sex.

My wife will do anything I want.

She loves me a great deal.

Relationship
We love each other.

We really get along.

We understand each other.

We used to like to make love.

When we made love it was great.

We used to like to experiment.

We could experiment again, and it would be fun.

We like to spend time together.

Weeks (1987) also used fantasy to increase desire, rehearse a particular behavior, and create a more positive sexual self-image. Loren and Weeks (1986) found that most individuals have sexual fantasies, and that these fantasies constitute a major component of the sexual appetite. We also found the content of normal sexual fantasies is extremely varied among individuals; many people are uncomfortable with their fantasies and worry that they are not "normal." Prior to initiating any work involving fantasies, the therapist should assess the partners' beliefs about their sexual fantasies. In actual practice, this consists of (1) asking partners whether they have fantasies; (2) asking how they feel about these fantasies; (3) asking whether they judge these fantasies to be normal or not; (4) determining whether the fantasies have been shared with the partner; and (5) asking whether they think amplifying their fantasy life will elevate their desire.

Corrective information is usually required because so little information is available about the range of fantasies experienced by "normal" individuals. Moreover, because couples rarely share their fantasies as a part of their sexual repertoire because of guilt, misinformation, or embarrassment, the idea of sharing sexual fantasies can be discussed. Sharing is an optional experience for the couple. Should they decide to talk about their fantasies, it is useful for them to understand that a fantasy does not necessarily mean that they want to *enact* it, and that fantasizing about other partners is one of the most common fantasies. The therapist can discuss the value of having an active fantasy life and further normalize the fact that having a fantasy about a person other than one's established partner and having fantasies during sex is normal. Additional techniques involve guiding the partners through a fantasy exercise in the session. The therapist gives suggestions in the form of a verbal outline of a sexual interaction while the partners fill in the details in their mind. The therapist gives the couple the following suggestions as they listen quietly. A long pause allows them to develop the fantasy material.

1. Think about the fact that you are feeling somewhat aroused. What does it feel like; what are you thinking?
2. You want to develop a fantasy of an ideal encounter with your partner.
3. Think about how you want to get this encounter started. How do you entice your partner?
4. What is the context for this encounter? How did you create it?
5. What happens at the very beginning of this encounter?
6. Think about who is in charge, what you want, what you want to give.
7. Imagine yourself in the sexual interaction. Who does what to whom?
8. How do these things feel and look as you imagine them?
9. How do you want the encounter to end? Are you together in each other's arms or doing something else?
10. When you look back over the encounter, what was most exciting, most loving, most romantic, most sexual?
11. Hold this image in your mind and play it over again and again, changing whichever parts you like. Be adventurous—try different things.

Finally, some partners are primed by reading books that contain fantasies such as the series written by Nancy Friday (1980) describing both men's and women's fantasies.

ASKING SPECIFIC QUESTIONS

In our experience, therapists are often reluctant to ask specific questions about what has or has not happened sexually and what is happening during the course of treatment. The therapist must keep asking very detailed questions from the beginning of therapy, explaining why such information is necessary, discussing how the clients feel about these types of questions, and letting them know that such questions may be initially embarrassing. Without very specific information, the therapist can only guess at what partners do and how they respond behaviorally and affectively. For example, a couple might assume that just a few seconds of genital stimulation is sufficient to produce an erection. Perhaps, in years past when the partners were young, this amount of stimulation worked. One young woman remarked that as soon as her husband got in bed to have sex he would have an erection. She commented she never had a chance to stimulate him to an erect state. As this couple grew older, this pattern changed, and now it took him a much longer period of time to establish an erection. The man confused this normal change with that of being impotent, became anxious as we have discussed earlier, and then developed a real erectile problem. Whenever faulty information or a lack of information is apparent, the therapist needs to intervene quickly to provide corrective facts.

Cognitive Therapy and Self-Defeating Sexual Thoughts

In order to eliminate or reduce these thoughts, cognitive (Beck, 1976; Clark, Beck, & Alford, 1999) or rational-emotive techniques (Ellis, 1962, 1999) can be used in conjunction with the behaviorally oriented treatment. Ellis and Harper (1961) have written a chapter describing the application of a number of cognitive techniques for erectile problems. The cognitive theory of psychotherapy proposes that human problems are the result of faulty thinking, cognitive distortions, or irrational thoughts. It has sometimes been called the A-B-C theory of psychotherapy. *A* stands for an action or an event; in other words, something happens. *B* stands for the belief we hold about the event; in short, it is our interpretation of the event. *C* is the consequence; how we feel (affective) and what we do (behavioral). In actual practice, the therapist goes from *C* to *A* to *B*. Patients are readily able to tell us what they felt and what they did. Then they can be asked ask about the event that triggered these feelings and behaviors. Now the task is to uncover the mediating thought(s). The patient may be able to identify this thought quickly or may need some help inferring what it might have been.

When the consequence is unpleasant, the task of therapy is to change the belief system. An unpleasant consequence might be unpleasant, greatly exaggerated feelings or self-defeating behaviors such as avoidance of sex or an erectile problem. The therapist can help to neutralize the negative thoughts simply by pointing out their existence and how they affect the patient's feelings and actions. Another technique is to develop counter-thoughts that directly compete with the self-defeating thoughts. This approach to therapy requires a good deal of self-monitoring of the negative thoughts and effort in replacing the negative thoughts with the counter-thoughts. The original thoughts are like well-worn tracks or cognitive habits. They continue in spite of the fact they are known to be counterproductive. Changing them takes time, deliberate effort, and continued acceptance of the fact that the new thoughts are "true" and will help to create a more workable reality for the patient.

CREATING A SEXUAL ENVIRONMENT

An erectile problem does not remain just an isolated sexual problem for most couples. The man experiences the problem as a failure, and his typical way of dealing with it is to avoid sex. His partner senses this dynamic and colludes in not pressing the issue and avoiding sex as well. Unfortunately, affection is often linked to sex in the man's mind, and he fears that sex will be expected if he shows affection. He also thinks that if his partner shows him affection, and he does not respond sexually, he has once again failed her. The upshot is that affection becomes less and less a part of the relationship.

Sexual interest and activity are most likely to occur when a relationship is characterized by affection. If affection has diminished, the therapist can explore the reasons why and suggest that the couple needs to work toward restoring or building a new level of affection. The therapist might ask about the feelings of affection each partner has for the other that are never or rarely expressed. Once it has been established that the feelings are present, it is now a question of learning to express them. We suggest that partners engage in at least one verbal and one physical show of affection each day. Feedback from couples has taught us that this is usually one of the first and most significant benefits of their therapy experience. The value of this simple discussion and assignment cannot be overstated.

Treating erectile dysfunction requires the couple to do a variety of exercises at home, ranging from taking a walk together to affectionate physical touch to sexual touch. They are designed to be undemanding in nature and to re-introduce the couple, in graduated increments, to the intimacy they desire in their relationship. The therapist should not convey the behavioral prescriptions in a cold and clinical manner, and the assignments should always be enacted in an environment that has sexual context.

Because the exercises should be fun and enjoyable regardless of the current circumstances, they must be carefully tailored to the couple and, obviously, with a nonthreatening outcome in mind. The therapist must present the assignments so that they make sense to the couple, and what makes sense to one couple will not work for another. This means the therapist must be attuned to the needs of the couple and begin the treatment exercises where they are likely to achieve success. Simple and easily understood exercises increase the likelihood of compliance. If the therapist only asks the couple to do certain behaviors without elaborating, explaining, and discussing relational issues, the couple may do the exercise and experience little that is enjoyable. The wording for giving these exercises is given later in the next chapter.

One task for the therapist is to discuss the conditions that contribute to experiencing an enjoyable exercise. As noted previously, most couples will need to schedule the exercise, coordinating their calendars in order to select days and times that are convenient. The term we use is "creating opportunities." There must be flexibility in the scheduling, however. We do not want the couple to make a date and then feel that they *absolutely* must do the exercise whether they feel like it or nor. A date is set to spend time together with the intent of doing the exercise. If they do not feel like it, they can reschedule or do something else together. The opportunity has been created to do *something* together. Whatever they do together helps build the intimacy in the relationship, which is the overall goal of therapy.

Prior to the scheduled opportunity, we suggest the couple create a state of "positive anticipation," analogous to planning a special vacation together. Days and weeks before the trip, the couple talks about what they want to do together, what they want to see, how much fun it is going to be, and how they cannot wait until they can get away. When both partners are looking forward to an upcoming event, there is a good deal of positive thinking and talking about it before it ever happens. In essence, they are "priming the pump" by creating positive anticipation.

In order to implement positive anticipation, two suggestions are given to the couple. The first is to think positively about their next opportunity: What would they like to get out of it? What kinds of good feelings would they like to experience? What would they like their partner to do for them? What would they like to do for their partner? These thoughts should be pondered during the day of the exercise. Secondly, partners are asked to verbalize some of these thoughts to each other prior to the exercise to "warm up" the relationship environment. Partners can call each other during the day or leave each other notes. Actually, this kind of thinking and talking is what makes dating so exciting, especially in the beginning stages. Partners are encouraged to be creative in their efforts to express their positive anticipation and emotionally build up to the exercise.

The selected exercise should be carried out when the partners are able to relax and not feel a pressure of time, and the scheduled time should be well protected. Children should be taken care of, answering machines turned on, and other distractions removed. Typically, we recommend that the television is turned off, and that they listen to soothing music or enjoy candlelight. Again, an environment is created in which the couple can enjoy the sensuality of their relationship. Some couples have a poor sense of boundaries and attempt to do the exercises under conditions that work against any kind of sexual interaction. One couple, for example, had a habit of having sex with two large dogs and two cats in their bed! The animals always interrupted them, and the wife had an ongoing resentment over the fact that the animals received more affection than she did.

The exercises are best carried out in a context in which *both* partners expect something. Couples understand that they are doing the exercises in order to help the man with his erection problem, but it is also made clear that the woman benefits by learning to relax and enjoy the undemanding assignments. It is essential to address *her* need for anxiety reduction. Every exercise should be two-sided in the sense of both partners getting something they want. We begin by prescribing the exercise that is needed at that time and then asking the couple what they would like to add to it to make it more fun, more enjoyable, pleasurable, and bonding for them, and that would give each one something they would like. Again, the therapist joins with the couple in designing the exercise rather than simply telling them what to do. In particular, we want the woman to identify and express some of her needs before they do the exercise. Setting up the exercise in this way also helps the man feel that it is less his problem, and that he is not imposing his needs on his partner. He will enjoy being able to give her something she wants, which also helps to reduce his sense of urgency in getting over the problem as soon as possible.

To further reduce the "coldness" of the exercise (the fact that it is assigned), we suggest that the partners consider several ancillary variables: the lighting in the room, using background music, taking a bath together before the exercise, using body lotions, doing something enjoyable together before the homework or just engaging in some light conversation, and doing anything else they might consider intimate or romantic or sensual. The main idea is to create an environment of give-and-take characterized by an intimate ambiance.

SENSATE FOCUS EXERCISES

The sensate focus exercises constitute a core part of the treatment of erectile dysfunction. Masters and Johnson (1970) developed these exercises with the express purpose of helping couples reconnect with their pleasurable sensory experiences. Kaplan (1979) used the same techniques but chose to call them Pleasuring-I and Pleasuring-II. The exercises and the way they are structured over time help to eliminate the performance anxiety associated with sex. The basic goal of the exercises is to create sensual and sexual experiences in a context that is free from anxiety. They are designed to produce a feeling of safety and an undemanding environment rather than a sense of pressure in the couple.

Since anxiety inhibits the erectile process, desensitizing the patient from this anxiety and re-establishing natural erectile functioning requires that he experience sensual and sexual behaviors in an anxiety-free context. Therefore, the design of the exercises must carefully fit the situation, and the process must proceed in an incremental or gradual fashion. That is, each exercise is designed to function as a small step in the direction of the larger goal. The graduated increments must be small so that each exercise is experienced as a success, not a failure. Since the emphasis is on feeling pleasurable sensations rather than producing an erection, success is much more likely. As we mentioned earlier, even failures can be viewed as successes if they have diagnostic utility. Just doing the exercise is a success because it breaks the cycle of sexual avoidance.

Purposes of Sensate Focus Exercises

Most descriptions of the sensate focus exercises overlook the multiple purposes that such simple exercises can have when properly implemented (Kaplan, 1979). The therapist who understands these purposes can communicate them to the couple, enhancing partners' appreciation of what they are striving to experience and the richness of an exercise that appears so simplistic on the surface. Such information helps improve compliance to treatment and creates a positive expectancy in the couple. In other words, they now *expect* certain experiences as a result of carrying out this assignment.

We have identified nine purposes for the sensate focus exercises:

1. To help the partners become more aware of their own sensations.
2. To help the woman become more in touch with her need for pleasure and worry less about her partner.
3. To facilitate an awareness of each other's sensual and sexual needs.
4. To expand the repertoire of intimate, sensual, and sexual behaviors.
5. To learn to appreciate foreplay, or non–goal-oriented sex, more fully.
6. To communicate sensual and sexual needs, wishes, and desires.
7. To create positive relational experiences.
8. To decrease sexual avoidance and enhance sexual desire.
9. To enhance the sense of cohesion, love, caring, commitment, intimacy, cooperation, and sexual interest between partners.

The first purpose is to help the patient become more aware of his own sensations. Men with erectile problems begin to lose touch with their bodily sensations. They are so busy worrying about and monitoring their performance during an interaction that they lose some sensory awareness. Also, the obsessional concern about failure further distances the man from his pleasurable sensations. One of the goals of therapy is to help him reconnect with his senses and disconnect from his obsessive, negative thinking. With each exercise, the man is told to focus solely on the pleasant sensations he is experiencing *in that moment* and put all other thoughts aside.

The second is to enhance the woman's awareness of her sensual experience. Because both partners are given some kind of sensate focus exercise, the woman partner becomes more in touch with her own pleasurable sensations and less worried about her partner. She therefore will be better able to tell him what is feeling good to her, which gives him a sense of physical competence. His past physical interactions have led him to feel incompetent. The feeling is now reversed as he feels a renewed sense of potency in the physical realm.

Most couples we have treated are too inhibited in their sexual communication to ask for what they would like. They are afraid to ask for too much, fearing that they will be viewed as selfish. The third purpose of the sensate focus exercises is to facilitate an increased awareness of what gives the other pleasure in order to increase the awareness of his/her own physical needs. The process promotes sensitivity to the other as well as the self. Specific suggestions promote this awareness. For instance, partners are always told to be creative and experimental during the pleasuring sessions. The therapists might say, "Try as many things as you can think of to give yourself and your partner pleasure. Be creative. Think about what you would like, tell your partner, and listen carefully to what your partner tells you."

The fourth purpose is to expand the repertoire of intimate, sensual behaviors in each couple. This occurs naturally as couples try different behaviors to enhance their sensory awareness and develop a fuller understanding of their sensory and sexual needs. Our experience in working with hundreds of couples has shown us that sexual behavior tends to become highly patterned over time. The couple falls into a rut with little variety and experimentation. When an erectile dysfunction is present, the pattern becomes even more limited in the effort to make the erection occur. Many couples also focus just on sexual intercourse. Men are more prone to just want intercourse after a perfunctory kiss and caress. Sometimes women will show the same pattern. The impact of the exercise is to open up many new physically intimate possibilities for the couple. This is another one of those early experiences in sex therapy that has an extremely positive significance for many couples.

Closely related to the above purposes, the fifth purpose is that the couple begins to appreciate foreplay as foreplay. It is not connected to a pressure-filled notion that any foreplay must and should lead to intercourse. Sex therapy couples may truncate foreplay, because the focus has been directed so much on solving the erectile problem. Men in general tend to undervalue and underappreciate the role of foreplay as an end in itself rather than a prelude to intercourse. Many men tend to view the sensual part of the experience as something to "get through" in order to get to the "main event." When couples are prohibited from having intercourse and instructed to work on developing their sensuality, they begin to discover the value of this experience.

Sixth, gaining more awareness and learning to appreciate the sensual aspects of being together needs to be communicated to the partner. We have observed that the vast majority of couples engage in very little sexual or sensual communication. In order to improve the overall quality and satisfaction of the couple's sexual life, they need to learn how to communicate with each other. The carefully graduated sensate focus exercises provide an ideal setting for practicing this communication; it is easier for the couple to discuss what they like during a back-rub than during genital stimulation. The two basic instructions given to the couple are: (1) notice what is feeling pleasurable from moment to moment, and (2) *verbalize* what is desired to keep the experience feeling good. Stating the obvious has a powerful effect when the therapist has been given a position of authority by the couple. In essence, the therapist is giving the couple permission to ask for what they want, sensually and sexually. This issue may need to be discussed at some length. The couple could be asked how they feel about communicating with each other in this way, why they haven't done so in the past, what early messages they got in their families of origin about sexual communication, and what the positive and negative outcomes of such communication might be. Bob and Julie were illustrative of a couple that did not communicate:

THERAPIST: When you do the touching exercises I want you to keep your minds focused on two things—what is feeling good and what you would like to keep it feeling good. This means you will need to communicate with each other. Let your partner know what feels good. Most couples don't do this, and it is much harder than you might think. How would you say you have communicated in the past about things you wanted sexually?

BOB: I don't know what she wants. I told her, tell me what you want me to do.

JULIE: But I feel like I'm giving him orders.

THERAPIST: But he is asking you to tell him.

JULIE: Yeah, but any time I ask him to do something he doesn't do it.

THERAPIST: Do you mean sexually?

JULIE: No (laughing); he listens better during sex.

THERAPIST: So, what stops you from telling him?

BOB: She always looks uptight.

THERAPIST: Let me hear more from Julie.

JULIE: I've just never been comfortable telling him. I dated several men before my husband and could never say what I wanted. It just seemed like it was being selfish, and men might be turned off by it.

THERAPIST: You think it will mean you are selfish and turn Bob off? Where did you get that idea?

JULIE: I don't know. It's always been my thinking.

THERAPIST: Bob, jump in here. Tell Julie how you would feel if she were to start telling you what she wanted.

BOB: I think it would be great. It would tell me she is interested. I never know what is going on in her head—maybe she likes what I do and maybe not.

THERAPIST: Say more; talk directly to Julie.

BOB: I want you to talk to me. It would help me if I knew you felt turned on, what you liked. The last thing I would think is that you are selfish. You would be giving me something I've wanted for years.

JULIE: I'll try.

THERAPIST: Just do your best. As I said, this won't be easy. Start with a few words next time and keep building up. If you start to feel uncomfortable about talking, then talk about that.

With every exercise prescribed, the therapist should always ask how their communication is going. It would be a major mistake to assume that partners gain this skill by simply doing the first exercise. Sometimes they will experience a successful week, and the next week forget the lesson of the prior week. Tracking this aspect of treatment requires great consistency on the part of the therapist.

In order for the couple to experience them as positive interactions, the sensate focus exercises need to be well-designed, well-timed, and well-sequenced. This positive relational experience constitutes the seventh purpose of the exercises. Unlike past experiences, which have been negative in terms of effect and outcome, these exercises are typically reported in positive terms. The therapist wants to help the couple generate as many positive interactions as possible. Gottman (1994) has empirically shown that couples who have happy, stable relationships are those who experience the most positive interactions (what he terms the "Dow Jones ratio of positive to negative experiences") These positive interactions give the couple the sense that they are moving in the right direction sexually and a good feeling about the relationship in general.

The eighth purpose is to rekindle some of the sexual desire that has been lost as a result of the performance anxiety, fear of failure, and all the other problems we have described as an integral part of having an erectile problem. Some men with an erection problem will eventually become so avoidant of sex that they lose their sexual appetite altogether. Most of the men we have treated have begun therapy with their desire significantly dampened; the exercises help to increase it. The therapist should inquire about their levels of desire at the beginning of therapy and keep checking in to see how each partner is being affected. Partners hear the other's report of their experience of doing the exercise and are always evaluating the interest level of the other in doing the exercises and of being sexually involved. They will frequently use participation as a measure of sexual desire.

The ninth purpose is to create a positive meta-message. The fact that the couple began therapy, continue therapy, and participate actively in the exercises creates an important meta-message about the relationship: It is a statement about the level of love, caring, commitment, intimacy, cooperation, and sexual interest felt by both. Making the time to do the exercises means the relationship takes priority over all other things at those times. Couples begin to experience this meta-communication as the therapy proceeds. The therapist may comment from time to time on this meta-message in order to make it more explicit and to praise the couple. Couples like hearing good news, and they like to be praised for their commitment and hard work. It also gives them a good feeling about the therapist and themselves.

The nine purposes of the sensate focus exercises reveal just how powerful they can be when properly implemented. We believe it is essential for the therapist to keep these points in mind as he/she begins to implement the exercises. In the next section, we will describe the sensate focus exercises and their application.

Structure and Application of Sensate Focus Exercises

The sensate focus exercises allow the therapist to organize all the various elements of treatment in a systematic fashion. At the outset of the process, the therapist has already described the treatment plan and is now ready to present the specific work. To carry out this plan requires that the couple be ready to suspend attempts at intercourse until asked to do so under prescribed conditions by the therapist. The rationale for not attempting intercourse is usually clear to partners, and they are usually willing to follow this directive. However, the therapist should always make sure the couple understands why it is necessary to suspend attempts at intercourse, and ask them how they feel about this prohibition. If necessary, the rationale can be further explained. Mostly, it is important to acknowledge the frustration that one or both partners may feel in putting on hold the very goal they are trying to reach. In some cases, one partner may have strong feelings that need to be validated and processed. For example, when one couple was instructed to put intercourse on hold, the wife responded by saying that she thought she would have to live without sex forever. What she meant was her husband had had the erectile problem for several years, and she believed putting intercourse on hold was just a way for the therapist to help her adjust to the fact that this was going to be her fate. It is prudent to reinforce the importance of removing all pressure and anxiety from the situation in which the exercises are to occur. Most couples will actually greet this proscription with relief. They have grown weary of trying to have intercourse, only to encounter their inability to do so. The therapist has already presented the rationale for starting with nonsexual exercises and explained how this will eventually help to restore erectile ability.

Step 1

The behavioral or sensate focus part of treatment begins with what has been termed sensate focus-I (Masters & Johnson, 1970). This exercise consists of sensual nongenital touching. As we mentioned earlier, the goal is to promote self-awareness, help the patient reconnect with his sensual feelings, and have a positive interaction with his partner. It is important to be very clear in giving the instructions for this exercise. The following statement is typical of how we set up this exercise:

> During the next week, your first task will be to do a touching exercise. It is not a sexual exercise but a *sensual* exercise. You will need to set aside about 20 minutes for the main part of this experience. During that 20 minutes, take turns massaging each other. This is not to be a therapeutic massage, but a sensual massage. Each of you will have about 10 minutes. Rather than massaging each other at the same time, please take turns. By taking turns, you will be able to focus either on what you are feeling or what your partner would like to

receive from you. The goal of this exercise is not to get an erection, nor is it to get sexually turned on. If you happen to get an erection or feel aroused, just take note of it.

[At this point, ask the partners how they would feel if he were to get an erection. They need permission to do nothing about it except let it be. A humorous comment, such as "No one ever died from not using an erection" or "It's okay to waste a good erection," is sometimes appropriate with some couples.]

When you are on the receiving end, allow yourself to experience as much pleasurable sensation as possible. Concentrate on what is feeling good. Think to yourself, "That is feeling good right now." Let your partner know what you would like to keep it feeling good. Communicating with your partner is important, and this will give you practice in learning how to ask first for sensual things and later for sexual things. Be creative and experimental. Ask your partner to try different things in order to give you different sensations. Do not worry about your partner when you are on the receiving end—just focus on yourself.

It would be better if you did not make this into a cold and clinical exercise. Try to get in the mood for it by thinking positive thoughts, remembering past pleasant experiences together, and saying things to each other during the day to create a positive mood. When you actually do the exercise, try to jazz it up some. You might turn on some music, light candles, or get some special body lotion or cream. You can be as creative as you would like to be in order to make it more enjoyable.

[To the man] Take note of any negative thoughts or feelings that occur during this exercise. Write them down later so we can discuss them here. You may have a tendency to monitor what is happening in your penis. At this point it is very unlikely you will gain an erection, and that is normal. Remember, getting an erection is not the point of this experience. You will succeed to the extent that you are able to give your partner and yourself pleasurable sensual feelings. Do you have any questions about how to do this exercise?

The instructions given above do not include specific behavioral information. The therapist then proceeds to ask the couple where they would be comfortable in beginning a sensual experience. Some couples have virtually not touched each other for months; they will not be ready to remove their clothes in the presence of the other and engage in a full body caress or massage (massage does not mean therapeutic massage but a light and gentle stroking of the partner's body). In this case, the sensual experience will need to be broken down into smaller, more comfortable units that fit the couple. The therapist might continue:

I am not sure where you should begin this type of sensual touching. Maybe you are ready to get in bed together naked and caress each other. Maybe you need to start in the living room, fully clothed, just giving each other a hand massage or foot massage. You can do anything in-between. The most important thing is that you are both comfortable with where you are when you start this exercise. Where do you think you would like to begin?

Sometimes the couple needs help in deciding which partner will give or receive. It is usually necessary to establish the order of who goes first before the couple tries the exercises for the first time. Subsequently, they can alternate to preserve a balance.

The therapist discusses where they would like to start and makes sure each is comfortable with the exercise. Use behaviorally objective language to establish the parameters of each assignment so that the couple knows exactly what is expected. Some couples try to advance too quickly and have to drop back. Selecting the right starting point is a difficult task for the therapist, and it is probably safer to be conservative in assigning the first exercise. The starting point is negotiated with careful attention paid to the partner who feels the most limited. In terms of a hierarchy, couples can go from a hand or foot massage (fully clothed), to a back massage (fully clothed), to a back massage (partially clothed), to a back and body massage (partially clothed, nongenital), to a back and body massage (nude), to a back, body, and breast massage (nude), to a body massage including genitals, to more focused genital stimulation.

At the beginning of the session following the first assignment, the therapist asks the couple how the exercise unfolded, gaining as thorough a picture as possible in order to optimally design the next exercise. Again, behaviorally objective language is necessary during the descriptions of the homework. The following questions are typical of what we ask in the follow-up:

To the couple
How did the exercise go? [Start with an open-ended question to see what they thought was most significant.]

How many times were you able to do it?

Was it difficult to find time?

Who initiated the exercises? [This can be important depending on who has initiated contact in the past.]

Was the experience enjoyable or pleasurable?

What did you like about it?

Was there anything you did not like?

What was it like being on the receiving end?

What was it like being on the giving end?

Did you let your partner know what felt good?

Did you let your partner know what you wanted? Why? Why not?

Did you feel turned on during the exercise?

To the man
Were you able to stay focused on just the sensual experiences and not think
    about getting an erection?

Were you able to stop the self-monitoring we talked about?

Were you able to stop any negative thoughts that occurred to you?

What was it like not to worry about getting an erection?

The couple continues the sensate focus-I exercises until both are comfortably able to give each other a full-body nongenital massage. The process can take from one to several weeks, depending on where they needed
to start. The exercises can be broken down into small behavioral units as
we just described to accommodate the couple's comfort level. Sometimes
partners will need to stay on the same exercise for two or three weeks, and
sometimes they may need to take a step back and do no exercises for a
week. It is important not to rush this process, even when the couple is
pressing ahead for more than they are able to achieve. Some couples are
anxious to get the problem fixed too quickly and will violate the prescription by trying to have intercourse. In the next session, they typically report
an erectile failure and wonder why it is still happening. The therapist can
explain why this event probably happened and ask that they get back on
track.

Step 2

The next step, sensate focus-II exercises (Masters & Johnson, 1970), is
similar in structure to the focus-I level, except that it involves genital stimulation. The prohibition against intercourse is still in effect. The intent of
sensate focus-II exercises is to help the man experience consistent erections
again. *This goal is never stated.* The therapist never prescribes an erection
or any other behavioral outcome (i.e., orgasm). This level is designed to
interrupt the cycle of negative thinking associated with gaining an erection.

In their review of studies on the role of performance anxiety, Wincze and Carey (1991) showed that it was not performance anxiety per se that inhibits erectile functioning but the negative thinking associated with it, the anticipation of the problem, and the self-monitoring that occurs. In other words, they believed it was not the *feeling* of anxiety as much as the negative *thinking* that really defines performance anxiety.

These instructions for sensate focus-II exercises are basically a modified version of the directions presented above. Nevertheless, we repeat the complete instructions. Sensate focus-II is usually divided into three sub-steps:

1. The couple is instructed to start with nonsexual touching and toward the end of the session move to genital stimulation. This exercise is exploratory. The goal is to find out which areas are most sensitive and to experiment with trying different ways of being touched.

2. The couple is instructed to start with nonsexual touching and move more quickly to genital stimulation. This exercise is more focused on the goal of experiencing pleasurable genital sensations. The man is cautioned that he probably will not get an erection and, if he does, he should just take note of it but not worry about having to do anything about it.

3. Again the couple begins nonsexually and then moves to genital stimulation. This time they are told to let the genital sensations build to whatever level they like. At this stage, the woman may choose to have an orgasm. Men are also permitted an orgasm, but only if they have a firm erection. Men can certainly ejaculate with a flaccid penis, but it is more likely that the man with an erectile dysfunction will ejaculate with a partial erection. Ejaculating with a partial erection may reinforce the erectile problem.

Moving through these sub-steps may take from three to several weeks. By the second sub-step, most men are beginning to experience the return of their erections. With continued practice, their erectile ability becomes more stable and consistent. It is normal to witness erratic performance at the beginning of this phase of treatment, and the man will need constant reassurance that his experience is normal, and that he is progressing as expected.

Learning to Lose an Erection

Men with an erectile dysfunction have become obsessed with getting and keeping an erection. It becomes one of the most important forces in their lives. Every time they have an erection, and it is possible to have inter-course, they will try to do so. We use an exercise described by Zilbergeld (1999) that helps to build sexual confidence over getting and keeping an erection. Although we are unaware of any empirical support for this exercise, our clinical experience with it has been very positive. The man with an erectile dysfunction develops the belief that if he does get an erection and loses it, it is gone forever—at least, for that particular encounter. What typically happens is that he gets the erection, then notices that he is losing some of the hardness, anticipates losing it entirely, and then does. He is now so lost in his negative thinking that regaining the erection is virtual-ly impossible. The purpose of this exercise is to help him experience the fact that erections can come and go and come. He can get an erection, lose it, and get it back again. We might give the couple the following instruc-tions:

> You have now reached a point in your therapy when mutual touching genitally usually leads to an erection. In fact, you have gained some confidence that this is probably going to happen, and you know it does not always happen, and that is okay too. This next exercise will sound strange to you. In the past, whenever you lost an erection, you could not get it back no matter how hard you tried. You learned that if you had an erection and lost it, it was gone. Now it's time to undo that lesson.
>
> During the next week, do exactly what you have been doing that's led to an erection. [*To the woman*] Stimulate your partner's penis for a while and, at some point [now *to the man*] ask her to stop and let the erection go away. What is different is that you are now making it go away on purpose. When the erection has subsided, ask her to stimulate you again. Focus on the pleasurable sensations, not on try-ing to get the erection back. Use everything you have learned up to now about not self-monitoring. Remember not to get caught up in those awful questions: Will I get an erection? How hard is it? Why isn't it getting harder faster? What happens if I lose it? How can I get it back? What will my partner think of me? Just start stimulating slowly to see what happens. If you get another erection, make that one go away too, and start the process over to see what happens.

The main mistake we have seen in doing this last exercise is assigning it prematurely. It should not be attempted until erectile ability, stability, and consistency have been restored. Mastering this exercise will give the man a great deal of confidence that he is ready to proceed to the next exercise.

Transitioning to Intercourse

The final phase of treatment involves having intercourse, which is also achieved in small steps. This is the moment of truth for men. Many of the men who present with an erectile dysfunction are able to get an erection but lose it at the point of penetration or within a very short time after penetration. This fact makes the transition to intercourse the most difficult part, because it is the point at which the men feel the most apprehension.

The therapist reminds the couple that the longer a man has an erection, the more stable it becomes. Rushing to penetration is to set himself up for failure. Furthermore, the exercise is worded in such as way as to reduce the demand for an erection. Never try to force an erection. The therapist might say the following:

> You have now reached a point in your therapy when it is possible to try intercourse under some very limited conditions. I know you have been waiting a long time to have intercourse naturally and normally, and I think you are getting close. For now, it will be necessary to do an exercise that you will probably find somewhat frustrating sexually. Begin the sensate focus-II exercise as you have in the past. [Remind the couple of the steps involved.] If you see that you are getting a good erection, then continue the stimulation for a period of time until you feel it is stable. If this does not happen, then just enjoy the pleasurable sensations as you did in the past. If the erection feels stable to you, then try a period of very brief penetration. To do this you will need to apply plenty of lubrication before you start this exercise and choreograph all of your movements in advance. [Lubrication is suggested for all couples because the therapist does not want the man to encounter any resistance during penetration. Given the clinical nature of the exercise, the woman may not be lubricated from any natural arousal that might occur.] In other words, [to the woman] you will stimulate him to erection and then [to the man] you will move quickly to penetration. You may need to stimulate yourself during the transition, and remember that it would be normal to lose some of the erection because you are getting less stimulation and you are moving around. Penetrate for just a few seconds and then withdraw and do some more manual stimulation. If the erection remains stable, try penetration again for a slightly longer period of time. You can penetrate three times, and if you are still erect, then you can ejaculate with manual stimulation. The next time you do this exercise, you can extend the period of penetration even longer. If you begin to lose the erection during penetration, pull out immediately, and see if it comes

back through manual stimulation. Use what you learned during the "lose" exercise. Do you have any questions?

This particular exercise can be frustrating for the female partner. Of course, she understands they need to do the exercise to help him regain his erectile ability and, in turn, she will benefit from that outcome. As we suggested earlier, the exercises should be designed such that both parties get something from it. The woman may tell her partner that she would like to be held, caressed, or that she might like to have an orgasm of her own through manual or oral stimulation or by using a vibrator.

In an ideal case, the treatment continues to work progressively, and the man is able to sustain longer periods of penetration. Once his confidence and performance have improved, the therapist gives permission for him to ejaculate inside provided his erection remains firm. In many cases, the man will need to back up to one of the prior exercises in order to regain some confidence. Once confidence has been re-established, he can go forward to the penetration exercises.

Kaplan (1979) discussed the importance of creating a context of nondemand intercourse for men with erectile problems. The idea is that intercourse is one of many sexual options. To emphasize this point, the therapist can create exercises that break down the final phase of intercourse. For example, the therapist might ask the man to lose his erection deliberately during penetration by ceasing movement, withdrawing, and then using manual stimulation to regain the erection.

Throughout both levels of sensate focus exercises, however, the therapist's attention should remain attuned to the foundational principles and strategies of treatment that turn these fairly common techniques into unique experiences of intimacy for the couple.

Suggested Readings for Clients

Barbach, L. (1982). *For each other: Sharing sexual intimacy*. Garden City, NY: Doubleday. A classic book for couples, we find it accurate and sensitive to the intimacy needs of both partners. This volume describes couples' sexual relationships from a broader perspective of helping couples develop a sense of eroticism.

Comfort, A. (1992). *The new joy of sex*. New York: Crown. One of the early books on sexual techniques, this second edition gives couples ideas about different ways of making love. It is quite literally an A-Z book of sexual ideas, ideal for couples searching for sexual variety.

Friday, N. (1980). *Men in love*. New York: Dell. A phenomenologically-oriented text that describes the sexual fantasy life of men, this book helps to normalize fantasies, gives men permission to fantasize, and reveals the range of content in fantasies.

Gottman, J. (1994). *Why marriages succeed or fail.* New York: Fireside. A bit more theoretical and research-oriented than Markman and Stanley's book (see below), this volume focuses on the need for positive behavioral interactions in couples. In addition, it presents information on communication styles that are highly destructive and predictive of divorce and couple dissatisfaction. This text is useful in helping couples assess their style of communication.

Gottman, J., & Silver, N. (1999). *The seven principles for making marriage work.* New York: Crown. Based on Gottman's long-term research on couples, this text discusses seven basic principles for making a marriage work: fostering fondness and admiration, turning toward, accepting influence, solving solvable problems, coping with the unsolvable problems, and sharing the same meaning. This book is practically written with simple ideas that are scientifically sound.

Markman, H., & Stanley, S. (1996). *Fighting for your marriage.* San Francisco: Jossey-Bass. A newer book that explores how to solve many of the common intimacy problems confronting couples. Very practical and readable, selected chapters may be used in understanding sexual difficulties.

Heiman, J., & LoPiccolo, J. (1988). *Becoming orgasmic: A sexual and personal growth program for women* (rev. ed.). New York: Simon and Schuster. A classic text for women, also enlightening for men, it is similar in format and style to Zilbergeld's text. The first half of this book provides information on sexuality in general, and the second half describes a program to treat women who have difficulty achieving orgasm or are anorgasmic.

Milsten, R., & Slowinski, J. (1999). *The sexual male: Problems and solutions.* New York: W.W. Norton. This book is an up-to-date, popular guide on male sexual function and dysfunction. It is academically and medically grounded, yet easy to read. The authors offer many useful tips on how to find help and what to expect from treatment. Psychoeducational information is given in an easy-to-assimilate style.

Zilbergeld, B. (1992b). *The new male sexuality.* New York: Bantam. This is a classic text for men to be read by men and women. The first part of the book gives the man an understanding of anatomy, how erections work, sexual mythology, male and female psychology, and chapters on communication and aging. The second half of the book describes the steps involved in treating the major sexual dysfunctions in men, including erectile dysfunction.

7

⌘ ⌘ ⌘ ⌘ ⌘

Integrating Psychological and Medical Treatments

THE MAJOR ADVANCES IN ASSESSING AND TREATING erectile dysfunction during the last two decades have occurred in the medical field. The recent development of an oral medication, Viagra, has revolutionized the way erectile dysfunction is treated and has changed our culture. Every newspaper, news show, and leading magazine in the country has run multiple pieces on Viagra. The effect has been to destigmatize erection problems in general. The population as a whole is much better informed about the extent of this problem and at least one effective treatment. People have become much more open about discussing the problem; today's couple coming for treatment of erectile dysfunction will be asking questions about their medical options.

Our task is to determine how to best treat the couple with an erectile dysfunction, using both treatment modalities in some cases. We remain alert to any bias toward viewing erectile dysfunction in strictly psychogenic terms or in strictly medical terms. The typical middle-aged couple coming for help with this problem will more likely than not present a mixed picture. For this reason, mental health professionals need to be aware of the medical side of treatment, the psychosocial effects of that treatment, and how to deal with the psychological issues surrounding an erectile dysfunction that may be primarily caused by a physical problem.

A couple of points are worth keeping in mind regarding cases where the etiology is organic. The psychological processes that follow from an organic problem are the same as those that follow from a non–organically induced erectile problem. An erectile problem may begin with a physical procedure or problem, such as surgery or a disease process. Once an erectile failure occurs, the man becomes anxious about his performance, which creates performance anxiety. He has now developed a *psychological overlay* to his organically induced problem. In addition, the couple typically responds to this change by making a number of psychological interpretations. Some of these interpretations will be injurious to the relationship, for example, "If I were more attracted to my partner, I would be able to get an erection" or, "If my partner were more attracted to me, he would be able to get an erection." These interpretations need to be corrected. The psychological overlay, which is actually independent of the medical problem, serves to maintain the problem. In fact, the medical problem might be corrected or improved, and the client may still have an erectile problem because of psychological factors.

Secondly, if the couple does begin a medical approach to treatment, it is not a simple matter of taking a medication or using a device (e.g., vacuum pump) to solve the problem. The fact that a drug or device must be used to induce or facilitate an erection has meaning to both partners. In some cases, the meaning is negative. For example, some men who use a drug feel they have failed to conquer the problem themselves, and they have to rely on a "crutch." Having a pharmacologically induced erection is just a reminder of their failure. Learning to use the drug or device may change the practical nature of the sexual interaction while triggering other psychological issues. These issues have not been adequately researched or described in the literature.

The purpose of this chapter is to describe what is known from the sparse research available and from our clinical experience in this area. We believe that learning to combine these treatments can advance the field of sex therapy. Sex therapists have much to offer couples who initially think a medical solution will solve an erectile problem and their other sexual difficulties. It is our contention that every couple who has experienced a medically treated erectile dysfunction would benefit from psychological intervention.

KNOWING WHERE TO START

An individual or a couple may begin treatment for some other reason and eventually begin to discuss the fact that an erection problem exists. Some clients have already started medical treatment and have been referred by their physicians. However, clients referred by a physician constitute the smallest percent of our caseloads in erectile dysfunction. Of patients referred by their urologists for help, we know that only a small fraction do so. It is much more likely that a therapist will refer a client to a physician for a medical evaluation and treatment. Assuming that the client is beginning to explore the erection problem initially with a therapist, our task is to determine whether the cause is psychological, and whether the couple will be good candidates for sex therapy. These two issues are separate but related. Through in-depth interviews, we need to assess the various psychological risk factors and try to rule out as many medical factors as possible. If we believe the cause(s) is psychological, then we might begin a course of sex therapy.

The safest or most conservative course of action would be to refer every client to a urologist for an evaluation. It is impossible for a sex therapist to have the knowledge to rule out all medical causes, and an interview alone will not reveal some causes no matter how thoroughly the interview is conducted. Some problems that look psychological actually have an organic basis and the therapist is seeing the psychological overlay. We can never be absolutely certain of our assessment. The client should always be given the option of seeing a urologist at the outset of treatment. The therapist may conduct an initial evaluation and report that several psychological risks are evident, but that nothing medical appears to be at work. However, a therapist cannot rule out all medical causes, and some situations that initially appear to be psychological turn out to have a medical cause. The client might then accept a referral to a urologist.

Just as some medical patients are reluctant to accept a referral to a psychologist, some erectile dysfunction clients are reluctant to accept a referral to a urologist. In these cases, the therapist can explain that they can begin a course of sex therapy but with the understanding that if it does not proceed in a way the therapist expects, a medical evaluation will be necessary. Within three to four weeks of the sex therapy, the therapist who has experience in treating this problem will know whether the client is responding. Usually by this time the client is able to achieve a stable erection using some of the sensate focus exercises. Although a fleeting erection may look promising to a sex therapist, it could actually represent a venous outflow problem requiring medical attention. In effect, the therapist has agreed to offer sex therapy on an experimental basis and shares this idea with the client at the outset of therapy.

Referring the Couple for Medical Intervention and Working with the Physician

If the therapist suspects the erectile dysfunction has an organic basis because of the absence of some of the primary psychological risk factors or the presence of some medical risk factor, the client should be referred to a urologist. If the therapist notes some organic risk factors, there is a need for thorough medical and psychological evaluations before beginning a course of treatment. Couples need to be educated about the complexity of assessing and treating erectile problems from the first session. They may have already made some decisions about the type of treatment they desire based on their own faulty assumptions. In some cases, the type of treatment they think they should receive is further compounded by the fact that they have been referred by another therapist *for sex therapy*, and they assume they will be getting therapy. Other couples may be referred by a physician, and they may assume their treatment will be medical in nature.

The referral to the urologist should be carefully considered. Not all urologists have training in erectile dysfunction and, in our experience, many also lack the personality predisposition to be effective. The most appropriate urologist is one who has received additional training in this area and has actively pursued treating men's sexual problems as a part of a larger practice. The urologists with whom we choose to work are often hard to distinguish from mental health professionals in their approach to patients. They are willing to spend a considerable amount of time doing a clinical interview, conducting the appropriate tests, providing feedback, and tracking the treatment over a period of time long enough to achieve results. Their ability to listen makes them effective at discerning when the erectile problem might result from psychological factors or which option for medical treatment might be more comfortable for a particular patient.

Once treatment begins, it is important for both the therapist and urologist to discuss how it is unfolding. Clients perceive this kind of communication to be important and appreciate the quality of care they are receiving. Even when treatment has not yet proven effective, it is reassuring to the client to know that his therapist and physician are coordinating their efforts on his behalf. When treatment consists of injections or oral medication, there is a dosing period during which the proper amount of medication is being determined. The physician will need to adjust the dose, depending upon the man's responsiveness and any side effects. The therapist is usually the first to hear about the man's erectile response to the medication and may choose to encourage him to contact his physician (or the therapist may choose to communicate directly with the urologist to discuss the patient's progress).

Any therapist who plans to treat erectile dysfunction should form a relationship with a urologist to whom he or she can refer. Most urologists are unfamiliar with what sex therapists do in treating erection problems and will need some education. Of course, this must be done in a subtle way or the physician may feel that his/her knowledge or competence is being questioned. The urologist is also likely to be unfamiliar with how sex therapy can be an invaluable adjunctive treatment. Discussions with the urologist regarding this matter can be helpful, as can providing the doctor with copies of articles that describe the psychosocial aspects of medical treatment for erectile dysfunction. These articles will be reviewed in the next section. Much of this education, however, will result from working on several cases together, wherein the urologist can actually see the benefit and read about the progress in the therapist's reports to the physician.

Some patients will enter treatment having already been evaluated and/ or treated by a urologist. The therapist should ask for the records from the physician and ask the client about what procedures were done. Since most urologists are often not well versed in this area, it may be necessary to have the client see another urologist who is qualified. We will often refer the client to another urologist with the simple explanation that he needs to see a specialist in order to get the best care possible. We have never had a patient reject the idea of getting the best care possible.

If Viagra proves to be as safe as initial claims and experience have demonstrated, it will be prescribed more and more by general practitioners and internists, who are even less likely to develop expertise in treating erectile dysfunction. Men who are treated unsuccessfully by their primary-care physicians will need to be referred to appropriate urologists; therapists may need to assume an advocacy role to obtain the proper treatment in light of managed-care restraints.

PSYCHOLOGICAL ISSUES IN MEDICAL TREATMENT

This section of the chapter focuses on the psychological issues involved in treating erectile dysfunction with vasoactive medications. From the early 1980s to the present, advances have been made in treating erection problems with drugs. The first generation involved drugs that were injected directly into the penis, the second generation (1996) involved inserting the medication into the urethra, and the third generation involved simply swallowing the oral medication Viagra (1998). A review of the medical literature shows that over 55 studies have been conducted on the efficacy of these medications. However, only two empirical studies have examined the psychological issues that are involved in the use of these medications. Thus, we have little empirically based research regarding the biopsychosocial effect of medical treatment on men and their partners.

Biopsychosocial Research

The first study was published in 1987 in the *Journal of Sex and Marital Therapy* (Althof et al.). The researchers investigated 82 patients who were using the injection treatment with papavarine or phentolamine. Of the patients in the study, 43 were organically impotent, 28 had mixed etiology, and 11 were psychogenically impotent. The average age of those with an organic problem was 57.9; those with mixed etiology, 58.4; and those with psychogenic etiology, 48.8. The men with organic and mixed etiology had had the erectile problem for 5 to7 years and those who were psychogenically impotent, up to 11 years. The drop-out rate after 6 months of treatment was 35% across all three groups, and the majority of these dropped out early in treatment. Of the patients who made it through the trial dosing phase, 96% experienced satisfactory erections. However, after 3 months 30% of the injections failed to produce an adequate erection. The researchers speculated that this drop in efficacy might be due to poor injection technique or the fact that, over time, the medication loses its potency. The men used injections 4.8 times per month. The patients reported improved erections, an increase in frequency of intercourse, decreased masturbation, and increased sexual satisfaction. Partners reported greater frequency of intercourse, more sexual arousal during intercourse, and greater satisfaction. They also found that half of the patients engaged in noncoital activities, which meant they had not become totally dependent upon the injection. Psychometric measures also showed that the men experienced greater relationship satisfaction, a sense of wellness, and enhanced self-esteem. In spite of this positive finding, the researchers noted that some men and their partners were offended by the idea of a drug-induced erection. The study also reported that "in some of the psychogenic patients in this study, self-injection has appeared to exacerbate interpersonal and intrapsychic conflict" (p. 165).

The same group of researchers (Althof et al., 1991) conducted a follow-up study that included 42 men, with an average age of 54.4. The men had experienced a dysfunction for an average of 6.8 years and were classified as 48% organic, 38% mixed, and 14% psychogenic. Sixty percent of the men who were referred for treatment or began treatment did not continue past the trial dose phase. The majority of these men could not accept the idea of using an injection and worried about possible side effects. One year later, the men who had continued with the treatment were using the injection 4.5 times per month with a success rate of 84.5%. The researchers found that men in this study were depressed at the beginning of treatment over their lack of performance, but after 12 months their depression had improved. The partners who participated in the study reported feeling more sexual satisfaction and arousal and an increased frequency of intercourse and coital orgasm.

The most striking feature of these studies is how well the treatment worked for those who used it, and how many patients dropped out during the early phase of evaluation or treatment. Unfortunately, no studies have been completed on the psychological issues surrounding Viagra, but we can extrapolate from the two previously mentioned studies and learn from our clinical experience. The men who did continue with treatment found that erectile ability usually improved. Those who were depressed over the problem felt better after a period of a few months, and the couples reported an increase in sexual satisfaction and activity. The focus of sex became less intercourse-oriented due to their renewed potency. The overall effect was positive for both the man and his partner.

SEX THERAPY AS AN ADJUNCT TO
MEDICAL TREATMENT

The purpose of this section is to examine ways in which sex/couple therapy can enhance the use of the medical therapies. The first and most obvious way the therapist can be helpful is to make the couple aware of the various medical options available today and refer the couple to a well-qualified urologist. Once the couple has begun the process of pursuing a medical option, it is useful to discuss how the couple feels about the treatment and their expectations. We have found that couples have mixed feelings about using a drug that induces or helps to induce an erection. Although they are excited by the possibility that a solution is available, they wonder how it will affect their sexual interaction. Their main concern is whether the decision reflects a lack of desire by one or both partners: He thinks that she does not believe he really desires her and must resort to a medication; she thinks that she isn't desirable enough and so he must resort to a medication. Unfortunately, they have used his erections as a measure of sexual desire and desirability and need to learn to differentiate between these. The best way to achieve this goal is for the man to verbalize his feelings of love and desire for his partner.

The couple's expectations for the treatment should also be explored. Couples may expect too much or too little. The majority of couples expect too much at the beginning of treatment and then shift to expect too little. This fact actually makes sense when the process is examined. The therapist and the physician tell the couple that the treatment induces an erection for the vast majority of men. This fact has the effect of elevating expectations. When the treatment begins, men are given the lowest dose of the medication and told to gradually increase it. Not only is this a medically sound procedure but it is also followed in order to reduce the probability of priapism. On the other hand, during this dosing phase in which the man is trying to find what works for him, he will experience many failures and, along with these, diminished hope. The couple then begins to believe this treatment will not work; they reduce the number of injections or pills ingested, begin avoiding sex again, and their anxiety escalates. Now they expect very little from the treatment. They become demoralized by the whole idea of using a medication and begin to question the therapist's optimism that this treatment could work.

This pattern of demoralization has been present in virtually every case we have treated using MUSE, Caverject, or Viagra. The couple must be prepared for this phase. They should be told to follow the urologist's orders and not to expect an erection to occur with any degree of stability until the dose has been significantly increased. The couple can be told, "The treatment won't work until it does, and then it should continue to work." Most of the patients we have treated also think they should begin the medication with the intent of having sexual intercourse the first time it is used. They prepare themselves, use the medication, and fail to get a response. We now advise men to go through a process of what we call "fast-track dosing": to use the treatment as frequently as is allowed without their partners and without the expectation that they will get an erection. They can then allow themselves to "fail," which eliminates the pressure of having to please the partner and reduces the worry that the treatment doesn't work.

An issue specific to the injection and transurethral insertion methods is that the medication almost automatically produces an erection that requires little or no stimulation. Typically, the man interrupts lovemaking to go to another room for 5–10 minutes (time to prepare the medication, inject, apply pressure to the puncture wound, and massage the penis to disperse the medication) to give himself the treatment—an interruption that is often frustrating. It is also a reminder to each partner that he is dependent on something to get an erection—and it's not his partner, who may begin to feel irrelevant or turned off by the fact that she was not involved in helping him get the erection. Both partners begin to wonder when sex is going to be natural again and consist of more than a test of his potency.

Viagra works in a way that is more natural. The drug does not produce an erection but facilitates the physiology of getting one. The man generally needs to have some physical stimulation for an erection to develop, which eliminates the above concern, but the concern over the use of a medication is still present. Partners wonder about how they will perceive each other when they make love. Viagra also has a relatively long half-life, which means that it lingers in the system for several hours and makes repeated episodes of sexual intercourse possible. The implications of the residual Viagra on further lovemaking are not clear at this time.

The therapist does not want the couple to become too focused on just having sexual intercourse. Lovemaking should not be reduced to *sex*making. We encourage couples to engage in noncoital activities and maintain a high level of physical interaction and affection that is *not* a prelude to intercourse. Even though the erection problem has been solved, other sexual problems, such as premature ejaculation, lack of desire, or anorgasmia, may still be present. Nor does restored erectile functioning solve any of the minor communication and relationship problems that most couples have, in one form or another. The couple may want to improve their relationship during the course of their work with the therapist. They may also want to enrich their sexual relationship with added variety, communication, new techniques, fantasy, and whatever else they think might be enjoyable.

As we have already mentioned, very little research has been conducted on partners' reactions to these medical treatments for erectile dysfunctioning. In our experience, women who have inhibited sexual desire and complaints about their partners are usually not very interested in the partner becoming sexually functional again. For those women who feel deprived and long for pleasurable sexual interactions, the clinician can expect to find a high level of interest in whatever restores function.

Sandy and Jack had been married for 23 years when they sought treatment for a variety of marital problems as well as parenting difficulties with their teenaged children. Sandy had many complaints about her husband: He was always distant, always working, and had never been an involved parent. Thus began an extended course of couple therapy. After a few months, Jack admitted that he had been having trouble maintaining erections for about 10 years. Sandy said that this disturbed her because every sexual interaction was focused on him being able to keep his erection. The therapy included work on their sexual relationship, but Jack did not experience any improvement in his erections. After some prompting he saw a urologist, and Viagra was prescribed. The Viagra enabled Jack to have the best erections he'd had in many years; Sandy's response, however, was unexpectedly negative. She said the Viagra had turned her husband into "an animal," that he had suddenly become sexually assertive and wanted to have intercourse for an extended period of time. In addition, she was experiencing discomfort and even pain during intercourse due to lack of sufficient lubrication. She was now worried that she would not be able to keep up with his newfound desire and that he would want to expand their sexual experiences even more. The purpose of the therapy was shifted to help them both deal with and adapt to the changes in their sexual life. Over a period of about three months, the couple learned how to work together sexually again. Treatment focused on communication, expectations, awareness, sensitivity, and sexual techniques that would be satisfying for each of them.

During the course of medical treatment, the possibility of noncompliance always exists. Partners may shift their thinking regarding the efficacy, safety, and meaning of treatment. They may begin to experience relational problems, which puts sex on hold. In general, the meaning of treatment for each partner is important to elicit and process at several stages along the way, but especially when one partner begins to feel treatment is a failure and becomes sexually avoidant.

INTEGRATING MEDICAL AND PSYCHOLOGICAL TREATMENTS

Combining medical and psychological treatments is necessary or potentially helpful in two general cases: those of mixed etiology and those in which there is no organic component but also no response to the sex therapy. In cases of mixed etiology, the goal is to resolve the psychological components through the sex/couple therapy and to provide a long-term medical treatment that will address the organic factor. The second situation is one in which the man does not have an organic problem, but the couple has not responded to sex therapy after a period of time long enough to warrant some progress. Kaplan (1990) first suggested a combined approach with those couples who were resistant or refractory to sex therapy. A third situation, which we have considered but have little experience with yet, is the use of Viagra to enhance the course of sex therapy; we suspect that using Viagra at the beginning of sex therapy might, indeed, accelerate the process.

Kaplan (1990) wisely observed that the use of medications (some of the early medications which were injected) is most useful when the couple is ambivalent about the *process* of sex therapy but not the outcome. In other words, these couples want the erection problem resolved, but they are uncertain about engaging in a process of *therapy* per se. Our experience is that these couples are willing to discuss and resolve their ambivalence with the therapist's support. They will also be willing to use a medication to help them push through any underlying resistance(s) commonly demonstrated when the partners claim there was no time to do the exercises, or they forgot to do them, did them incorrectly, did them but did not respond, or when they cancel therapy appointments or repeatedly bring up issues that distract them. Those couples who are conflicted about the outcome have a poorer prognosis. Unconscious forces are at work, undermining the restoration of potency. These couples actively resist both processing their underlying conflicts and using a pharmacological method to help promote erections. In many of our cases, the years of failure have produced an intractable performance anxiety.

Psychotherapeutic techniques normally used to deal with anxiety fail to provide relief, and some men with whom we have worked have tried anti-anxiety medications, without success. The best way to break the cycle of performance anxiety is with erectile success, but erectile success is impossible because of the level of performance anxiety.

In those cases where we believe the problem persists in spite of efforts to do sex therapy, because of performance anxiety and negative cognitions, we will suggest breaking the cycle with medication. We point out that once he has used the medication successfully, he will begin to gain a sense of sexual confidence and sexual competence. These feelings and the new underlying positive cognitions will motivate him to proceed with the sex therapy. When the couple begins to use one of the medical options, the therapy now focuses on how to best use this treatment as we described in the section above. Within a matter of a few weeks, the couple has hopefully achieved intercourse using one of the medications.

Once the couple begins to feel more confident about being able to have intercourse with the medication, they then go back to the sensate focus-II exercise without the medication. The man has now had the experience of getting and keeping an erection for a sustained period of time. He knows his problem is not organic, and he knows his body is capable of supporting an erection. He has also had intercourse with his partner and knows it is something they both want, in spite of earlier avoidance. The sensate focus-II exercise should now produce the desired effect—an erection. The remainder of treatment is the same as described in the last two chapters. The exception is that the couple is told they may keep the medication nearby as a safety net. Knowing they have a method of predictably and reliably producing an erection has a tremendous effect on lowering fear and anxiety. They can now anticipate that every sexual encounter will be a success. Many men have reported they feel much better just knowing they can use the medication and report that because it is there they do not need to use it.

We have discussed what happens when the urologist fails to find an organic component and how medication is combined with the sex therapy. Now assume the man does have an organic component to his erection problem. The problem is one that will require the use of a medication indefinitely in order to achieve an erection. The couple should be educated about the nature of the physical problem and the effect the physical problem has had on creating what we have called the psychological overlay. Treatment is now focused on helping the couple integrate the medication into their lovemaking. The couple may still do the sensate focus-II exercises to help reduce the performance anxiety and negative thinking with the aid of the medication (unless they are using MUSE or Caverject, which tend to produce an erection immediately). The main goal of treatment is to help the couple resume their sexual life after several years of failure and sexual avoidance. A systematic approach that includes some of the traditional sex therapy exercises is beneficial because it takes some of the focus off intercourse while also helping them gain more comfort in being able to have intercourse again.

8

⌘ ⌘ ⌘ ⌘ ⌘

Pitfalls in Dealing with Couples' Problems

THE PREVIOUS TWO CHAPTERS WERE DEVOTED to working on the erectile dysfunction in the individual and with the couple. The couple work was directly focused on the erectile dysfunction and did not deal with some of the issues that commonly emerge during the course of sex therapy. As we have already indicated, it is rare for a couple to present with just one sexual dysfunction. It is also rare for a couple to have no other relational issues. Interestingly, some couples can be treated for their sexual difficulties without addressing the other issues. These couples may have problematic relationships, but they still find a way to relate to each other sexually. The only form of intimacy they still share may be sexual; some couples readily admit that sex is the primary bond in their relationship. Most couples, however, find it difficult to do the sex therapy when there are problems in the relationship. These problems include communication issues, different expectations, anger, and conflict. These issues become major obstacles to the closeness and cooperation required to being sexual with one another, making it difficult to resolve their sexual problems. In some instances, the therapist may need to resolve these types of issues before attempting the sex therapy, while in others the sexual and relational problems may be treated concurrently.

The purpose of this chapter is to discuss some of the basic processes involved in working with couples, rather than describe some of the basic techniques. Process refers to how the therapy is conducted and is essential if therapy is to proceed and for the techniques to work. Much of what is covered in this chapter deals with some of the common pitfalls therapists encounter and how to avoid them. The reader should consult prior books on couple therapy for a detailed explanation of the process and problems in this treatment (Weeks, 1989; Weeks & Hof, 1987, 1995; Weeks & Treat, 1992).

Our theory, the intersystemic approach, is the foundation for all our process considerations, ranging from whom is seen, to which problem(s) is treated and when, to how to keep a balanced perspective on the couple. Couples form interlocking and dynamic systems of behavior. A basic assumption of couple work is that it takes two to create the problem. Each partner contributes something to the pathology in the relationship, and each is considered equally healthy or unhealthy, differentiated or undifferentiated, pathological or nonpathological. This assumption may be ruled out, but it is the starting assumption.

Sometimes the problem or the pathology "jumps out" from one partner; it is obvious and unmistakable. The pathology in the other partner may be more subtle and difficult to see because it is more acceptable. A prime example is a couple in which both partners have a personality disorder. The man has an obsessive-compulsive personality disorder, and the woman has a histrionic personality disorder. The therapist is probably going to hone in on her problem first because it is more apparent. His problem may be masked by hers, or be less obvious, because his problem has traits that are less socially offensive or off-putting.

Working with couples is extremely challenging. The therapists in our institute have all done years of individual, couple, and family work. They all agree that working with couples is the most difficult, because they form such stable systems of behavior. Although they may appear to be unstable, those who come for treatment have found some way of being together that meets their deeper needs. Yet their system of relating distresses them. It appears they can't live with each other, and they can't live without each other. The way they relate is all they know how to do, and they feel threatened when the therapist suggests a change in these well-trodden relational pathways. Although the couple requests help and ostensibly wants behavioral change, helping both partners achieve desired changes is not an easy task for the therapist. The main obstacle is the homeostasis or "status quo" of the couple system that has become familiar, albeit miserable, for the partners. Fear of the unknown is more intimidating than the unpleasant patterns of interaction.

Couple work is filled with pitfalls. The therapist must keep a number of factors in mind or the couple will probably drop out of treatment. These factors deal with the therapist's stance toward the couple and are process-oriented rather than content-oriented.

AVOIDING COMMON PITFALLS

The couples therapist must be attentive to a number of issues that are not relevant in individual work. Inattention to these matters can be disruptive to the work and cause the couple to leave treatment or render it ineffective. Similar to the need for careful implementation of the sex therapy techniques already discussed, it is essential to utilize the couple therapy techniques within a context that is controlled by the therapist. The therapist needs to pay particular attention to these issues in the first few sessions in which he/she is attempting to join with the couple. Joining with two people who are in conflict and see the relationship from different perspectives is much more difficult than joining with one person. Once the therapist has joined with the couple, he/she may purposefully choose to overlook some of these guidelines. Such a strategy should be carefully planned and considered from each partner's perspective, and the potential risks weighed against the possible advantages.

Don't take sides. Nothing can kill a course of couple therapy more quickly than taking sides with one partner against the other. The therapist must be extremely careful to avoid even the appearance of side-taking. When partners begin therapy, each has a hidden agenda of getting the therapist to take his/her side or getting the therapist to see things his/her way—the right way. If one of the partners believes the therapist is taking sides against him/her, he/she will probably not return to therapy (if he/she does return, it is only to go through the motions). From that partner's point of view, the therapist has lost neutrality and credibility.

It is much easier to avoid side-taking if the therapist understands the basic assumption that each partner contributes to the pathology of the relationship. The therapist must also be careful with his or her use of language. Of course, at the beginning of treatment the therapist listens and reflects back what is being offered by making statements that merely acknowledge rather than agree with what is said. For example, the therapist might say, "You perceive that your husband is always angry with you because . . . " rather than, "Your husband is always angry with you." Partners are exquisitely sensitive to language and how it might express—or even hint at—side-taking. Empathic restatements are more easily tolerated when the emotions of each partner are so fragile.

Don't intervene too quickly. Most couples express the idea that they wanted the problem fixed yesterday (even when they've had the problem for years) but then sabotage the therapy if it moves too quickly. Going slowly in the beginning is in everyone's interest. The couple has formed a stable system, living for years within a homeostatic world that is familiar even if distressful. At the beginning of therapy, the clinician does not know what forces have kept the couple stuck and together. Treatment can begin with small steps to test the couple's motivation, readiness to change, and resistances. Predictably, small steps produce small "failures," and the underlying resistance can be processed without having to deal with a big "failure." It is prudent for the therapist to expect or even to welcome the smaller resistances, because they represent fear of change from what is known to the unknown.

Don't answer questions until you are ready. Therapists expect certain questions at the beginning of treatment about cost, insurance, frequency and length of meetings, who is to come, the therapist's experience in treating their problem before, and so on. Some questions have a hidden agenda along the lines of getting the therapist to take sides or proving the other partner is wrong, crazy, stupid, inept, or bad. Even innocent-sounding questions can be loaded. Partners may have debated the seemingly neutral question for years, but the therapist is unaware of the fact that it has been a focal point for their conflict. One woman recently asked, "Doctor, don't you think far too much emphasis is placed on sex in this culture?" What she was really saying was that her husband placed too much emphasis on sex, and she wanted me to tell him to stop pressuring her for it. When the therapist suspects a question has a hidden agenda, it is best to deflect it, ask why she/he wants to know, what he/she thinks, what the partner thinks; or the therapist can say that he/she would like to think about it some and get to know them better before offering an opinion.

Don't proceed until the problem(s) and goal(s) have been identified clearly. Couples usually present with a host of problems with which they want or need help. They may not initially be aware of the real or underlying problem about which they want to talk but feel too much fear or shame. Part of proceeding slowly is to get a sense of (1) all the problems confronting the couple, (2) what they want to change, and (3) the order in which they want these areas to change. How the therapist views these three categories may be greatly at odds with the couple's view. In the case of Mary and Bill, the husband wanted his erectile problem solved immediately. Mary believed other problems such as conflict and different parental expectations were more important than his erections. She also described having no desire for sex anyway, which meant she would not be invested in Bill getting better. In such a case, the therapist would begin to pursue one course of action while the couple is becoming more and more frustrated that they aren't getting what they want. The process of defining the problems, goals, and order of problems treated should be done in collaboration with the couple.

Don't discuss problems in abstract terms. Couples are not therapists and usually have trouble describing their interactions in behavioral terms. They need assistance in elaborating and/or clarifying what they mean by expressions such as "communication problems," "losing control," or "drinking too much." The therapist may have to probe by asking the couple to describe an example of a behavioral sequence, from beginning to end, in order to get a clear picture of what happens when they have "communication problems." An interesting example was the wife who complained that her spouse had "only one drink" each night upon returning from work, but that he routinely proceeded to fall asleep and as a result, the couple had sex infrequently. When asked to measure the amount of alcohol in this "one drink," he reported at the next session that he was consuming over three ounces of vodka per drink! A similar process can be utilized when asking the couple about sexual behaviors involved in foreplay. It is essential to have the couple describe the method, duration, intensity, and focus of their touching.

Don't discount problems, even small ones. Some partners are experts on ignoring, discounting, minimizing, and denying that a problem exists in their relationship. Those who were constantly disregarded as children and continue to be discounted by their partners will typically fail to bring up a problem or will present it in such an indirect way that it is barely noticeable. The therapist must listen with a "third ear" for significant communications that are embedded in the apparently mundane conversation. For example, one client with inhibited sexual desire was talking about her lack of desire and, in the middle of her monologue, very quietly mentioned that her husband's parents were always around. She immediately returned to her main point and continued without pause. It turned out that the husband was very enmeshed with his parents, and the couple had been fighting about this issue for years. He had her agree prior to coming to therapy that they would not talk about this issue in therapy!

Don't allow conflict and differences to escalate. The level of emotional intensity can escalate very quickly—in fact, instantly, in some couples. Other couples will slowly escalate their anger or conflict in a session. The therapist must maintain control over the process, asking the partners to slow down or cool off when necessary. This task can usually be accomplished by getting the partners to talk to the therapist, rather than each other, and asking cognitively oriented questions. This process gets the partners to think more and feel less, thereby diffusing the emotional intensity in the session. When couples fight in therapy they begin to lose confidence in the safety of the therapeutic setting, in the therapist as a source of help, and in the therapist as a referee of what happens between them.

Do not assume that partners will perceive the problem or their relationship in the same way. If the partners were able to agree on what the problem was and perceive how they worked together or failed to work together in similar ways, they might not need therapy in the first place. Most couples have some disagreement about the problem and/or the state of their relationship. Their differences in perception may be the product of fundamental categorical differences or different projective processes. One of the most common manifestations of these differences is the response to a question about how the prior week was experienced. One partner might say it was one of the best ever, while the other might say it was one of the worst. Or one partner might think that a fight during the last week was awful, and the other was unaware of even having a fight. It is useful to normalize these categorical differences and talk about working toward finding a common understanding. Determine the areas of agreement and work from there. It is sometimes useful to have each partner describe the problem from the other's frame of reference. Discuss how one partner's perception might be different from the other's. In addition to making the assumption that differences exist, it is important to describe the differences in behavioral terms. A behavioral description sometimes reveals to each partner that things were not as they had recalled.

Don't be seduced by one partner's truth. A point closely related to partner's perceptions is how each partner begins therapy by telling the therapist his/her version of the truth. In most cases, each partner is convinced of the utter rightness and correctness of his/her perception. Both want to tell the therapist "what really happened." These truths can be very convincing. Of course, as one partner is telling his/her truth, the other partner is preparing his/her rebuttal in order to make a convincing statement. To avoid this game, we ask about each one's "theory" so that it becomes clearer that whatever follows is no longer the truth but one partner's theory or explanation.

Don't cause imbalance in the system. In addition to avoiding taking sides, it is also important not to show favoritism or give one partner more time and attention than the other. For example, seeing one partner individually is one way the system may become imbalanced. The therapist may begin to accept one partner's version of how the relationship works, and the other partner may worry that he/she is now "one-down" because the partner has had time to "brainwash" the therapist. An innocent conversation with one partner about some mutual interest that does not include the other partner can be perceived as "liking" the other partner more. The potential for imbalance is especially risky when the one of the partners is a mental health professional. In this instance, using professional language or jargon is likely to leave the nonprofessional partner feeling left out of the communication, one-down, and wounded as a result.

Don't make interpretations prematurely. The concept of an interpretation is as old as psychoanalysis. In an interpretation, the therapist makes a statement that he/she believes captures the essence of a behavior. Couple therapists must be very cautious about interpretations. When the couple's dynamics are not well understood, an interpretation could be perceived as siding with one partner or suggesting that one has a deep problem and the other does not. In couples therapy, it is better to make *systemic interpretations*, such as, "The two of you are very protective of the relationship, and that's why you avoid fighting," or *bilateral interpretations*, such as, "John, you avoid fights because that's what you learned to do growing up; and Mary, you can't stop a fight until everything is okay because that's what you learned to do growing up." These kinds of systemic interpretations are central to bringing each partner into the process. The interpretation implies that they both play a part in the problematic interaction.

Don't get lost in stories about the past. Partners will sometimes want to begin therapy by telling every hurtful story they have stored away from the beginning of the relationship. These stories can be recounted in great detail and with great emotional intensity. The point of them is usually to prove just how terrible the other partner has been in the past. The therapist must redirect the partner who wants to tell these stories by asking what these past interactions mean to him/her, how he/she feels about them, and how current interactions have been affected by them. The past is important, but it is how the past influences the present that is therapeutically useful.

Don't allow emotions to rule the session. Partners can use their emotions to manipulate the session by distracting attention from the issue at hand, attempting to gain sympathy, and so on. These outcomes might not be intentional; but they nonetheless happen if the emotional climate of the session is not carefully monitored and controlled. One partner might use his/her hurt to dramatize how terrible the other partner has been. When this happens, the feelings should be acknowledged appropriately so that they can be used by the partners as the basis for developing empathic understanding of the other. If one partner feels hurt, what did the other do that was hurtful? What is the partner who feels the hurt doing that might make the hurt persist? Sometimes a feeling has deep roots in the past that must be explored if it is to be understood. It is well known that partners tend to recreate old patterns experienced in their family of origin in their current relationship. When the pattern is re-enacted, it carries a great deal of emotionality—much more than would be expected from the situation at hand.

Don't let the couple take charge of the session. In some approaches to individual therapy, sessions are less structured, and the client is allowed to take the lead. In our experience, couple therapy needs to be much more structured, and the therapist must take a more active role than in individual therapy. The therapist needs to develop and stick to a plan for the evaluation and treatment, unless there is a good rationale for departing from it. We are not suggesting that the therapist be rigid or controlling but that the therapy provided be thematic and programmatic. The couple is not the expert on how to solve their problem. They are asking the therapist to provide knowledge and skill. Couples can get lost in the same argument they have had over and over again. Providing a structure helps them escape their endless loops and shows them that effective problem solving involves a systematic application of some basic principles.

Individual and family therapists sometimes assume that marital therapy is just adding another person to the therapy room or subtracting a person or two. Although individual and family therapy may be guided by theoretical notions that are very similar to those used in couples therapy, the techniques and unique challenges of couple work can be difficult to master. In this chapter, we focused on the process of working with couples in terms of some of the common problems or pitfalls. Even the most astute and experienced therapist will sometimes fall prey to these pitfalls. All of us must remain vigilant and mindful of these ideas; otherwise, we lose the couple to premature termination, or imbalance the system and lose the investment of one partner.

9

⌘ ⌘ ⌘ ⌘ ⌘

Dealing With Couples' Problems: Common Issues

THIS CHAPTER WILL PROVIDE A BRIEF OVERVIEW of some of the more common problems a therapist is likely to encounter in treating a couple with an erectile dysfunction. These problems include communication issues, different expectations, and anger and conflict. In some instances, the therapist may need to resolve these types of issues before attempting the sex therapy, while in others, the sexual and relational problems may be treated concurrently.

PROBLEMS IN COMMUNICATION

In order to solve any problem a couple must be capable of communicating effectively. Effective interpersonal communication is a skill; consequently, much of what is done in the communications area of a relationship is psychoeducational in nature. The therapist offers new ideas about how to communicate and then coaches the couple in mastering those skills. A few basic skills can help solve many problems confronting the couple. Unfortunately, partners have usually suffered through so much miscommunication that it is hard to get them back on track. The miscommunication has led to the development of several maladaptive assumptions that impedes them from trying anything new.

164

Assumptions Facilitating
Effective Communication

We begin our communications work by discussing the five foundational assumptions required to communicate more effectively. The first assumption is that of *commitment*; the partners must be committed to each other and to the therapeutic process. If they know they are committed, they will stay engaged with each other even when the communication becomes difficult again. The level of commitment to the relationship needs to be evaluated as early as possible in order to establish whether the couple is appropriate for conjoint therapy. The level of commitment is evaluated by asking each partner how committed they feel to the relationship. Three common permutations occur—both are very committed, both are tentatively committed or uncommitted, and one is committed and the other is not. Having two committed partners from the outset is an ideal way to begin therapy. When this is not the case, the therapist must spend time on this issue prior to beginning sex therapy.

The second assumption is that of *good will* or good intent. Each partner needs to have a fundamental belief that the other holds him/her in high regard and wishes to express good will and good intent toward him/her. In many relationships, communications in the past have had bad effects, leading partners to assume there is bad *intent*. But bad effect does not necessarily imply bad intent. This assumption needs to be accepted by both partners before they are willing to check out statements with each other.

The third assumption is that of *understanding*. The couple has experienced so much miscommunication and misunderstanding that they give up at the first sign of trouble. They believe that they will only dig themselves into a deeper hole if they continue to communicate. The new assumption is that they can only achieve understanding through continued efforts at effective communication, and they may experience confusion and misunderstanding along the way. This assumption requires ongoing reinforcement by the therapist to overcome the couple's fear of failure.

The fourth assumption is that *communication is more than expressing some idea about an object or person*. Most couples are familiar with communication at the content level—a discussion about something concrete. Couples must be educated about the process level of communication that requires mature, differentiated, and abstract thinking and reflecting. Being able to communicate about how they communicate requires that they step back and observe the process. Many of the problems between partners are not what they say but how they say it. Without the ability to recognize and process this level of communication, there is no way to address the real problem.

The fifth assumption of *circularity* is the most difficult one for couples to grasp. This is the assumption that pervades the thinking of systems thinkers. We automatically assume each partner contributes to the problem and is a part of a reciprocal and spiraling process. For example, we look for the interlocking aspect of each partner's individual pathology; an over-functioner coupled with an underfunctioner, an emotionally overcontrolled partner with an emotionally undercontrolled one. In essence, the partners have a predictable system of interaction with prescribed behaviors for each partner. Couples do not think systemically; they tend to think in discrete and linear (cause and effect) terms and have difficulty connecting or linking their behaviors. The assumption can be explained at the beginning of treatment and the couple asked to think along these lines. The therapist might give the following instruction: "When you are interacting or communicating with each other, try to see how your behaviors fit together. Look for the connections and links between what you do and what your partner does when a problem occurs; it's much easier to think about your partner's role than it is to think about your own. Try to put yourselves in the picture to see how you influence each other in covert and overt ways." This process of therapy itself slowly teaches them this concept of circularity.

Creating a Context for Communication

Sometimes therapy deals with the obvious: Many couples simply do not create a context that facilitates effective communication. They either don't make time or try to squeeze in a quick talk during a "station break." Otherwise, they never communicate with each other. This type of communication is too telegraphic is be effective. In the therapist's office, they need to practice talking directly to each other. Some therapists have partners direct their communication through them. In our experience, this is not an effective strategy for working with couples, because the partners need to practice speaking directly to each other in the office with the therapist coaching. Then they can practice these skills at other places where no mediating influence is present, no amiable therapist available to interpret and translate. The skills acquired in the office hopefully generalize and are used at home.

Second, the environment should be relatively free of distraction. They may need to set aside time *just for talking* without distractions or interruptions from children, chores, television, phone calls, and so on. A direct conversation about feelings cannot be effective if the television is on, or kids are skidding in and out of the room. Third, it helps if they are physically close, even touching each other. We recommend sitting together on a couch or love seat so they are touching hand to hand or side to side. Eye contact is also essential.

Finally, communication is a process that takes time. Part of setting aside time is to set aside *enough* time. When the couple is just starting this practice the time should be tailored to what both partners can successfully do. We typically prescribe ten minutes in the beginning of treatment and gradually increase the time as they learn the concepts.

Levels of Communication

Many couples complain that they do talk, but it is only superficial. They are frustrated because this type of communication doesn't reveal the other person to them. For the most part, this issue has been handled poorly in the communications field. Basically, couples need a way of assessing the level at which they are communicating and a cognitive schema for moving to a deeper level. If you were to ask a couple to communicate at a deeper level without explaining what this idea involved, most couples would not know where to begin.

Bernal and Barker (1979) described a straightforward schema that we find helpful to couples. We describe this schema to couples by defining each level of communication and offering a brief description.

Level 1: *Objects.* The couple focuses on issues outside of self. They talk about the events in their lives and other people's actions. It is like giving a newspaper account of events—no feelings, no interpretations, no personal meaning. For example, Harry would come home from work each day and give his wife a detailed account of his day. He would just report on the events in chronological order without conveying any sense of what things meant to him, or how he felt about various happenings.

Level 2: *Individual.* Each partner talks about his/her behavior as a reaction to something or someone else. This level is limited to linear cause-effect thinking in which responsibility for one's own actions is disowned and projected onto others. A husband, for example, might tell his wife he was angry because she said something critical. He does not see his part in the transaction.

Level 3: *Transactional.* The reciprocal and circular nature of the relationship is discussed. Each partner can talk about self as a feeling, thinking being. I statements are made at this level. There is a greater degree of responsibility for one's action and emotions; for example, a man might say to his wife that he understood why she was so upset because he used a harsh tone of voice in expressing an otherwise small complaint.

Level 4: *Relational.* This level builds on the preceding one. The partners can now discuss process as well as underlying rules, roles, and communication processes or meta-communications. The couple can follow the directive, "Talk about how you talk." When Rachael and Mark entered therapy, they constantly interrupted each other, and it was apparent that neither listened to the other. After some coaching and a good deal of feedback from the therapist, the couple could interrupt themselves to talk about how they were falling back into the same pattern. Gradually, they were able to change their old patterns by becoming self-reflective and verbally explicit about their communication.

Level 5: *Contextual.* The added dimensions of history and explanation bring us to the final level. The couple can now discuss how their earlier experiences influence them to behave in various ways in the relationship and offer explanations for why they behave the way they do. For example, as in the case of the partners who constantly interrupted each other, exploration of their family histories revealed that neither one was given a voice in his/her family of origin. The only way they had learned to be heard was to interrupt others and to do so in an aggressive manner.

We also explain these levels are not hierarchical: No one level is better than another. Limitations in communication occur only when couples are unable to engage in a particular level when it is needed. It is a matter of being able to utilize all the levels. Some discussions are simple, straightforward, and on the surface. Other discussions require much more depth and self-disclosure. The first two levels do not offer much in the way of self-disclosure. In order for the partners to feel close to and known by each other, their communication must have deeper hues from time to time.

Obstacles to Communication

Couples typically have a number of communication patterns that are ineffective and block mutual understanding. The couple can be made aware of these types of communications and instructed to avoid them by monitoring their statements in order to prevent these old habits from creeping back into play. Progress is usually incremental as couples slowly begin to replace the old habits with those newly acquired.

One of the most common communication problems is *mind-reading*, which occurs whenever one partner assumes he/she knows what the other is thinking, feeling, etc., without checking it out. Typically, the mind-reader insists that he/she knows the other's thoughts whenever the other's behaviors and verbal statements contradict the assumption. This incorrect assumption about the partner's thoughts, behavior, or feelings serves to complicate a situation and prevent resolution of problems. Instead of mind reading, assumptions should be openly discussed and clarified.

A second problem is *personalizing* issues. Instead of discussing or even disagreeing with one's partner about a certain behavior, the personalizing partner will criticize the *personhood* of the responsible partner. The issue becomes one of who the *person* is, rather than what the person *did*. The *problem* should be attacked, not the person.

A third problem is that of *distraction*. The distracting partner fails to respond to a statement but makes some kind of comment that serves to change the focus. This problem causes partners to feel misunderstood or estranged from each other. In the worst case, the individual fails to acknowledge his or her partner's needs and immediately expresses his or her own needs. This obstacle to communication must be interrupted as soon as possible to prevent further disconfirmation and alienation.

Fourth, many couples use *polarizing language*. This kind of language creates distance and divides the partners. Common polarizing words include "right" and "wrong," "good" and "bad," "truth" and "lie," "crazy" and "sane." The use of black-and-white descriptors should be minimized or eliminated. Words such as "perceptions," "beliefs," "opinions," and "impressions" can be substituted. Rather than proclaiming something to be "right," the partner can talk about what he/she would like or prefer.

Gottman (1994, 1999) has studied couples' communication patterns for many years and has identified four styles of communication that are highly destructive in couples and predictive of divorce. The therapist should monitor for these communications, teach the couple about them, and suggest their elimination. Gottman's (1994) book is also useful for couples to read who are having these types of communication problems. The four negative types of communications are:

- *Criticism*: Attacking someone's personality or character rather than a specific behavior. A criticism needs to be differentiated from a complaint.

- *Contempt*: Making statements intended to insult or hurt one's partner. Contemptuous expressions include insults, name-calling, hostile comments, mockery, and nonverbal body language (especially facial expressions).

- *Defensiveness*: Avoiding responsibility for one's actions. It can include denial, rationalizations or excuses, cross-complaining, "yes-butting," and talking over the person.

- *Stonewalling*: Not listening to the partner. The stonewalling partner may walk away, change the subject, or withdraw into silence.

Techniques Facilitating Communication

A few simple techniques can lead to a vast improvement in communication. These techniques can be taught and coached in the session and then practiced at home.

- *I-Statements:* The partners are asked to speak for themselves by making an I-statement rather than a you- or we-statement. The I-statement is self-disclosing, communicating the partner's thoughts, feelings, needs, wishes, hopes, etc.

    WIFE: He doesn't help with anything.

    HUSBAND: That's not true.

    THERAPIST: [*To wife*] Please back up and say what you did a moment ago, but use an I-statement.

    WIFE: I don't mean to be critical. I'm overwhelmed and need more help from you. I keep asking for things, and they don't happen.

    HUSBAND: I want to help—I just don't know what to do and then you get angry.

    THERAPIST: This is much better—keep going.

- *Reflective listening:* Listening needs to be an active process. First, one partner speaks, and the other listens attentively. The listening partner then reflects back both the content and the feelings that are embedded in the statement. The listening partner does not respond to the statement until he/she has clearly understood the content and affective part of the message. When a message is communicated, problems can occur on both ends. The sender's message may not be very clear, and it could possibly have contradictory elements. The receiver may not interpret the message as it was intended to be received. They may need to keep restating the message back and forth until the intent is clearly understood. Reflective listening helps couples gain a mutual understanding that communication is an imperfect process, and miscommunications will inevitably occur. They should also be able to separate *effect* from *intent*: Just because a statement is received in one way does not mean it was intended to be received in that way. The following illustrates reflective listening:

    HUSBAND: I don't like the way the babysitter was watching the children yesterday. Dave was walking toward the pool, and she didn't notice. I had to stop him.

    WIFE: You're concerned the babysitter wasn't watching Dave.

    THERAPIST: How do you think he felt?

WIFE: He said concerned, but I think he was afraid for Dave and angry with me and the babysitter.

HUSBAND: That's right.

THERAPIST: Say more.

HUSBAND: I didn't want her to hire this babysitter; she's too flaky.

THERAPIST: Are you angry with your wife?

HUSBAND: Not angry but annoyed that she didn't listen to me.

WIFE: Okay, he's not angry but annoyed.

- *Validation:* Couples often discuss the need to be validated. Validation is often confused with agreement with the other. Validation does not necessarily include agreement, but it always includes respectful acknowledgment. One partner is able to understand the other's feelings and thoughts from that partner's perspective. In order to validate another person, one partner would have to put aside his/her ego or needs and focus on the other.

    THERAPIST: Hold on—would you validate what your wife just said before going on?

    HUSBAND: I think she wants me to understand that I have let my parents have too much influence over my life.

    THERAPIST: Do you feel he understands what you're saying?

    WIFE: Part of it. I want him to know that I always feel like the third wheel when we're with his family.

    HUSBAND: She feels left out when we're all together. I've heard her say that plenty of times, but she's usually so angry about it that all I want to do is get away from the thing.

PROBLEMS IN EXPECTATIONS

Every person begins a relationship with a set of expectations about what it means to be dating, engaged, married, and parents. Partners carry expectations about rules, roles, rituals, and virtually every aspect of couple life. Sager (1976) pointed out that these expectations exist at three levels. At one level, the expectations have been explicitly expressed; for example, a husband might say to his wife that he wants her to learn to play tennis with him. The expectation is explicit and consciously aware to each partner. At the second level, each partner has expectations of the other that he/she is aware of but does not openly communicate. Somehow the other partner is supposed to automatically know about the expectation and fulfill it; for example, a man expects his wife to initiate sex more often but does not tell her of this expectation. This level is more problematic than the first level where the couple can negotiate their expectations; at the second level the source of the conflict or disappointment is not clear. At the third level, the expectation cannot be communicated because its holder is not consciously aware of it; its existence can only be *inferred* from behavior. When a partner repeatedly sets up situations that implicitly require that a need be met for him/her, it is clear that he/she is asking for something indirectly; for example, when a wife sets up a situation in which the children are always present or need attending, she is indirectly saying she does not want to spend time with her husband.

Some needs or expectations are healthy while others are not. For example, partners who enact, in essence, a parent-child relationship will hold unhealthy expectations that eventually lead to a great deal of conflict. Partners who form relationships based on unhealthy expectations may avoid being sexual with each other in order to avoid having to deal with their underlying sexual problems. Each spouse may bring unconscious conflicts about sex into the marriage. They collude with each other to avoid some or all sexual activities in order to protect themselves.

The therapist can help the couple identify and understand their expectations by asking each to write out a list of what he/she expects to give and get. These expectations can then be negotiated in the sessions to their mutual satisfaction. Most couples will be able to pull up some of their heretofore unconscious expectations and, with the therapist's help, begin to understand their origins. One woman exploring the origins of her expectation that her husband should be there for her and help her at all times came to the realization that, although she could never get her father's attention or love when she was young, she could get boys' attention by being helpless. Later in life she used the same strategy in her marriage, believing that she had to be incompetent in order to receive her husband's help and attention.

Another way to uncover expectations is to ask about ways in which partners feel disappointed or let down by one another. Sometimes a disappointment follows on the heels of a failed conscious expectation; other times, one partner might feel disappointed by the other in a given situation but not know why. The therapist can begin to ask about what was wanted in a situation and in what ways the partner felt disappointed.

One case involved a couple in their sixties who had been married for almost 30 years. They had a traditional marriage. Preretirement, the husband had been consumed by his business, and his wife had been rearing three children. As the years progressed, they began to realize how little they had in common. The wife had also developed back problems that frequently prevented them from having sex. While they both tried to overlook or at least minimize the problems between them, they had become increasingly dissatisfied and detached from each other. As one might suspect, their interest in sex with each other diminished. While the husband still had some interest in sex, he had very little interest in his wife. From his perspective, she constantly disappointed him by not sharing his interests, expectations, or wanting to spend time with him. Somewhere along the way he had also developed an erectile problem. Evaluation by a urologist showed the problem was unlikely to be organic, despite his age. He decided to try Viagra, because neither one had the motivation for doing sex therapy as a couple. The Viagra proved effective but did nothing to improve the quality of the sexual relationship or in the overall relationship. Ultimately, this couple decided to divorce due to a lack of compatibility.

In the area of sex, couples carry many implicit or unexpressed expectations. This is because many people find it difficult to talk about sex, especially to ask for the kind of stimulation they desire. In addition, there is the assumption that all partners should be experts in lovemaking, intuitively knowing what to do to please the other. In turn, partners may feel frustrated, disappointed, and even sexually rejected because they aren't getting what they want. In one case, a man did not like the way his wife kissed. He felt he could never tell her that she wasn't kissing him the way he liked because she would interpret his request as a criticism.

PROBLEMS IN ANGER AND CONFLICT

Anger and conflict are inevitable in every close relationship, yet in our experience very few couples have been taught how to deal with these issues optimally. Most muddle through, finding solutions of their own. Some couples attempt to deny anger and conflict; others go to the opposite extreme and express it vigorously—if not viciously. The question is not whether anger and conflict occur between partners, but how they manage it when it does occur. Unresolved anger and conflict corrode the relationship, leaving little to work with in a therapy context. Partners who are openly fighting with each other or engaged in covert warfare will not cooperate with each other, and attempting to do sex therapy with such a couple is doomed to fail.

Intersystemic Approaches to Anger and Conflict Resolution

We will only present an overview of the intersystemic approach to dealing with this issue. For a more detailed discussion see *Integrative Solutions* (Weeks & Hof, 1995). The first step in helping the couple to deal with this issue is to normalize it. Some couples think they should never be angry or fight with each other, especially if they have only experienced destructive fights in the past. They need to learn that anger is normal, and conflict is inevitable because each partner brings his or her own set of needs to the relationship. From time to time these needs will be in conflict. This discussion is intended to change the couple's attitude toward anger and conflict so that they don't try to avoid it. It is also intended to suggest that when these issues are handled well, the relationship is strengthened and grows. Being able to confront a difference and, at the same time, affirm the priority of the relationship gives the couple a stronger sense of cohesion.

In one of our cases, the man was unable to assert his wants and needs. He always felt he was one-down in a relationship. He had been married twice and he believed he was the problem in both marriages. In this relatively new relationship, he was unable to assert himself or set any limits with his partner. As far as his partner knew, he was happy with the relationship. The partner had clear ideas about what she did and didn't want. She readily took charge in such things as selecting activities and deciding when to spend time together. His unexpressed anger over his inability to express the simplest likes and dislikes was reflected when he began to develop problems initiating lovemaking and maintaining an erection. After dating for about six months, he decided to terminate the relationship and work on understanding himself before trying to find a more suitable partner. His pattern had been to develop relationships with women who were assertive, demanding, and critical. Because of the insight gained in therapy, his next relationship proved to be much more successful. His choice of a partner was more appropriate, and he utilized the knowledge he had gained about himself. His erectile problem vanished.

Along with this discussion about the role and meaning of anger and conflict, the therapist may want to provide some bibliotherapy. We usually recommend *The Dance of Anger* (1989) by Harriet Goldhor-Lerner and *Your Perfect Right* (1983) by Alberti and Emmons. The first text, written for women but equally useful for men, discusses the role of the family of origin in the development of attitudes about anger and conflict. The second text is about assertiveness but contains an excellent chapter on anger and also covers communication and negotiation. These texts can help the couple gain more insight into their relationship and also contain a number of useful techniques.

The literature on conflict resolution contains several major behavioral approaches (Kassinove, 1995; L'Abate & McHenry, 1983). Unfortunately, the behavioral approaches share the assumption that couples will be able to resolve their conflict and work through the anger once they have the techniques. But we have found that couples often *resist utilizing these tech-*

niques because of their attitude toward anger. They may deny or avoid anger because they believe it can only have destructive consequences. Their thinking goes, *it can only be destructive; why do anything that would bring it out in the open?* The first task is to help them see that anger has a potentially constructive benefit for them.

The second step in the process is to help the couple understand the meaning and function of anger in their relationship and the attitudes they have acquired from their families of origin. The following questions are used to uncover this information. We keep them as open-ended as possible in order to elicit all possible responses.

- What is anger to you?
- What does it mean when you are angry?
- What does it mean when you are angry with your partner?
- What does it mean when your partner is angry?
- What does it mean when your partner is angry with you?
- How do you respond to your partner's anger?
- How do you respond to your own anger?
- How do you let your partner know you are angry?
- How long does your anger usually last?
- What other feelings are associated with or underlie your anger?

These questions require considerable discussion, and an entire session is required in order to do a thorough exploration—for example, the last question usually requires a full session. To answer the last question, clients are asked to pay attention every time they get angry in order to access the deeper feelings. What happens for many partners is that anger is used as a shield or a defense against the expression of more unresolved feelings, such as fear, hurt, depression, guilt, shame, sadness, insecurity, and low self-esteem.

Nine more questions constitute what we call the "focused anger genogram" (DeMaria, Weeks, & Hof, 1999). These questions help partners better understand how their experiences in their families of origin have shaped their current attitudes. It often provides clues about why partners behave the way they do and thereby enables the therapist to challenge some of their historically based beliefs.

- How did your parents deal with anger/conflict?
- Did you see your parents work through anger/conflict?

- When members of your family (name each one) got angry, how did others respond?
- What did you learn about anger from each of your parents?
- When your parents became angry with you, how did you feel and what did you do?
- How did members of your family respond when you got angry? For example, who listened or failed to listen to you?
- Who was allowed/not allowed to be angry in your family?
- What is your best/worst memory about anger in your family?
- Was anyone ever hurt as a result of someone's anger? Who?

An argument occurs when partners' needs or perceptions are in conflict. Couples need a set of guidelines to follow during a fight to help them preserve the integrity of the relationship even as they engage in conflict over their current difference. Following are the intersystemic guidelines we use:

1. Explore the feelings and underlying emotions first.
2. Make a clear complaint without blaming.
3. Take responsibility for your feelings.
4. Take time-outs as needed.
5. Maintain an attitude of negotiation and compromise.

When a partner feels angry, the first task of therapy is to explore the feelings and the underlying emotions experienced by the partners. This process can take anywhere from a few seconds to a few hours. Sometimes the argument is about something entirely different from what it appears to be about. Most often, it is about some underlying issue, and the current argument is just another example or symbol of that issue. One clue that something else is really the problem is when the anger appears to be disproportional to the situation. For example, a husband arrived from work one day to find that his wife was in a rage over the lawn being unmowed. The real issue was not the lawn, but the fact that he did not carry his share of household responsibilities and rarely completed anything he promised her he would do. How does the therapist get to the real issues? First, he/she will probably note the overreaction and wonder what it means. The most obvious tactic is to ask the wife why she is so angry about this particular behavior. If she cannot immediately answer this question, then the therapist may ask what this behavior means to her, or how it is similar to other behaviors or interactions between them. The husband can also be asked to guess what might be happening, or whether it is like past interactions. Sometimes the therapist can infer from several similar interactions (fights over things not being done) what the underlying issue might be.

The partner who is making the complaint should be clear about what he/she wants in the future. It is implicit in any argument that some change is desired, but the partner who is on the receiving end should not have to guess what that change is to be. This reflective period has two purposes: to examine and discuss the constellation of feelings around the anger, and to cool down enough so that the anger can be talked about rather than acted out.

Some partners act out their anger in an uncontrolled and destructive manner. The therapist can explain that each partner is responsible for his/her anger, and that if he/she wants to be heard and get some of what he/she wants, it will be necessary to control the anger. Couples who have engaged in explosive outbursts and an unmodulated expression of anger probably need a time-out rule. We give the following instructions: "Either one of you can call a time-out if you feel that the level of anger is getting too intense. You can call a time-out for yourself if you are getting too angry, or you can call a time-out if you cannot listen to your partner because he/she is getting too angry. When you call the time-out just say, 'I want a time-out for (specify time).' Once the time-out is called, nothing else should be said. Go your separate ways or, if you need to, we will agree on exactly where you should go."

Both partners should agree to the time-out, and it should be made clear that this is an ironclad agreement. The minimum period for a time-out needs to be at least twenty minutes (Gottman, 1994). Once the time has elapsed, the couple reconnects and tries to continue the conversation. We suggest that if anger intensifies again, the couple wait until the next therapy session to deal with the issue. In past fights, invariably one partner has shut the fight down and refused to discuss it further. With this history, the other partner might be reluctant to accept a time-out. The couple should agree to work on the argument later and use the time-out period to reflect on why the anger became so intense and what each can do to manage it.

Partners also need to be reminded that in order for a fight to be constructive they must enter the process with an attitude of negotiation and compromise. If one wins, the other loses—and, ultimately, that means that the relationship loses. Partners must be willing to give up something to gain something. If the process has gone well, each one will feel they have given up something in the larger interest of preserving the relationship.

Fighting is a skill that is not mastered easily. When couples begin to practice fair fighting or conflict resolution, they will get stuck and make some of their old mistakes. Both therapist and couple must learn to be patient. We have the couple practice the specific steps in the office with our coaching, starting with the low-concern issues and progressing to the serious ones. Some couples need to role-play totally fabricated issues before they can begin to deal with an issue of real concern.

Couples typically want a quick fix and do not give the issue the time it deserves. Explain that when they are on their own at home they will need to schedule time to talk about the issue that is at the core of their argument. The couple may schedule half-hour to one-hour segments. Some couples spend too much time and burn themselves out, whereas others spend far too little time during each argument. Issues which are difficult, complex, and long lasting usually require many hours of discussion. The couple needs to break the argument down into smaller segments. Following each segment, they need to congratulate themselves for taking on the task and plan for the next meeting. Of course, these times should be well protected. Couples need to learn that disputes can be like work tasks. With each day a little more of the task is completed. Some disputes take many hours to resolve.

Earlier we mentioned that partners typically incorporate a number of bad habits into their fighting. We give couples a list (shown below) of some of the do's and don'ts of fighting and ask them to note which habits they have, both good and bad. Next, we ask them to think of a plan that would help them not fall into the bad habits. Since the list is not exhaustive, we ask them to identify any other bad habits we haven't covered and ask each partner to comment on the other. Each partner is asked to be responsible for avoiding his/her bad habits. We explain that both of them will invariably slip and ask them to develop a way of quickly recovering so as not to make the slip the new focus of the argument. We begin the process of establishing basic ground rules by asking the couple to abide by the following ideas. Additionally, we review each ground rule to determine whether each partner has had trouble in that area in the past, and, if so, how they might avoid this habit.

Essential do's
1. Be specific when you introduce a complaint.
2. Confine yourself to one issue at a time. Otherwise, you may skip back and forth, evading the harder issues.
3. Always consider compromise. Remember that your partner's view of reality is just as real as yours, even though you may differ. There are no totally objective realities.

Essential don'ts
1. Don't just complain, no matter how specifically; ask for a reasonable change that will resolve or reduce one gripe at a time.
2. Don't discuss counterdemands until the original demands are clearly understood, and there has been a clear-cut response to them.
3. Never assume that you know what your partner is thinking until you have checked out the assumption in plain language; never assume or predict how you partner will react or what your partner will accept or reject.
4. Don't make sweeping, labeling judgments about your partner's feelings, especially about whether or not they are real or important.
5. Do not use sarcasm or contempt to convey your feelings.

After the couple is clear about their habits and how to take responsibility for them, we move on to the core of fair fighting. This involves having the couple follow very specific guidelines, which we explain during the session:

> The person who has the problem is responsible for bringing it up as soon as possible. But before you bring up the problem, think it through in your own mind. Have an idea about what you want and present the idea without allowing emotion to take over. If you need to calm down first, take the time to do so and think about why you are feeling so much emotion about the problem.
>
> State the problem to your partner as clearly and concretely as possible. It is important to state how you feel and why you feel the way you do. For example, you might say, "I'm feeling angry because I felt put down by the comment you just made."
>
> It is important that you both understand the problem being brought up in the way it was intended to be understood. The partner who is on the receiving end should reflect back what was said using reflective listening. This is done by saying, "I hear you saying you feel _____ because of _____."
>
> After reflecting back what was said, ask clarifying questions so you know exactly what was meant. When both partners agree on what was initially said, the other partner may respond in terms of his or her feelings and ideas about the problem. Perhaps the partner with the problem misunderstood the intent of the message that caused the problem, or the message that was sent *was* intended and has caused hurt feelings.
>
> The partner who brings up the problem should take responsibility

for offering a possible solution in terms of changes both can make. This solution should be discussed, and then the other partner may offer a countersolution. Again, solutions should be couched in terms of what both can do, and focus on negotiation and compromise. Discuss the various proposals until you both agree on one solution. Remember that solutions are neither right nor wrong. You are trying to find something that works for both of you.

Once you have agreed on an idea, talk about how you will implement it. Who is to do what, when, and how? Solutions frequently don't work because attention to detail has been overlooked.

Now that you have a plan, think about things that would undermine it. What could go wrong? How might each of you unconsciously sabotage it? Working through a difficult problem usually stirs up a lot of negative feelings. Focus on the fact that you have worked together and been successful. Point this fact out to each other along the way and congratulate yourselves for the work you are doing. Celebrate your successes, even if it is in some small way. Agree to reexamine the problem in a reasonable period of time to assess how things are going. Keep your mind open to making changes or finetuning it. Don't let minor slips destroy all the work you have done.

The first few steps of this model for fair fighting are concerned with expressing feelings and understanding the nature of the complaint. One of the most common problems in fighting is that the feelings (whatever they may be) are not given enough attention. The rule is: *Feelings first*. Couples often try to skim over this stage and then get stuck in the next stage because the emotional work has not been fully processed. Partners should not proceed to the next stage until they both agree that the feelings have been discussed enough, and that they understand each other's point of view.

The second stage is the problem-solving or practical part of the model. Partners generate solutions to the problem, sort out the implications of the solutions, and tentatively agree on a course of action. They also agree to evaluate how well their solution is working within an agreed-upon period of time.

The therapist can help partners practice this model in the office until they begin to see how it works. At first, going through the steps will seem mechanical and awkward, but this disappears with practice. The therapist might praise partners for their cooperative spirit and invite the couple to congratulate each other when they have had a successful experience. Celebrating their successes is an important part of an inherently tense process. Partners need to acknowledge and celebrate the fact that they can come to terms with the differences that exist within their relationship.

This chapter addressed just a few of the possible problems couples who are in sex therapy might experience. They might be confronting an affair, an addiction, in-law problems, financial woes, parenting conflicts, depression, and so on. As we stated earlier, the focus should remain on the presenting problem to the extent that is possible. In some cases, it is not possible because the other issues distract from or interfere with addressing the problem that was defined as primary. In other cases, the couple will be quite willing to deal with the other issues before attempting the sex therapy. Sex and couple therapy can frequently be combined: Part of the session is devoted to the sexual problem and the other part to the couple problem. In a typical scenario, a couple will report they did not do any of the homework, or even try, because they had a big fight during the last week. Such a statement provides an opportunity for the therapist to explore what the fight was about and why it had such a dampening effect on their relationship. The couple might choose to work on their fighting behavior and put the sex therapy temporarily on hold. In other cases, couples may report marital problems such as fighting but still be able to carry out their assignment. These couples are good candidates for mixing couple and sex therapy. The therapist can literally split the session into two parts—one part dealing with the sexual issues and the other with the marital issues. Sue and Ben were typical of this type of couple. They entered therapy because of Ben's erectile problem. However, the focus shifted quickly. They were an older remarried couple. Each one had adult children. Ben was anticipating retirement and was doing some estate planning. Sue did not believe her children were going to be treated fairly which evoked in her a strong sense of loyalty toward her children and a sense of mistrust toward Ben. The therapist shifted focus to deal with these larger family issues. For a period of several weeks, the therapy mixed these two issues in every session. Whatever the mix, the therapist needs to flexibly utilize a wide range of skills, and the couple needs to feel some ownership in the treatment plan in order for both therapist and couple to cocreate a successful therapeutic experience.

References

Adams, K. M. (1991). *Silently seduced*. Deerfield Beach, FL: Health Communications.

Alberti, R. E., & Emmons, M. L. (1983). *Your perfect right: A guide to assertive living*. San Luis Obispo, CA: Impact.

Allen, R., & Brendler, C. B. (1990). Snap-gauge compared to a full nocturnal penile tumescence study for evaluation of patients with erectile impotence. *Journal of Urology, 143*, 51–54.

Althof, S., Turner, L., Levine, S., Risen, C., Bodner, D., Kursh, E., & Resnick, M. (1987). Intracavernosal injection in the treatment of impotence: A prospective study of sexual, psychological, and marital functioning. *Journal of Marital and Sex Therapy, 13*, 155–167.

Althof, S., Turner, L., Levine, S., Risen, C., Bodner, D., Kursh, E., & Resnick, M. (1991). Sexual, psychological, and marital impact of self-injection of papaverine and phentolamine: A long-term prospective study. *Journal of Sex and Marital Therapy, 17*, 101–112.

American Medical Association. (1988). *House of delegates resolution regarding AIDS*. Chicago: Author.

American Psychiatric Association. (1954). *Diagnostic and statistical manual of mental disorders*. Washington, DC: Author.

American Psychiatric Association. (1980). *Diagnostic and statistical, manual of mental disorders* (3rd ed.). Washington, DC: Author.

American Psychiatric Association. (1987). *Diagnostic and statistical manual of mental disorders* (3rd ed., rev.). Washington, DC: Author.

American Psychiatric Association. (1994). *Diagnostic and statistical manual of mental disorders* (4th ed.). Washington, DC: Author.

Anderson, K. V., & Bovim, G. (1997). Impotence and nerve entrapment in long distance amateur cyclists. *Acta Neurologica Scandinavica, 4,* 233–240.

Andersson, E. K., & Wagner, G. (1995). Physiology of the penile erection. *Physiological Reviews, 75,* 191–276.

Apfelbaum, B. (1989). Retarded ejaculation: A much-misunderstood syndrome. In S. R. Leiblum & R. C. Rosen (Eds.), *Principles and practice of sex therapy: Update for the 1990s* (pp. 168–206). New York: Guilford.

Barbach, L. (1982). *For each other: Sharing sexual intimacy.* New York: Doubleday.

Barlow, D. H. (1986). Causes of sexual dysfunction: The role of anxiety and cognitive interference. *Journal of Consulting and Clinical Psychology, 54,* 140–148.

Beck, A. (1976). *Cognitive therapy and the emotional disorder.* New York: International Universities.

Berman, E., & Hof, L. (1987). The sexual genogram: Assessing family-of-origin factors in the treatment of sexual dysfunction. In G. R. Weeks & L. Hof (Eds.), *Integrating sex and marital therapy: A clinical guide* (pp. 37–56). New York: Brunner/Mazel.

Bernal, G., & Barker, J. (1979). Toward a metacommunication framework of couples intervention. *Family Process, 18,* 293–302.

Birchler, G. R., & Webb, L. J. (1977). Discriminating interaction behavior in happy and unhappy marriages. *Journal of Consulting and Clinical Psychology, 45,* 494–495.

Blumstein, P., & Schwartz, P. (1983). *American couples: Money, work, sex.* New York: William Morrow.

Bowen, M. (1976). Theory in the practice of psychotherapy. In P. J. Guerin (Ed.), *Family therapy: Theory and practice* (pp. 42–90). New York: Gardner.

Bradley, W. E., Lin, J. T., & Johnson, B. (1984). Measurement of the conduction velocity of the dorsal nerve of the penis. *Journal of Urology, 131,* 1127–1129.

Broderick, G. A. (1998). Evidence-based assessment of erectile dysfunction. *International Journal of Impotence Research, 10,* 564–573.

Carey, M. P., Wincze, J. P., & Meisler, A. W. (1993). Sexual dysfunction: Male erectile disorder. In D. H. Barlow (Ed.), *Clinical handbook of psychological disorders* (2nd ed., pp. 442–480). New York: Guilford.

Clark, D., Beck, A., & Alford, B. (1999). *Scientific foundations of cognitive theory and therapy for depression.* New York: Wiley.

Comfort, A. (1992). *The new joy of sex.* New York: Pocket.

Costabile, R. A., Spevak, M., Fishman, I. J., Grovier, F. E., Hellstrom, W. J., Shabsigh, R., Nemo, K. J., Rapport, J. L., Tam, P. V., Weldon, K. L., & Gesundheit, N. (1998). Efficacy and safety of transurethral alprostadil in patients with erectile dysfunction following radical prostatectomy. *Journal of Urology, 4,* 1325–1328.

Crenshaw, T. (1996). *The alchemy of love and lust.* New York: G. P. Putnam.

Crenshaw, T., & Goldberg, G. P. (1996). *Sexual pharmacology.* New York: W. W. Norton.

Davidson, J., & Rosen, R. (1992). Hormonal determinants of erectile functions. In R. Rosen & S. Leiblum (Eds.), *Erectile disorders* (pp. 72–95). New York: Guilford.

DeMaria, R., Weeks, G., & Hof, L. (1999). *Focused genograms: Intergenerational assessment of individuals, couples, and families.* Philadelphia: Brunner/Mazel.

Dozier, R. M., Hicks, M. W., Cornille, J. M., & Peterson, G. W. (1998). The effect of Tomm's therapeutic questioning styles on therapeutic alliance: A clinical analogue study. *Family Process, 37,* 189–200.

Drawz, B., Drawz, G., Kittner, C., Seiter, H., & Schuemichen, C. (1998). Penile perfusion and functional scintigraphy: Preliminary clinical results before and after microsurgical revascularization. *British Journal of Urology, 2,* 241–245.

Eid, F., & Pearce, C. (1993). *Making love again.* New York: Brunner/Mazel.

Ellis, A. (1962). *Reason and emotion in psychotherapy.* New York: Lyle Stewart.

Ellis, A. (1999). *How to make yourself happy and remarkably less disturbed.* Atascadero, CA: Impact.

Ellis, A., & Harper, R. (1961). *A guide to successful marriage.* North Hollywood, CA: Wilshire.

Engel, J. D., & McVary, K. T. (1998). Transurethral alprostadil as therapy for patients who withdraw from or failed intracavernous injection therapy. *Urology, 5,* 687–692.

Ernst, E., & Pittler, M. (1998). Yohimbine for erectile dysfunction: A systematic review and meta-analysis of randomized clinical trials. *Urology, 159,* 433–436.

Feldman, H. A., Goldstein, I., Hatzichristou, G., Krane, R. J., & McKinlay, J. B. (1994). Impotence and its medical and psychosocial correlates: Results of the Massachusetts male aging study. *Journal of Urology, 151,* 54–61.

Fogarty, T. F. (1976). Marital crisis. In P. J. Guerin, Jr. (Ed.), *Family therapy theory and practice* (pp. 325–334). New York: Gardner.

Frank, E., Anderson, C., & Kupfer, D. J. (1976). Profiles of couples seeking sex and marital therapy. *American Journal of Psychiatry, 133,* 559–562.

Frank, E., Anderson, C., & Rubinstein, D. (1978). Frequency of sexual dysfunction in "normal" couples. *New England Journal of Medicine, 299,* 111–115.

Frankl, V. E. (1952). The pleasure principle and sexual neurosis. *International Journal of Sexology, 5,* 128–130.

Frankl, V. E. (1991). Paradoxical intention. In G. R. Weeks (Ed.), *Promoting change through paradoxical therapy* (pp. 99–110). New York: Brunner/Mazel.

Friday, N. (1980). *Men in love.* New York: Dell.

Friday, N. (1991). *Women on top.* New York: Pocket.

Froelich, R., & Bishop, M. (1977). *Clinical interviewing skills* (3rd ed.). St. Louis: CO: Mosby.

Fulgham, P. F., Cochran, J. S., Denman, J. L., Feagins, B. A., Gross, M. B., Kadesky, K. T., Kadesky, M. I., Clark, A. R., & Roehrborn, C. G. (1998). Disappointing initial results with transurethral alprostadil for erectile dysfunction in a urology practice setting. *Journal of Urology, 6,* 2041–2046.

Gagnon, J. H. (1974). Scripts and the coordination of sexual conduct. In J. K. Cole & R. Deinstbier (Eds.), *Nebraska Symposium on Motivation.* Lincoln, NE: University of Nebraska.

Gagnon, J. H., Rosen, R. C., & Leiblum, S. R. (1982). Cognitive and social aspects of sexual dysfunction: Sexual scripts in sex therapy. *Journal of Sex and Marital Therapy, 8,* 44–56.

Gill, H. (1997). Urological evaluation of sexual disorders. In R. Charlton & I. Yalom (Eds.), *Treating sexual disorders* (pp. 110–122). San Franscisco: Jossey Bass.

Gladue, B. A., Boechler, M., & McCaul, K. D. (1989). Hormonal response to competition in human males. *Aggressive Behavior, 15,* 409–422.

Goldhor-Lerner, H. (1989). *The dance of anger.* New York: HarperCollins.

Goldstein, I., Lue, T. F., Padma-Nathan, H., Rosen, R. C., Steers, W. D., & Wicker, P. (1998). Oral sildenafil in the treatment of erectile dysfunction. *The New England Journal of Medicine, 338,* 1397–1459.

Gottman, J. (1994). *Why marriages succeed or fail and how you can make yours last.* New York: Fireside.

Gottman, J. (1999). *The marriage clinic: A scientifically-based marital therapy.* New York: W. W. Norton.

Gottman, J., & Silver, N. (1999). *The seven principles for making marriage work.* New York: Crown.

Govier, F. E., Gibbons, R. P., Correa, R. J., Pritchett, T. R., & Kramer-Levien, D. (1998). Mechanical reliability, surgical complications, and patient and partner satisfaction of the modern three-piece inflatable penile prosthesis. *Urology, 2,* 282–286.

Guinguis, N. (1998). Oral treatment of erectile dysfunction from herbal remedies to designer drugs. *Journal of Sex and Marital Therapy, 24,* 69–73.

Hackney, H., & Nye, S. (1973). *Counseling strategies and objectives.* Englewood Cliffs, NJ: Allyn & Bacon.

Haley, J. (1976). *Problem solving therapy.* San Francisco: Jossey-Bass.

Heiman, J., & LoPiccolo, J. (1998). *Becoming orgasmic: A sexual and personal growth program for women* (Rev. ed.). New York: Simon & Schuster.

Heiman, J. R., & Meston, C. M. (1997). Empirically validated treatment for sexual dysfunction. *Annual Review of Sex Research, 8,* 148–194.

Hellstrom, W., Bennet, A., Gesunheit, N., Kaiser, F., Lue, T., Padma-Nathan, H., Peterson, G., Tam, P., Todd, L., Varady, J., & Place, V. (1996). A double-blind, placebo-controlled evaluation of the erectile response to transurethral alprostadil. *Urology, 48,* 851–856.

Hof, L., & Berman, E. (1986). The sexual genogram. *Journal of Marital and Family Therapy, 12,* 39–47.

Howard, B., & Weeks, G. (1995) A happy marriage: Pairing couples therapy and treatment of depression. In G. Weeks & L. Hof (Eds.), *Integrative solutions: Treating common problems in couples therapy* (pp. 95–123). New York: Brunner/Mazel.

Jarrow, J. P., & Lowe, F. C. (1997). Penile trauma: An etiologic factor in Peyronie's disease and erectile dysfunction. *Journal of Urology, 4,* 1388–1390.

Kaplan, H. S. (1974). *The new sex therapy.* New York: Brunner/Mazel.

Kaplan, H. S. (1979). *Disorders of sexual desire.* New York: Brunner/Mazel.

Kaplan, H. S. (1990). The combined use of sex therapy and intrapenile injections in the treatment of impotence. *Journal of Marital and Sex Therapy, 16,* 195–207.

Kaplan, H. S. (1995). *The sexual desire disorders: Dysfunctional, regulation of sexual motivation.* New York: Brunner/Mazel.

Kaplan, S. A., Reis, R. B., Kohn, I. J., Shabsigh, R., & Te, A. E. (1998). Combination therapy using oral alpha-blockers and intracavernosal injection in men with erectile dysfunction. *Urology, 5,* 739–743.

Karadeniz, T., Topsakal, M., Aydogmus, A., & Beksan, M. (1997). Role of RigiScan in the etiologic differential diagnosis of erectile dysfunction. *Urology International, 59,* 41–45.

Kassinove, H. (Ed.). (1995). *Anger disorders: Definition, diagnosis, and treatment (The series in clinical and community psychology).* New York: Taylor & Francis.

Kinsey, A. C., Pomeroy, W. B., & Martin, C. E. (1948). *Sexual behavior in the human male.* Philadelphia: W. B. Saunders.

Kolodny, R., Masters, W., & Johnson, V. (1979). *Textbook of sexual medicine.* Boston: Little Brown.

L'Abate, L., & McHenry, S. (1983). *Handbook of marital interventions.* New York: Grune & Stratton.

Laumann, E. O., Gagnon, J. H., Michael, R. T., & Michaels, S. (1994). *The social organization of sexuality.* Chicago: University of Chicago.

Leiblum, S. R., & Rosen, R. C. (1991). Couples therapy for erectile disorder: Conceptual and clinical considerations. *Journal of Sex and Marital Therapy, 17,* 147–159.

Levine, S. B. (1992). Intrapsychic and interpersonal aspects of impotence: Psychogenic erectile dysfunction. In R. C. Rosen & S. R. Leiblum (Eds.), *Erectile disorders: Assessment and treatment* (pp. 198–225). New York: Guilford.

Lewis, R., & Mclaren, R. (1993). Reoperation for penile prosthesis implantation. *Problems in Urology, 155,* 918–923.

Linet, O. I., & Ogring, F. G. (1996). Efficacy and safety of intracavernosal alprostadil in men with erectile dysfunction. *The New England Journal of Medicine, 334,* 873–876.

LoPiccolo, L., & Heiman, J. (1978). Sexual assessment and history interview. In J. LoPiccolo & L. LoPiccolo (Eds.), *Handbook of sex therapy* (pp. 103–112). New York: Plenum.

LoPiccolo, J., & LoPiccolo, L. (Eds.). (1978). *Handbook of sex therapy.* New York: Plenum.

Loren, R., & Weeks, G. R. (1986). Comparison of the sexual fantasies of undergraduates and their perceptions of the sexual fantasies of the opposite sex. *Journal of Sex Education and Therapy, 12,* 31–36.

Lue, T. F., Hricak, H., Schmidt, R. A., & Tanagho, E. A. (1986). Functional evaluation of penile veins by cavernosography in papaverine-induced erection. *Journal of Urology, 135,* 479–483.

Lue, T. F., & Tanagno, E. A. (1987). Physiology of erection and pharmacological management of impotence. *Journal of Urology, 137,* 829–836.

Mahlstedt, P. P. (1987). The crisis of infertility: An opportunity for growth. In G. Weeks & L. Hof (Eds.), *Integrating sex and marital therapy: A clinical guide* (pp. 121–148). New York: Brunner/Mazel.

Maltz, W. (1988). Identifying and treating the sexual repercussions of incest. *Journal of Sex and Marital Therapy, 14,* 116–144.

Manning, M., Junemann, K. P., Schepe, J. R., Braun, P., Krautschick, A., & Alken, P. (1988). Long-term follow-up and selection criteria for penile revascularization in erectile failure. *Journal of Urology, 5,* 1680–1684.

Markman, H., & Stanley, S. (1996). *Fighting for your marriage.* San Francisco: Jossey-Bass.

Marziali, E. (1988). The first session: An interpersonal encounter. *Social Casework, 69,* 23–27.

Masters, W. H., & Johnson, V. E. (1966). *Human sexual response.* Boston: Little, Brown.

Masters, W. H., & Johnson, V. (1970). *Human sexual inadequacy.* Boston: Little, Brown.

McCarthy, B. (1995). Bridges to sexual desire. *Journal of sex education and therapy, 21,* 132–141.

Mellion, M. B. (1991). Common cycling injuries: Management and prevention. *Sport Medicine, 1,* 52–70.

Michael, R. T., Gagnon, J. H., Laumann, E. O., & Kolata, G. (1994). *Sex in America: A definitive survey.* Boston: Little, Brown.

Milsten, R., & Slowinski, J. (1999). *The sexual male: Problems and solutions.* New York: W. W. Norton.

Minuchin, S. (1974). *Families and family therapy.* Cambridge: Harvard University.

Morales, A., Condra, M., Owen, J., Surridge, D., Fenemore, J., & Harris, C. (1987). Is yohimbine effective in the treatment of organic impotence? Results of a controlled trial. *Journal of Urology, 137,* 1168–1172.

Morokoff, P. J., Baum, A., McKinnon, W. R., & Gillilland, R. (1987). Effects of chronic unemployment and acute psychological stress on sexual arousal in men. *Health Psychology, 6,* 545–560.

Mosher, D. (1979). Sex guilt and sex myths in college men and women. *Journal of Sex Research, 15*(3), 224–234.

Mulcahy, J. (1998). Review of penile implants. *Journal of Sex Education and Therapy, 23,* 220–225.

Nerthman, P., & Raifer, J. (1997). MUSE therapy preliminary clinical observations. *Urology, 5,* 809–811.

Nukui, F., Okamoto, S., Nagata, M., Kurokawa, J., & Fukui, J. (1997). Complications and reimplantation of penile implants. *International Journal of Urology, 3,* 335–338.

Odell, M., & Quinn, W. (1998). Therapist and client behaviors in the first interview: Effects on session impact and treatment duration. *Journal of Marital and Family Therapy, 24,* 369–388.

Padma-Nathan, H. (1988). Neurologic evaluation of erectile dysfunction. *Urologic Clinics of North America, 15,* 77–80.

Padma-Nathan, H., Hellstrom, W., & Kaiser, F.(1997). Treatment of men with erectile dysfunction with transurethral alprostadil. *The New England Journal of Medicine, 336,* 1–7.

Padma-Nathan, H., Steers, W. D., & Wicker, P. A. (1998). Efficacy and safety of oral sildenafil in the treatment of erectile dysfunction: A double-blind, placebo-controlled study of 329 patients. *International Journal of Clinical Practice, 52*(6), 1–4.

Parys, B. T., Evans, C. M., & Parsons, K. F. (1988). Bulbocavernosus reflex latency in the investigation of diabetic impotence. *British Journal of Urology, 61,* 59–62.

Perelman, M. (1998). Commentary: Pharmacological agents for erectile dysfunction and the human sexual response cycle. *Journal of Sex and Marital Therapy, 24,* 309–312.

Pfeiffer, E. (1974). Sexuality in the aging individual. *Journal of the American Geriatrics Society, 22,* 481–484.

Pinsof, W. M., & Catherall, D. R. (1986). The integrative psychotherapy alliance: Family, couple, and individual therapy scales. *Journal of Marital and Family Therapy, 12,* 137–151.

Porst, H. (1997). Transurethral alprostadil with MUSE (medicated urethral system for erection) vs. intracavernous alprostadil: A comparison study in 103 patients with erectile dysfunction. *International Journal of Impotence Research, 4,* 187–192.

Rako, S. (1996). *The hormone of desire.* New York: Harmony.

Renshaw, D. C. (1988). Profile of 2,376 patients treated at Loyola Sex Clinic between 1972 and 1987. *Sexual and Marital Therapy, 3,* 111–117.

Rogers, C. (1951). *Client-centered therapy.* Boston: Houghton Mifflin.

Rosen, R. C., & Leiblum, S. R. (1992a). Couples therapy for erectile disorder: Obsevations, obstacles, and outcomes. In R. C. Rosen & S. R. Leiblum (Eds.), *Erectile disorders: Assessment and treatment* (pp. 226–254). New York: Guilford.

Rosen, R. C., & Leiblum, S. R. (Eds.). (1992b). *Erectile disorders: Assessment and treatment.* New York: Guilford.

Rosen, R. C., & Leiblum, S. R. (1992c). Erectile disorders: An overview of historical trends and clinical perspectives. In R. C. Rosen & S. R. Leiblum (Eds.), *Erectile disorders: Assessment and treatment* (pp. 3–26). New York: Guilford.

Rosen, S. R., & Leiblum, R. C. (Eds.). (1999). *Principles and practice of sex, therapy: Update for the 1990s.* New York: Guilford.

Rossi, D., Ayuso, D., Rattier, C., Bladou, F., Hermanowicz, M., & Serment, G. (1997). Clinical experience with 80 inflatable penile prostheses. *European Urology, 3,* 335–338.

Russell, L. (1990). Sex and couples therapy: A method of treatment to enhance physical and emotional intimacy. *Journal of Sex and Marital Therapy, 16,* 111–120.

Sager, C. (1976). *Marriage contracts and couples therapy.* New York: Brunner/Mazel.

Sarramon, J. P., Bertrand, N., Malavand, B., & Rischmann, P. (1997). Microrevascularization of the penis in the vascular impotence. *International Journal of Impotence Research, 3,* 127–133.

Schiavi, R. (1988). Nocturnal penile tumescence in the evaluation of erectile disorders: A critical review. *Journal of Sex and Marital Therapy, 14,* 83–96.

Schiavi, R. (1992). Laboratory methods for evaluating erectile dysfunction. In R. Rosen & S. Leiblum (Eds.), *Erectile disorders* (pp. 141–170). New York: Guilford.

Schnarch, D. (1991). *Constructing the sexual crucible: An integration, of sexual and marital therapy.* New York: W. W. Norton.

Schnarch, D. (1997). *Passionate marriage: Love, sex, and intimacy in, emotionally committed relationships.* New York: W. W. Norton.

Segraves, R. T., Schoenberg, H. W., Zarins, C. K., Knopf, J., & Camic, P. (1981). Discrimination of organic versus psychological impotence with the DSFI: A failure to replicate. *Journal of Sex and Marital Therapy, 7,* 230–238.

Segraves, K. A., Segraves, R. T., & Shoenberg, H. W. (1987). Use of sexual history to differentiate organic from psychogenic impotence. *Archives of Sexual Behavior, 16,* 125–137.

Segraves, R. T., & Segraves, K. A. (1992). Aging and drug effects on the male sexuality. In R. Rosen & S. Lieblum (Eds.), *Erectile disorders.* New York: Guilford.

Sexton, W. J., Benedict, J. F., & Jarrow, J. P. (1998). Comparison of long-term outcomes of penile prostheses and intracavernosal injection therapy. *Journal of Urology, 3,* 811–815.

Shields, C., Sprenkle, D., & Constantine, J. (1991). Anatomy of an initial interview: The importance of joining and structuring skills. *American Journal of Family Therapy, 19,* 3–18.

Spector, I. P., & Carey, M. P. (1990). Incidence and prevalence of the sexual dysfunctions: A critical review of the empirical literature. *Archives of Sexual Behavior, 19,* 389–408.

Sprecher, S., & McKinney, K. (1993). *Sexuality.* Newbury Park, CA: Sage.

Sternberg, R. (1986). A triangular theory of love. *Psychological Review, 93,* 119–135.

Sternberg, R., & Barnes, M. (Eds.). (1988). *The psychology of love.* New Haven, CT: Yale University.

Strong, S., & Claiborn, C. (1982). *Change through interaction: Social psychological processes of counseling and psychotherapy.* New York: John Wiley.

Sundaram, C. P., Thomas, W., Pryor, L. E., Sidi, A. A., Billups, K., & Pryor, J. L. (1997). Long-term follow-up of patients receiving injection therapy for erectile dysfunction. *Urology, 6,* 932–935.

Talmadge, L., & Wallace, S. (1991). Reclaiming sexuality in female incest survivors. *Journal of Sex and Marital Therapy, 17,* 163–182.

Teloken, C., Rhoden, E., Sogari, P., Dambros, M., & Souto, C. (1998). Therapeutic effects of high-dose yohimbine hydrochloride on organic erectile dysfunction. *Urology, 1,* 122–124.

Tiefer, L., & Melman, A. (1987). Adherence to recommendations and improvement over time in men with erectile dysfunction. *Archives of Sex Behavior, 16,* 301–309.

Tomm, K. (1988). Interventive interviewing: Part III—Intending to ask linear, circular, strategic, or reflexive questions? *Family Process, 27,* 1–15.

Trapp, J. (1998). External vacuum therapy: A historical review. *Journal of Sex Education and Therapy, 23,* 217–219.

Turner, L. A., Althof, S. E., Levine, S. B., Kursh, E., Bodner, D., & Resnick, M. (1990). Treating erectile dysfunction with an external vacuum device: Impact on sexual, psychological, and marital functioning. *Journal of Urology, 144,* 79–82.

Turner, M. (1995). Addictions in marital/relationship therapy. In G. R. Weeks & L. Hof, *Integrative solutions: Treating common problems in couples therapy* (pp. 124–147). New York: Brunner/Mazel.

Verhulst, J., & Heiman, J. R. (1979). An interactional approach to sexual dysfunction. *American Journal of Family Therapy, 7,* 19–36.

Vermeulen, A. (1991). Androgens in the aging male. *Journal of Clinical Endocrinology and Metabolism, 73,* 221–224.

Vermeulen, A. (1994). Clinical problems in reproductive neuroendocrinolgy in men. *Neurobiology of Aging, 15,* 489–493.

Wagner, G., & Kaplan, H. S. (1993). *The new injection treatment for impotence.* New York: Brunner/Mazel.

Watzlawick, P. (1978). *The language of change: Elements of therapeutic communication.* New York: Basic.

Weeks, G. R., (1987). Systemic treatment of inhibited sexual desire. In G. Weeks & L. Hof (Eds.), *Integrating sex and marital therapy: A clinical guide* (pp. 183–201). New York: Brunner/Mazel.

Weeks, G. R. (1989). An intersystem approach to treatment. In G. R. Weeks (Ed.), *Treating couples* (pp. 317–340). New York: Brunner/Mazel.

Weeks, G. R. (1994). The intersystem model: An integrative approach to treatment. In G. Weeks & L. Hof (Eds.), *The marital-relationship therapy casebook: Theory and application of the intersystem model* (pp. 3–34). New York: Brunner/Mazel.

Weeks, G. R. (1995). Inhibited sexual desire. In G. R. Weeks & L. Hof (Eds.), *Integrative solutions: Treating common problems in couples therapy* (pp. 215–252). New York: Brunner/Mazel.

Weeks, G. R., & Hof, L. (Eds.). (1987). *Integrating sex and marital, therapy: A clinical guide.* New York: Brunner/Mazel.

Weeks, G. R., & Hof, L. (Eds.). (1995). *Integrative solutions: Treating, common problems in couples therapy.* New York: Brunner/Mazel.

Weeks, G., & Treat, S. (1992). *Couples in treatment: Techniques and approaches for effective practice.* New York: Brunner/Mazel.

Weiss, D. L. (1998). Conclusion: The state of sexual theory. *The Journal of Sex Research, 35,* 100–114.

Werthman, P., & Rafker, J. (1997). Muse therapy: Preliminary clinical observations. *Journal of Urology, 5,* 809–811.

Wiederman, M. W. (1998). The state of theory in sex therapy. *The Journal of Sex Research, 35,* 88–99.

Wilke, R. J., Glick, H. A., McCarron, T. J., Erder, M. H., Althof, S. E., & Linet, O. I. (1997). Quality-of-life effects of alprostadil therapy for erectile dysfunction. *Journal of Urology, 6,* 2124–2128.

Williams, G., Abbou, C., Amar, E., Desvaux, P., Flam, T., LycKlame a Nijeholt, G., Lynch, S., Morgan, R., & Muller, S. (1998). Efficacy and safety of transurethral alprostadil therapy in men with erectile dysfunction, MUSE study group. *British Journal of Urology, 81,* 889–894.

Wincze, J. P., & Carey, M. P. (1991). *Sexual dysfunction: A guide for assessment and treatment.* New York: Guilford.

Wolpe, J. (1958). *Psychotherapy by reciprocal inhibition.* Stanford, CA: Stanford University.

Wolpe, J. (1973). *The practice of behavior therapy.* New York: Pergamon.

Woody, J. D. (1992). *Treating sexual distress: Integrative systems, therapy.* Newbery Park, CA: Sage.

Zilbergeld, B. (1978). *Male sexuality.* New York: Bantam.

Zilbergeld, B. (1992a). The man behind the broken penis: Social and psychological determinants of erectile failure. In R. C. Rosen and S. R. Leiblum (Eds.), *Erectile disorders: Assessment and treatment* (pp. 27–54). New York: Guilford.

Zilbergeld, B. (1992b). *The new male sexuality.* New York: Bantam.

Zilbergeld, B. (1999). *The new male sexuality* (Rev. ed.). New York: Bantam.

Index

Abbou, C., 34
Adams, K. M, 86
addictions
    drug, as a contraindication to sex
        therapy, 94–95
    sexual, interactional factors in,
        57
adrenalin, effect on erectile dysfunc-
    tion, 24
affairs
    as a contraindication to sex therapy,
        94
    as interactional factors in sexual dys-
        function, 57–58
affective facets, in case formulation for
    therapy including, 112–13
age/aging
    changes in sexual functioning related
        to, 18–21
    fear of, as a risk factor for sexual
        dysfunction, 49–50
    and level of dehydroepiandrosterone,
        18
    and prevalence of erectile dysfunc-
        tion, 6–7

as a risk factor in sexual dysfunc-
    tion, 78–79
Alberti, R. E., 174
alcohol, effects of, on sexual arousal,
    22
Alford, B., 126
Alken, P., 34–35
Allen, R., 27
Althof, S. E., 30, 33, 148, 149
Amar, E., 34
Anderson, C., 7, 8
Anderson, K. V., 22
anger
    as a common issue, 173–81
    fear of, interactional factors in,
        59
anxiety
    physical changes caused by, 21
    reducing, case formulation for,
        107–8
    risk of erectile dysfunction related
        to, 44
    sensate focusing exercises to reduce,
        129–30
Apfelbaum, B., 54

apomorphine, effect on sexual arousal, 37
arousal
    changes in, with age, 19–20
    as a phase of the sexual response cycle, 15
assessment
    early in treatment, 73–75
    initial medical, 24–26
    preliminary, case formulation, 102–3
    of psychological risk factors, 62–87
assumptions, that facilitate communication, 164–65
attachment interactions, 51
attention deficit disorder (ADD), as a risk factor for erectile dysfunction, 44–45
Aydogmus, A., 27
Ayuso, D., 32

Barbach, L., 19
Barker, J., 167
Barnes, M., 3
barriers, to seeking help, 8–10
Baum, A., 44
Beck, A., 126
Beksan, M., 27
Benedict, J. F., 33
benign prostatic hyperplasia, 22
Berman, E., 60, 73, 85
Bernal, G., 167
Bertrand, N., 34
bibliotherapy, 119–21, 174
Billups, K., 33
bipolar disorder, 43
Birchler, G. R., 55
Bishop, M., 66
Bladou, F., 32
blood pressure, penile, measuring, 28
Blumstein, P., 55
Bodner, D., 30, 33, 148, 149
body image, men's and women's embarrassment over, 76
Bovim, G., 22
Bowen, M., 58, 88
Bradley, W. E., 29
Braun, P., 34–35
Brendler, C. B., 27
Broderick, G. A., 28, 29

Camic, P., 89
Carey, M. P., 7, 8, 43, 88, 104, 113, 139
case formulation, 102–17
case studies
    Alex, enmeshment, 60–61
    Derrick, contraindications to sex therapy, 95–96
    Doug, sexual script, 53–54
    Harry, recovery from prostate surgery, 41–42
    Henry, bipolar illness, 43
    Marge and Harry, unconsummated marriage, 115–17
    Maryann and Bob, sexual attraction risk factors, 53
    Max and Mora, cognitions and anxiety, 81–82
    Michael, divorce, 50
    Rich and Barbara, contraindications to therapy, 92–93
    Rick and Rachel, questions in assessment of the sexual problem, 74–75
    Sandy and Jack, Viagra, 152
    Shirley and Mark, favorable indicators for sex therapy, 97–98
    Steve and Margo, contraindications to therapy, 93–94
    Sue and Ben, mixing couple and sex therapy in the same session, 181
Catherall, D. R., 65
Caverject (alprostadil), for medical treatment of erectile dysfunction, 2, 33
cavernosography, for diagnosis of causes of erectile dysfunction, 29
central nervous system, role in sexual response, 16
    specific conditions affecting, 21–22
change, rate of, controlling in couple therapy, 158–59
choice, and likelihood of compliance in therapy, 111
circularity, of communication, 165–66
Claiborn, C., 111
Clark, A. R., 34, 66
Clark, D., 126

Cochran, J. S., 34
cognitions
  case formulation for integrating into
      therapy, 112
  for countering negative attitudes,
      121–25
  in risk factors
    individual, 76
    relational assessment of, 81–83
  see also negative cognitions
cognitive therapy, and self-defeating
      sexual thoughts, 126–27
collusion, of a couple, for maintaining
      erectile dysfunction, 101
commitment
  defined, 3
  as a foundation for communication,
      165
  lack of, as a contraindication to sex
      therapy, 95
  and resolution of sexual concerns,
      84–85
communication
  components of, recognizing as more
      than content, 165
  destructive styles of, 169
  problems with
    as a common issue, 164–71
    and sexual dysfunction, 56–57
  schema for evaluating levels of,
      167–68
  sensual, sensate focus exercises in, 132
  about sexuality, 4–5
  by the therapist, without abstract lan-
      guage, 160
compliance, in therapy, 110–11
Condra, M., 35
conflict
  escalating, control by the therapist in
      couple therapy, 160–61
  intersystemic guidelines for engaging
      in, 176–77
conflict resolution
  difficulty with, and individual con-
      current therapy for couples,
      84–85
  lack of skill in, as an interactional
      factors in sexual dysfunction,
      56–57

negative actions contributing to, 179
observing a couple's skills in, initial
    interview, 67–68
positive actions contributing to, 178
consistency, in the pattern of erection,
    11
Constantine, J., 66
contempt, in destructive communica-
    tion pattern, 169
context, for communication, creating
    through therapy, 166–67
contextualizing the problem, reframing
    to accomplish, 99
contraindications
  to sex therapy, 91–96
  to vacuum pump use, 30
  to vascular surgery, 34
control, fear of, interactional factors
    in, 59
Cornille, J. M., 67
Correa, R. J., 32
Costabile, R. A., 34
couples
  emphasis on, in sex therapy, 13
  erectile dysfunction as a problem for,
      3–5
  pitfalls in dealing with the problems
      of, 156–63
  sex therapy with, basic principles,
      88–117
  sexual dysfunction in, 7–8
Couples in Treatment: Techniques and
    Approaches for Effective Prac-
    tice (Weeks & Treat), 102
Crenshaw, T., 17, 18, 21, 22, 35, 52,
    81
crisis, creation of, by Viagra, 2
criticism, destructive, in a communica-
    tion pattern, 169
culture
  communication about sex in, 61
  limitation on sexual dialogue in, 4–5

Dambros, M., 35
The Dance of Anger (Goldhor-Lerner),
    174
Davidson, J., 18, 19
defensiveness, in a communication pat-
    tern, 169

dehydroepiandrosterone (DHEA), ef-
    fects of, on sexual arousal, 18
DeMaria, R., 87, 103, 175
Denman, J. L., 34
dependency, fear of, 58
depersonalization, in assigning home-
    work, 111
depression, effect on erectile perfor-
    mance, 43–44, 57
desire, sexual, 15
Desvaux, P., 34
distraction, as an obstacle to communi-
    cation, 169
divorce, anxiety during, and erectile
    dysfunction, 50, 78
Dozier, R. M., 67
Drawz, B., 34
Drawz, G., 34
drugs
    dose adjustment in medical treat-
        ment, 150–51
    effects of, on sexual arousal, 22
    nonprescription, 35

For Each Other (Barbach), 19
Eid, F., ix, 23, 29
electrocardiogram, for identifying car-
    diac problems, 26–27
Ellis, A., 126
embarrassment, as a barrier to help, 9
Emmons, M. L., 174
emotion, controlling expressions of, in
    therapy sessions, 162
empathy, open-ended questions to
    foster, 66
Engel, J. D., 34
enmeshment, as a risk factor for sexual
    dysfunction, 60–61
environment
    sexual, technique for establishing in
        therapy, 127–29
    supportive, in the initial interview,
        64–70
Erder, M. H., 33
erectile dysfunction, defining, 5–6
erections
    instructions in losing, 139–40
    misconceptions about, 10–13
    physiology of, 15–18
Ernst, E., 35

Evans, C. M., 29
exercises, sensate focus
    step 1, 135–38
    step 2, 138–39
expectations, common issues related to,
    171–73
exploratory and sensual interactions,
    51
exposure, fear of, interactional factors
    in, 59

family of origin
    development of sexual identity in,
        60–61
    learning about sex in, 73
    learning sexual scripts in, 85–87
fantasies, sexual, technique for utiliz-
    ing, 124–25
Feagins, B. A., 34
fear
    of dependency, 58
    of intimacy, as a risk factor in sexual
        dysfunction, 58–59, 79
    reducing, case formulation for,
        107–8
feelings
    expressing in disagreement, 180
    fear of expressing, 58–59
Feldman, H. A., ix, 7, 20
Fenemore, J., 35
fighting
    constructive, negotiation in,
        177–78
    fair, 180
    see also conflict
Flam, T., 34
flow chart, for treatment, establishing
    priority in a case formulation,
        104–6
Fogarty, T. F., 53
foreplay, valuing, sensate focus exer-
    cises in, 132
Frank, E., 7, 8
Frankl, V. E., 107
Friday, N., 125
Froelich, R., 66
Fukui, J., 32
Fulgham, P. F., 34, 66
functions of erectile dysfunction, re-
    framing of, 99, 101–2

Gagnon, J. H., 7, 8, 20, 85
generalized erectile disorder, 6
genital stimulation, in sensate focus
     exercises, 138–39
genogram
     focused anger, 175–76
     sexual, 87
Gesundheit, N., 34
Gibbons, R. P., 32
Gill, H., 23, 24
Gilliland, R., 44
Glick, H. A., 33
goals, defining with clients,
     159–60
Goldberg, G. P., 17, 18, 21, 22, 35,
     52, 81
Goldhor-Lerner, H., 174
Goldstein, I., ix, 7, 20, 30, 35, 36
good will, as a basis for facilitating
     communication, 165
Gottman, J., 56, 134, 169, 177
Govier, F. E., 32
Gross, M. B., 34
guilt, and sexual response, 47
Guinguis, N., 35, 36

Hackney, H., 66
Haley, J., 69
Harper, R., 126
Harris, C., 35
Hatzichristou, G., ix, 7, 20
health, and testosterone level, 18
Heiman, J. R., 51, 79, 85, 104, 108,
     112, 118
Hellstrom, W., 30, 34
help, barriers to seeking, 8–10
Hermanowicz, M., 32
Hicks, M. W., 67
Hof, L., x, 51, 56, 60, 73, 85, 87, 91,
     99, 103, 104, 157, 173, 175
homework, case formulation,
     108–12
homosexual couples, working with, x
hope, communicating to patients, 91
hormonal system
     laboratory tests to determine func-
          tioning of, 26–27
     role in erectile dysfunction, 23–
          24
     role in sexual response, 17–18

Howard, B., 57
Hricak, H., 29
Human Sexual Response (Masters &
     Johnson), 16

implicit directions, and compliance
     with homework, 111–12
incest
     case example, 116
     as a risk factor for sexual dysfunc-
          tion, 48–49, 61, 86–87
individuals, psychological risk factors
     of, 42–46
individual therapy, need for, 95–96
information, diagnostic, from pre-
     scribed exercises that fail to
     work, 109
inhibited sexual desire (ISD), 45–46
     interactional factors in, 54–55
initial interview, telephone, 62–64,
     89–90
initial session, assessment of psychologi-
     cal risk factors in, 64–71
injection therapy
     individualized prescription of, 32–33
     phentolamine for, 37–38
     study of, 148–49
Integrative Solutions (Weeks & Hof),
     173
interactional risk factors, 80–81
intercourse
     emphasis on lovemaking separately
          from, 151–52
     transitioning to, 141–42
intergenerational assessment
     of factors in sexual dysfunction,
          60–61
     learning about sex in the family of
          origin, 73
     of psychological risk factors, 85–87
interpretation, by the therapist, 162
intersystemic approach
     to anger and conflict resolution,
          173–81
     in case formulation, 102–17
     and the pitfalls of couples' therapy,
          157
     to risk factors
          for erectile dysfunction, 39–61
          framework for assessment, 62–87

intimacy
  defined, 3
  differences between men and women
    in need for, 52–53
  fear of, as a risk factor in sexual dys-
    function, 58–59, 79
  issues, overview, 1–11
  common, in dealing with couples,
    164–81
I-statements, for facilitating communication, 170

Jarrow, J. P., 23, 33
Johnson, B., 29
Johnson, V. E., 1, 13, 14, 16–17, 40,
  42, 45, 54, 88, 105, 107, 108,
  118, 129, 135
joining, in couple therapy, 158
Journal of Sex and Marital Therapy,
  148–49
Junemann, K. P., 34–35

Kadesky, K. T., 34
Kadesky, M. I., 34, 66
Kaiser, F., 30, 34
Kaplan, H. S., ix, 13, 15, 17, 20, 21,
  23, 38, 40, 42, 51, 80, 88, 104,
  129, 130, 142, 153
Karadeniz, T., 27
Kassinove, H., 174
Kinsey, A. C., 6
Kittner, C., 34
Knopf, J., 89
Kohn, I. J., 38
Kolata, G., 7, 8
Kolodny, R., 17
Kramer-Levien, D., 32
Krane, R. J., ix, 7, 20
Krautschick, A., 34–35
Kupfer, D. J., 7
Kurokawa, J., 32
Kursh, E., 30, 33, 148, 149

L'Abate, L., 174
laboratory tests, for medical evaluation, 26–27
Laumann, E. O., 7, 8, 20
Leiblum, S. R., ix, 13, 16, 39, 52, 53,
  85, 88, 104
Levine, S. B., 30, 33, 42, 51, 148, 149

Lewis, R., 32
life-cycle changes, as risk factors, 58,
  78–79
lifelong versus acquired erectile dysfunction, 5–6
Lin, J. T., 29
Linet, O. I., 30, 32, 33
location, of homework performance, 110
LoPiccolo, L., 79, 85, 118
Loren, R., 124
love, components of an adult relationship, 3
lovemaking versus sexual intercourse,
  151–52
Lowe, F. C., 23
Lue, T. F., 29, 30, 32, 35, 36
LycKlame a Nijeholt, 34
Lynch, S., 34

McCarron, T. J., 33
McCarthy, B., 15
McHenry, S., 174
McKinlay, J. B., ix, 7, 20
McKinney, K., 55
McKinnon, W. R., 44
McLaren, R., 32
McVary, K. T., 34
Mahlstedt, P. P., 58
Malavand, B., 34
male erectile disorder, defined, 5–6
Maltz, W., 86
Manning, M., 34–35
Martin, C. E., 6
Marziali, E., 64
Massachusetts Male Aging Study, 7
Masters, W. H., 1, 13, 14, 16–17, 40,
  42, 45, 54, 88, 105, 107, 108,
  118, 129, 135, 138
mechanism of action, sildenafil
  (Viagra), 35–37
medical assessment
  of benign prostatic hyperplasia, 22
  concern about health, and sexual dys-
    function, 49–50
  of erectile dysfunction, 14–38, 72
  penile blood pressure, measuring, 28
medical model of illness, 3
medical treatment
  integrating with psychological treat-
    ment, 144–55

psychological issues in, 148–50
sex therapy as an adjunct to, 150–52
working with the physician, 146–48
Meisler, A. W., 43
Mellion, M. B., 22
Melman, A., 89, 110
Meston, C. M., 104, 108, 112
Michael, R. T., 7, 8, 20
Michaels, S., 20
mind-reading, as an obstacle to communication, 168–69
Minuchin, S., 64
Morales, A., 35
Morgan, R., 34
Morokoff, P. J., 44
Mosher, D., 46, 47
Mulcahy, J., 32
Muller, S., 34
MUSE (alprostadil), for medical treatment of erectile dysfunction, 2, 33–34, 151
myths
dispelling, techniques for, 121–25
about erections, 11–12

Nagata, M., 32
narcissism, as a contraindication to therapy, 94
naturalism, myth of, 121
negative cognitions
eliminating, 121–25
of men with erectile problems, 47–48
neutralizing in therapy, techniques for, 126–27
negotiation, in constructive fighting, 177–78
Nemo, K. J., 34
neurological testing, of the penis, 29
The New Male Sexuality (Zilbergeld), 19
nitric oxide, release in response to Viagra, 36
nocturnal penile tumescence (NPT), studies of, in medical assessment, 27
Nukui, F., 32
Nye, S., 66

obstacles, to communication, 168–71
Odell, M., 64
Ogring, F. G., 30, 32, 33
Okamoto, S., 32
organic causes of erectile dysfunction, 21–24,
see also medical assessment
orgasm
changes in, with aging, 20–21
as a phase of the sexual response cycle, 15
Owen, J., 35
oxytocin, excretion during sexual arousal, 18

Padma-Nathan, H., 29, 30, 34, 35, 36
Parsons, K. F., 29
partner
implications of involvement of, 90
refusal to engage in sex therapy, 94
see also couples
Parys, B. T., 29
passion, defined, 3
past, recounting in therapy, limitation placed by the therapist, 162
Pearce, C., ix, 23, 29
penile implants, 31–32
penis, neurological testing of, 29
perceptions, differing between partners, responses of the therapist to, 161
Perelman, M., 36
performance anxiety
in aging males, 20
case formulation for treatment of, 107–8
origins of, 42–43
as a risk factor, 76–77
personality disorder, as a risk factor, 44–45
personalizing issues, as an obstacle to communication, 169
pessimism, about therapy, origins of, 90–91
Peterson, G. W., 67
Peyronie's disease, 23
Pfeiffer, E., 19
phases, of the sexual response cycle, 15
phenolamine (Vasomax), 37–38

physical examination, general, information from, 26,
  see also medical assessment
physicians, preferences in treatment, surgical and medical, 2
Pinsof, W. M., 65
Pittler, M., 35
polarizing language, as an obstacle to communication, 169
Pomeroy, W. B., 6
Porst, H., 34
positive regard, fostering with empathetic questions, 66–69
positive thinking, technique for developing, 123,
  see also cognitions; negative cognitions
premature ejaculation, performance anxiety over, 45
prevalence, of erectile dysfunction, 6–7
priapism, as a side effect of some medications, 33
priority, setting for multiple problems in treatment, case formulation, 104–6
Pritchett, T. R., 32
problems
  attention to, by the therapist, 160
  integrating facets of, 112–13
problem-solving skills
  fair fighting using, 180
  lack of, as a risk factor in dyadic interactions, 56–57
  see also conflict resolution
process, of therapy, importance in case formulation, 113–14
prolactin, effect on erectile dysfunction, 24
prostaglandins, role of, in vasodilation, 18
Pryor, J. L., 33
Pryor, L. E., 33
psychiatric problems, as risk factors
  for erectile dysfunction, 43–46
  for sexual dysfunction, 80
psychoeducational information, in sex therapy with couples, 118–19
psychological issues
  in erectile dysfunction, 39–61
  in medical treatment, 148–50

serious psychopathology, as a contraindication to therapy, 94
psychological treatment, integrating with medical treatment, 144–55

questions
  for accurate assessment of the sexual problem, 70–72
  about anger, 175–76
  from clients, wary answers to, 159
  for determining sexual ignorance, 77–78
  about the functions and meaning of anger, 175
  about intergenerational factors, 86
  about life-cycle stages, 78–79
  for reframing erectile dysfunction, 99–100
  about sex education in families of partners, 85–86
  specific, technique for asking, 125–26
  therapeutic
    for dispelling negative thoughts, 122–25
    in the initial interview, 66–69
    from the therapist, about homework exercises, 137–38
Quinn, W., 64

Rafker, J., 34
Rako, S., 17
rank-order interactions, 51
Rapport, J. L., 34
Rattier, C., 32
readings, suggested for clients, 142–43,
  see also bibliotherapy
rectal examination, 27
referral
  information from, in the initial telephone interview, 63–64
  by and to physicians, 145–46
reflective listening, for facilitating communication, 170–71
refractory periods, changes on aging, 10–11, 20–21
reframing
  for assessing psychological risk factors, 69–70, 73
  in the initial session, 99–102

Reis, R. B., 38
rejection, prior, as a risk factor in inter-
    action, 59
relational issues, as a contraindication
    to sex therapy, 95
relationship issues
    case formulation for treating, 106
    and sexual dysfunction, 55–56
religious beliefs, respecting in therapy,
    121–23
Renshaw, D. C., 7
Resnick, M., 30, 33, 148, 149
Rhoden, E., 35
RigiScan, device for detecting sleep erec-
    tions, 27
Rischmann, P., 34
Risen, C., 33, 148, 149
risk factors
    defined, 39
    dyadic, 52
    interactional, 50–61
    nonpsychiatric, 46–50
    psychological, 40–46
        assessing in therapy, 75–87
    relational, 95
Roehrborn, C. G., 34, 66
Rogers, C., 64, 66
Rosen, R. C., ix, 13, 16, 18, 19, 30,
    35, 36, 39, 52, 53, 85, 88, 104
Rossi, D., 32
Rubinstein, D., 7, 8
Russell, L., 56

Sager, C., 171
Sarramon, J. P., 34
satisfaction, sexual, as a goal of
    therapy, 104
scheduling, of homework assignments,
    109–10
Schepe, J. R., 34–35
Schiavi, R., 27, 28, 29
Schmidt, R. A., 29
Schnarch, D., 15, 51, 80, 88, 104
Schoenberg, H. W., 89
Schuemichen, C., 34
Schwartz, P., 55
secrecy
    power of communication through, 86
    as a risk factor for erectile dysfunc-
        tion, 48–49

Segraves, K. A., 16, 20
Segraves, R. T., 16, 20, 89
Seiter, H., 34
sensate focus exercises, 129–42
    after medication success, 154–55
    structure and application of, 134–39
Serment, G., 32
sex
    erections as a condition for, myth of,
        10
    negative attitudes surrounding,
        12–13
Sex in America study, 7, 8
sex therapy
    as an adjunct to medical treatment,
        150–52
    favorable conditions for, 96–98
    prevalence of erectile dysfunction in
        men presenting for, 7
Sexton, W. J., 33
sexual attraction, explaining, 53
sexual bill of rights, technique for
    developing, 123
sexual desire
    age-related changes in, 18–19
    erection as an indication of, 10
    lack of, 55
    level of, as a risk factor, 83–84
sexual difficulties
    accurately assessing, 70–73
    multiple, and interactional risk
        factors, 54
sexual equilibrium, components of,
    51–52
sexual genogram, 87
sexual identity, development in the fam-
    ily of origin, 60–61
sexual ignorance, as a risk factor for
    erectile dysfunction, 46–47,
    77–78
sexuality, components of, 4
sexual orientation
    assessing as a risk factor, 79
    uncertainty about, and sexual perfor-
        mance, 45
Sexual Pharmacology (Crenshaw &
    Goldberg), 17
sexual response cycle, 14–15
sexual scripts, 53–54
    learning in the family, 85–87

Shabsigh, R., 38
shame, as a barrier to help, 9
Shields, C., 66
Shoenberg, H. W., 16
side effects
    of apomorphine, 37
    of injection therapy, 33
    of Viagra, 36
    of yohimbine, 35
Sidi, A. A., 33
sildenafil, see Viagra
situational erectile disorder, 6
skepticism, about therapy, origins of,
    90–91
sleep
    erection during, 16
    monitoring as part of medical assess-
        ment, 27–28
smoking, effects on vascular disease,
    23
Snap-Gauge, device for detecting sleep
    erections, 27
Sogari, P., 35
Souto, C., 35
spectatoring/hyperreflection, case for-
    mulation dealing with, 107–8
Spector, I. P., 7
Sprecher, S., 55
Sprenkle, D., 66
Steers, W. D., 30, 35, 36
Sternberg, R., 3
steroids, effect on erectile dysfunction,
    24
stonewalling, destructive, in a commu-
    nication pattern, 169
Strong, S., 111
structure, in couples therapy, need for,
    163
Sundaram, C. P., 33
suppository, transurethral, 33–34
surgery
    penile implants, 31–32
    vascular, 34–35
Surridge, D., 35
symptom, focus on, 104
systems
    balanced, maintaining by the thera-
        pist, 161–62
    couples', 51–54
    interactional risk factors in, 50–54

psychological risk factors in, 69–70
    see also intersystemic approach

Talmadge, L., 86
Tam, P. V., 34
Tanagno, E. A., 29, 32
Te, A. E., 38
techniques
    basic, for sex therapy with couples,
        118–43
    for facilitating communication,
        170–71
    for managing anger, couples' resis-
        tance to, 174–75
    see also questions
Teloken, C., 35
territorial interactions, 51
testosterone, levels of
    and feelings of power, 52
    and sexual arousal, 17–18
therapeutic relationship, establishing,
    64–70
therapists
    availability of, 9–10
    bias of, and identification of risk fac-
        tors, 40
    gender of, implications to the client,
        65–66
    identification with patients, pitfalls
        of, 119
    joining with two people in conflict,
        158
    monitoring by
        of destructive communication in
            therapy, 169
        of progress in homework, 133–34
        of success in homework, 137–38
    quality of treatment provided by, 9
    professional qualifications, 113
    sex and couple, territories of, 3
    working with physicians, 146–48
therapy, implementation of, case formu-
    lation for, 113–14
Thomas, W., 33
thyroxin, effect on erectile dysfunction,
    24
Tiefer, L., 89, 110
time-out, when anger is out of control,
    177
timing, of erections, 10–11

Tomm, K., 67
Topsakal, M., 27
touching, nongenital, exercises using, 135–36
transitions, assessment questions concerning, 78,
    see also life-cycle changes
Trapp, J., 30
Treat, S., 91, 102, 157
treatment
    medical, 29–37
    plan for, case formulation, 103–7
    psychological, integrating with medical treatment, 144–55
trust
    role of, in a sexual relationship, 58
    in the therapist, 65
Turner, L. A., 30, 33, 148, 149
Turner, M., 57

ultrasound studies, Doppler, for evaluating vascular problems of the penis, 28–29
understanding, as a basis for facilitating communication, 165
urology tests, for evaluating organic causes of erectile dysfunction, 28

vacuum pump, prescription, 30–31
validation, to facilitate communication, 171
vascular surgery, 34–35
vascular system
    effects of problems on erectile dysfunction, 22–23
    role in erection, 16–17
vasopressin, role in sexual arousal, for males, 18

venous flow controller, 31
Verhulst, J., 51
Vermeulen, A., 18
Viagra (sildenafil)
    advantages of, 151
    effect of
        destigmatizing, 144
        on view of causes of erectile dysfunction, 9
    release of, 1–2
    as a temporary expedient, 98

Wagner, G., 17, 23
Wallace, S., 86
Watzlawick, P., 69
Webb, L. J., 55
websites, for information about medications, 38
Weeks, G. R., x, 15, 51, 55, 56, 57, 58, 62, 69, 87, 91, 99, 102, 103, 104, 123–24, 157, 173, 175
Weldon, K, L., 34
Werthman, P., 34
Wicker, P., 30, 35, 36
Wilke, R. J., 33
Williams, G., 34
Wincze, J. P., 8, 43, 88, 104, 113, 139
Wolpe, J., 77
women, sexual dysfunction in, 8
Woody, J. D., 51, 104

yohimbine, studies evaluating, 35
Your Perfect Right (Alberti & Emmons), 174

Zarins, C. K., 89
Zilbergeld, B., 10, 12, 19, 61, 77, 121, 140